# LEAVES FROM MY PERSONAL LIFE

# LEAVES FROM MY PERSONAL LIFE

V.R. KRISHNA IYER

*Justice, Supreme Court of India*

GYAN PUBLISHING HOUSE

NEW DELHI-110002

Leaves from My Personal Life

ISBN: 9788121208376



Published in 2004 in India by
Gyan Publishing House
5, Ansari Road, Darya Ganj, New Delhi-110002
Phones : 011-47034999, 9811692060
E-mail : books@gyanbooks.com
Website : http://www.gyanbooks.com

*Laser Typesetting at* : Shree Vaishnavi Creations, Delhi
*Printed at* : Mehra Offset Press, Delhi

# Contents

# Preface

'It is a hard and nice subject for a man to write of himself: it grates his own heart to say anything of disparagement, and the readers' ears to hear anything of praise for him'.

I have lived on this planet for four score and eight years and filled many positions relatively insignificant, but curiously creating an illusion that I do matter in some measure in public life. Friends from various strata of society have been pressing me to write my autobiography. But I have consistently dismissed the idea as an elite enterprise and expression of veiled vanity. Autobiographies by mediocrities mushroom in bookshops and those who wish to project themselves as larger than they are write their megalo-stories. I never wish to add to their number knowing as I do that anything I write of myself may be a wee-bit of boast which I should sensitively avoid.

I know of great and glorious autobiographies. Gandhiji's Experiments with Truth, Nehru's magnificent Autobiography, the spiritually elevating Autobiography of a Yogi by Yogananda, Edward Gibbon's fine Autobiography and other world classics which stand on a lofty footing. Great lawyers like M.C. Setalvad, great judges like Chagla and Mahajan, great writers like R.K. Narayan and yet other illustrious and intellectual giants have enriched the treasury of English literature. Of course, the great Winston Churchill wrote the most inspiring wonder of war literature in his 'The Second World War' the like of which no Nobel prize winner has written. In a different vein, Lord Denning, among the greatest judges of the commonwealth, has delectably written, with anecdotal illustration, his fascinating Family Story.

How dare I consider, playing the author of a self-centred

book, knowing how little I matter, how small has been my contribution to the story of India in its executive, legislative and forensic dimensions. Humility banished from my mind all thought of writing about my own career from childhood to old age, aware of glaring shortcomings. But responding to the gentle persuasions from well-meaning friends, I decided to put pen to paper to produce some micro-writing relating to episodes in my life not spectacular to narrate, but give glimpses from my life. By themselves they are unimportant events but may interest those who come across me and my judgements in court, me and my mini creativity as minister in the first Communist Ministry in Kerala nearly half a century back. I did not want to write for an audience as such, but, of course, addressed myself to a generation which has not seen me at work. Glimpses from personal life picked up at random, incidents from vicissitudes of fate selected to be representative, events which had made some impact on public affairs when they occurred and have since passed into oblivion—these ripples and eddies constitute this book. I confess that this is no work of historic value or memoir which has lasting interest. The only assurance I can give the reader is that what is written is, to the best of my knowledge and memory (at my advanced age), a frank statement with no exaggeration or bias. If it is readable I shall be thankful. If it is dull, drop reading it. The book is written not for pleasure or profit but out of courtesy since many have shown interest in my writing this book. What they wanted was an autobiography. What I give is glimpses here and there, not even a coherent story. My life is not worth telling, but anecdotes and episodes may still be informative. That is the only justification for spending my time and claiming the time of the reader.

I have been a lawyer, a minister, a judge and one who has been engaged in public issues after superannuation, for two decades now. The various chapters of the book relate to different facets of my life and unless one has some patience to know the background and read the message, the pages may well be tedious. Therefore, I appeal to those who care first to acquaint themselves with a little bit of me so that what is written gains pertinence. After all, these are leaves from an Indian's life and have therefore, some meaning for other Indians. I offer only a sketchy, personal and incomplete account of my past verging on the present but largely irrelevant for those who look for a biographical narrative.

There is a glut of midget memoirs in the market and many merit early oblivion. I do not wish to compete for this fate and so choose to select only a few events from my personal life. I am aware of the ephemerality of my random anecdotes. Even so, there is a pleasure in the telling although I confess it is rambling. But in the words of Walt Whitman:

*Camerado, this is no book,*
*Who touches this touches a man.*

April 7, 2003

**V.R. KRISHNA IYER**

# 1
# Some Recollections of My Days in the Annamalai University on the Occasion of Doctorate

I was once an alumnus of the Annamalai University (1933-35). Those two years did shape my culture and gave direction and dimension to my mental development. A marvellous library, professors whose personality moulded the character and yearning for learning of the students and a University Union which did leaven my love of public speaking and fearless debate make me nostalgic and look back to those long-ago days with academic patriotism. When a doctorate was conferred on me decades later I made what has been described as an Alumni Day Address. I present it to the reader, not because there is anything of oratorical excellence or fair rare but because it is a narration which is part of my life and an event which I deeply cherish. With these introductory words I crave leave to repeat the speech for the readers to learn curiosity.

***Mr. Vice-Chancellor; Brothers and Sisters of that*** invisible, far-flung and yet affectionate Annamalai fraternity, friends.

All of us gathered here have a certain institutional patriotism which is the instinctive tribute that we, the Annamalai alumni, continue to pay to our alma mater so long as the light of learning, kindled by this University, burns bright in our bosoms and illumines our value-laden life in these items of encircling gloom. I do not wish to convict myself of dotage by regaling you with anecdotage, for Benjamin Disraeli has righty said – and our politicians must listen to him – that.

"When a man fell into his anecdotage it was a sign for him to retire from the world"

You will, therefore, forgive me for forsaking that fashionable bluff usually indulged in on festive occasions of romancing and recounting, with ersatz humour, how the world was great when we were young, how geniuses walked the campuses then but goofy successors and goonda usurpers have brought things to a lamentable pass now and how the peaceful splendour of Union eloquence and Miscellany elegance gave place to student unrest and revolutionary slogans and how a hundred other graces of the past succumbed to the disgrace of later years. I decline to dig from that great dust-heap called history or play the customary game of each generation calling the next a scapegrace. A mock battle of the tenses is but empty witticism for which I have no mood and you have no mind. Even so, memory stirs up story after story when I see old places, revive old longings and wistfully come upon some surviving old faces or remnant landscapes. It is ingratitude to wear disdainful silence masked by self-importance where discriminating remembrance is the expression of affection screened by the distance of time. Therefore, do give me the indulgence to gossip a little on 'old forgotten things and battles long ago!' After all, the flash and splash of colours on the sunset sky are Nature's gossip with the celestical world about the beaming events of morning, noon and afternoon. I have Nature's alibi for testing your patience with my tremendous trifles in the evening of my life.

A word about the man whose name is immortalised by this University. There are two types of millionaires in our country. Many of them are human warehouses of huge bank balances. They die counting and crying. On the contrary, there are private trustees of immense national resources who husband and spend for developmental needs. They are counted among the few and lamented when they leave. The first species are miserly and miserable wealthy in the coffers, but penurious in the coffins. At best, their ugly parsimony stains the soul, invites the assassin, antagonises relatives and paralyses society by cornering to themselves what belongs to the community. Social justice demands their liquidation by law, not by Naxalites. The other category whom I may call Princes of Abundance, live, perhaps in luxury, but patronise the arts, foster cultural pursuits, direct their resources to life the people's level of education and leave, by discriminating benefactions geared to higher values and goals, a better world than they were born in. Such a satwic aristocrat blessed by Indo-Burmese riches, who possessed a dynamic vision and capacity for action, was Raja Sir Annamalai Chettiar, the Founder who, with his influence, eminence and munificence, lit this lamp of higher education in Chidambaram – that hallowed spot from where the cosmic dance of Nataraja, in cyclic patterns, sustains, destroys and re-creates this Universe with the vibrancy of wisdom and the rhythm of ordered movement. The Divine Founder, who is manifest and unmanifest, is the final cause and course of all terrestrial events but a human agent figures on the Earth as the cause when something happens. Raja Sir Annamalai Chettiar was that instrument of enlightenment – proud Tamil Enlightenment, the ancient glory of which had lain dormant for too long and needed a philanthropic midwifery to bring into re-incarnation that cultural magnificence which to-day takes a high place in the world treasure of sublime learning. The Annamalai University, in the heart-land of Tamil country, was the first and foremost to raise the academic status of Tamil language and literature from the vernacular servitude to which it had been condemned in the past.

The legendary wealth and fabulous philanthropy of Raja Sir Annamalai Chettiar thus accounts for this noble institution. He was a friend of my fathers', if a big man can be regarded as a friend of a small man like my father. But I must hasten to add that that was not the reason for my joining this then not-so-prestigious educational marvel. The truth was that there were many Malayalees in this University in those days; living there was cheap, teaching then was good, courses offered were diverse and attention to students was personalised. Equally importantly, degrees were not difficult since students were not swarming armies as in the Madras University but restricted to the size of a single college.

I spent two halcyon years in Annamalainagar, in 1933-35, when academic tumults and radical tempests had not arrived, and the cool, sequestered value of life warmed up into convulsive activity by fits and starts only when the flames of nationalism showed up all around in that era of S.Satyamurthi's spell-binding peals of eloquence and Somasundara Bharathi's patriotic presence. Student marches, with Bharathi songs chanted, were a great experience and Gandhiji's visit to the campus was episodic, even epic. Two things, then engraved on the marble of my blurred memory, may bear mention because of contemporary relevance.

One was the unique visit of the then nationalist dynamite called Mahatma Gandhi. Gandhiji came to the campus and spoke to a respectable crowd. Many had foregathered, rich and poor, high placed and low-placed, teachers and students. He talked straight without the decorative eloquence, noisy gesticulation and interminable length of contemporary leaders. He came on time, stopped on time and did business like a bania without loss of time. He accused the British for holding India slave and accused Indians for not rising in united revolt. Sedition was his religion since Government was satanic. His presence was charismatic; his word dynamic; his deeds honest; his demands resistless. He belongs to the ages now and is claimed as part of our political heritage. And yet, when any Government goes satanic few of his followers dare to turn seditious. Genuflection is the new culture of our politicians. Gandhiji maintained that consistency which was not always a virtue. His descendants have refined this sentiment into a fine art by practising defection as a daily homage to the Father of the Nation. He spoke in simple language so that his thoughts would be transparent and his appeal direct. His successors, identified by dress, express themselves in decorative circumlocution, so that their words may hide their thought behind dazzling diction. A few of these imitate him by playing the role of public moral weight-lifters, but while he was transparent and was always amenable to investigation, his high-placed disciples resist discovery. We are not concerned here with the moral gap between Gandhi and Gandhians, but with my adolescent impressions of the Mahatma's short sojourn in this hallowed campus. At the end of the speech, he auctioned the garlands and demanded higher bids because the proceeds were to finance the freedom struggle. There were some bidders, but the patriotic misers loved their lucre more than their mother-land and so, Gandhiji did not get the best price for his garlands. To-day, tycoons crowd around his political legatees in office to offer the highest bid in fantastic sums handed up in deepest secrecy because now it is a business investment for political dividends. But then it was risky evidence of national sympathy! Indeed, currently, the only act of patriotism is to drive away these bidders for political favours although no party nor leader-not even those who swear by revolution and socialism – has the courage to refuse these bid. The 30s when Gandhi came were days of police dossiers because Gandhi was a dangerous man and many in the affluent bracket obeyed the rule that discretion was the better part of valour. Those were times when the Mahatma was the Nation's omniscient Ombudsman and once did not permit a great leader with supreme credentials of sacrifice to become Chief Minister because he was not above suspicion in the matter of some public collection. Now that Gandhiji has been assassinated and safely rests in Rajghat, public morals in public life have been interred with his bones or set aflame with his body. Undoubtedly, Gandhian values, as precious as Gandhi himself, have been assassinated many times.

At the same meeting, the frail but firm leader argued that when people were dreadfully poor and India needed resources to be free, it was a sin to wear jewellery. "Give me your gold, I will use it for freeing this country" – he demanded at that meeting. Women are made of softer stuff and many in the crowd yielded up their bangles and necklaces. In our corrupt times, many business-men may, on the slightest hint, present bangles and necklaces to officers' wives and ministers' darlings may be. When I think of the perversions in morals and distortions in norms which have over-powered the nation's soul within 45 years of that simple event, I wonder whether the spirit of our Freedom Founder will spare any strutting leader 'dressed in a little brief authority' for the national deception which many thinking men feel is the reality of Indian politics.

Another impressionable event of my undergraduate years was a peroration Sri Satyamurthi delivered to the University students. His gruff voice, his instant wit, his patriotic fire and his inspirational sentiments had received All-India fame. When the crescendo of his eloquence was reached, even commonplace things and catchy claptraps were invested with such dignity and power that they had incendiary effect. As he worked himself up, punctuated by applause, he quipped that the British boasted that the Sun never set on the British Empire but this was because, roared Satyamurthi, the Sun never trusted the British. He continued in the same strain and, at his fighting best, climaxed with the demand for the supreme sacrifice; who lives if India dies? Who dies if India lives? Many of us were excited then. Most of us of the present day are too cold-blooded to warm up on hearing such hortative exercises. And there are two reasons, if not more, for this indifference. Burning sincerity is the authentic signature of convincing exhortation. And, almost without exception, leaders in politics have lost their credibility because many of them and their parties have helped themselves to such an extent at public expense that when their campaigners and great orators heave that their heart bleeds for their country the hearers know that there is no uneasy feeling in their bosom. No cardiologist need be called. It is only a professional exercise like that of an advocate who sheds tears for his client. Secondly, the speakers and the addresses are unconcerned about the country. India is individual for each of them. There never was a time in Indian history when the politics of corruption and the corruption of politics became so utterly integrated and ubiquitous as now when public life has become the cartoonist's paradise. Who lives if India dies? Perhaps every V.I.P., be he public official, legislator servant of the people, will privately say: "I live even if India dies because I have made enough and it is in Switzerland". The more relevant question may be, who lives if the Swiss franc or American dollar is devalued? India is only a means for personal ends. The old patriotism has died down and India Private Limited is coming to stay. Oh! The pity of it, that our public men are competing against each other to prove Dr. Johnson's definition of patriotism! Yet others, in considerable numbers, are testifying to Bernard Shaw's cynical insight in Major Barbara where he says:

He knows nothing, and he thinks he knows everything. That points clearly to a political career.

Bribery is so pervasive that in practice that act has been de-criminalised, the Penal Code notwithstanding. Who will police the police?

I should have abstained from these sardonic expressions but we are living in times when Lord Acton's famous dictum on Power is too mild for Indian realities and, amidst the sound and fury of developmental achievements since I left Annamalai, the major one is the progressively expanding and stable base of the Poverty Sector! Who takes credit for this? Aren't we among the four poorest countries?

Dissociating myself from political overtones, I recall how in the year after my batch left Annamalai, many revolutionary trends and leftist demonstrations showed up in this campus. Assuming them to be the authentic voice of Left politics, ideology had thus acquired academic residence in this University. One should have thought, regardless of political sympathies, that the integrity of the student ideologue would keep his later politics principled and ardour for the proletariat intense. Even on this front, ahs polemics shot-down dialectics? When millions live next-door neighbours of starvation, privation and death, even those who swear by Revolution forget their basics and swear at each other, practising a violent cult of untouchability and civil war of ideology. Who millions live next-door neighbours of starvation, privation and death, even those who swear by Revolution forget their basics and swear by Revolution forget their basics and swear at each other, practising a violent cult of untouchability and civil war of ideology. Who would have thought that the hot left cult of those days was so soft and easy of self-division? May be, the political pathology of India that is Bharat spares none-not even the disciples of

Lenin, from the syndrome of division, defection and self-cum-sectarian squabbles. Maybe, history has some untold story yet. Let us be optimists but realistic in wishing Indian Public life dominance over parties, personalities and lesser interests. Perhaps, we may have to come full circle back to the proposition that secular politics divorced from spiritualised ethics is self-defeating, whatever the doctrine.

When I hear these days some songs of Subramania Bharati as a tail-piece in music concerts' my mind travels back to Chidambaram, because my student days were charged with the revolutionary patriotism of Bharati songs. The major difference that I have always noticed between then and now is but this; to-day the militant music and the revolutionary incitement enwombed in the inspirational poems of Bharati are forgotten or buried five fathoms deep. His lilting, innocuous folk songs which do not incite the masses against the suppressive economic order have become the entertainment tail-piece of the elite in carnataka sangeeth. This is reflective of the decadent mood of the Establishment to keep the masses away from direct action. Symptomatic of this disease is the interpretation of socialism in the Constitution by lawyers and judges, by politicians and big businessmen. The tragic truth is that in the 30s this University and its alumni had been cradled in indignant nationalism but, all over the country, the decades that have gone by have domesticated and caged the wild potential of those days. We are now genteel, and insensitive and believe tat the dogs may bark, the caravan will pass. Many of the alumni of that vintage have occupied responsible positions and lived through life's fitful fever, gathering experience, learning lessons, reading omens and getting ready for the consequence. May be, we may pool our thoughts, and mature fruits may come therefrom.

Many of my friends belong to the Annamalai University fraternity. The periodic academic elections remind us of this living institution. I have felt – so have many of my friends of those days from this campus – that we have had tremendous opportunities for development which many students in more pretentious institutions of proud heritage did not enjoy. The great facilities for games were almost unparalleled in the

South. A residential university has a remarkable intellectual atmosphere and academic advantage. Learning, enquiry, discussion, meting together, eating together and a whole host of other collective activities had an impact on the student community, which I have not found elsewhere. Perhaps, Oxford or Cambridge, Harvard or Yale or other Universities in the West and some in India, possess such opportunities for self-development.

But two institutions moulded my life and that of many others like me which I may mention is passing.

Among the meaningful influences which have shaped my humble life was the University Library merely to walk through which was sheer enlightenment, with the window of the world's wisdom flung open for eyes to see, minds to devour and souls to soar. I have not read much from that universal congregation of great authors in every department of human knowledge; but the titles themselves taught, the shelves whispered and the latest arrivals looked like the footsteps of wise men on the march. Great men, dead or alive, became good friends and even without opening a page one could hold conversation with the Past, Present and Future. My dwarfed mind broadened and marks in examinations became things of inconsequence beside the eclectic fellowship and encyclopedic scholarship that a vast, were -arranged library vouchafed. Once you have become a frequent visitor to such a secular shrine you can never be small.

The University Union was a lovely institution of Victorian vintage debates, where the art of public speaking, the magic of rhetoric, the spice of repartee and the cult of fearless thought received fillip. When you recall the thrill of the spoken word at its best, with perfect masters of fine diction, correct pronunciation, hot rebuff, rhythm and cadence, like Rt. Hon. Srinivasa Sastry, S.E. Ranganathan, Sir C.P. Ramaswamy Ayyar and S. Satyamurthi, you transport yourself to a bye-gone Satyuga of oral splendour. The spirit of debate, the freedom of expression, the equal combat regardless of personalities, the creative thought and spontaneous retort of which the Union was witness, made Saturday nights memorable events. Of course, the spells of superb orators were punctuated by the insufferable shallowness of bores, bullies, braggarts and belligerents. Don't be carried away by the exciting impression that India's Burkes and Churchills were all from Annamalai – not at all. From the sublime to the ridiculous, was the performance of the Union, at times; for, various debates went on about themes like 'baldness is a sure sign of wisdom', 'science must take a holiday and what not. True, some Union Presidents had a winsome command and of one of them a Vice-Chancellor had said: Send him to hell or babel, he will command a silent audience". There were others who were so supreme in the verbal torrent of sound and fury signifying nothing, that unshaken by shouts and uncowed by boos, their stentorian spouts would swashbuckle along. They were the forerunners of the present parliamentarians. The age of symbol of a nation's cultural refinement and poetic sensitivity. Great thoughts, expressed in great words, elevate the soul with satvic effulgence; but vulgar strings of words flung violently at each other to the accompaniment of gesticulations and direct action, are the most damaging environmental pollution which over powers judgement by tamasic negativity. Just listen to Romain Rolland on Swami Vivekananda.

> His words are great music, phrases in the style of Beethoven, stirring rhythms like the march of Handel choruses. I cannot touch these sayings of his, scattered as they are through the pages of books at thirty years distance, without receiving a thrill through my body like an electric shock. And what shocks, what transports must have been produced when in burning words they issued from the lips of the hero!

On occasions when Sastri, C.P., Jerome D'Souza or other luminary spoke, we had that feeling. But now, get a pass and listen to a parliamentary debate or legislative duel – verbal assaults and violent tantrums, sometimes black – guardly, at other times blockheadly, - and you will realise what a serious handicap it is to be a polished speaker, clear thinker, cool debator or brilliant Demosthenes. In a Convocation Address then delivered, the distinguished speaker deplored: look at our streets and our legislatures! Today, if I may adapt a great lawyer's wit at a recent lecture: It will be defamatory of the street squabblers to be compared with legislative boxers. Reasons seems to have fled to brutish beasts, relevance seems to have deserted the Houses and loyalty to principle seems to have defected from all, all honourable members, where, then, is the effect of good speech? Why, then, is the gift of the gab? When, then, do we value reason? How, then, can truth expose falsehood? Mill and Voltaire, Gandhi and Nehru, Lincoln and Lenin and the World's best exponents of Humanity's causes must fall victim to the totalitarianism of vituperation and overthrow of persuasion, if speech has no place in public affairs and noise can stifle voice.

I have spoken without restraint although my office enjoins, through judicial lockjaws the strictest constraints. The reason is that I have thrown myself back to the flippant years, forty-four years ago. They were days of classical music with the savants of the Music College filling the air with sweet concords, of hectic elections with peaceful canvassing and choice on merits, (I, myself, unwittingly got elected as Student Editor of the Annamalai Miscellany), of good food and lovable company. No distractions invaded the educational island and our teachers were great scholars. I have read little but learnt much because the classes were more than an hour's oral expenditure but an exchange, a rapport, an exercise in cross-fertilisation and striven for perfection. If education is the manifestation of the perfection already in man, Annamalai proved it for many at least in partial measure.

The omega of my homage to my alma mater has come. No human homage to this House of Higher Teaching can excel the promise that we will be humane. The need today is not great heads but goods hearts, not loaded learning but deep love, not superintelligence but utter integrity. We want *Man*, not brilliant beast.

That University is best which cultures the heart more than it cultivates the head, which teachers the art of living and the science of being and demands nothing in exchange for precious learning save graduation into an integrated Indian. One's title to be an Annamalai alumnus is dignity, humility, a little morality and veracity in public and private life. To deepen and broaden Consciousness is to enliven the

Creative Potential and that is Education, not books coexisting with crooks.

There is widespread drought in our land. Its distressing dimension is drought of basic character. We have disastrous flood in our country. Its fury is most in the human area of the political mafia. There is ubiquitous starvation in India today. Its source is the starvation of the human spirit. The cumulative effect is that expensive developmental exercises have proved endless experiments in Untruth.

> "Remember" said John Adams, remember', democracy never lasts long. It soon wastes, exhausts and murders itself. There never was a democracy that did no commit suicide"

From this University we must send our anti-suicide squads called Annamalai alumni.

> Sir Winston Churchill, in a magnificent burst of eloquence, said:
>
> "At the bottom of all tributes paid to democracy is the little man, walking into a little booth, with a little pencil, making a little cross on a little bit of paper – no amount of rhetoric or voluminous discussion can possibly diminish the overwhelming importance of the point"

That little man, having read the unmanifest part of manifestoes, enters the little booth to search in vain for a little Indian who will live a little up to his word 'to wipe every tear from every eye', but returns in tears because the ballot does not contain such a name. Who lives if India dies? Who dies if India lives? Does it ring a bell now? We must solemnly resolve to be men. The virtue of men is hard to acquire. They are found only:

Where the mind is without fear and the head is held high;

Where words come out from the depth of truth;

Where the clear stream of reason has not lost its way into the dreary desert sand of dead habit.

Where is that India?

Let us reflect why in India home economics survives fitter than homo sapiens.

I am profoundly grateful to the Vice-Chancellor for having given me this long-distance opportunity to remember by University. My sister spent several years here. My cousin taught chemistry here. Rajah Sir Muthiah Chettiar – that perfect gentleman –and I, have been friends for decades with five years together in the Legislative assembly although obviously on opposite sides. My poignant memory wanders back to the last visit my wife and I made to this dear University. She is now no more on the physical plane. So also that gem of a man, Sri M.P. Damodaran, who had spent long years in the good administration of this institution, has been my life-long friend. He too is on the other side, thanks to Death's irrevocable demand. Life and Death are a continuum, a cultural, astral, spiritual continuum. What we acquire, good or evil, is not lost. And if in the Annamalai University, an institution whose contribution to the people-oriented study of Tamil at University level will be double-loaded when the cultural history of India comes to be printed, we, alumni, who have gained thirst for knowledge, value of wisdom, love or art, patriotic pride, parliamentary tolerance and, above all, strength of character, we must forever be grateful. The most endangered species of our time is men of character; the extinct species are public spirited, people-oriented, selfless souls. Shall we re-learn what we imbibed from this hallowed spot and remake Indian man?

I thank you all with feelings too deep for expression and pray to be forgiven for truthful irreverence. I close with the profound wish that it be given to the Annamalai University to contribute its portion to the nation's redemption of its cultural tryst with ultimate destiny.

# 2
# I was a Prisoner

*I know not whether Laws be right,*
*Or whether Laws be wrong;*
*All that we know who lie in gaol*
*Is that the wall is strong;*
*And that each day is like a year,*
*A year whose days are long.* *(OSCAR WILDE)*

As a young lawyer I picked up a lucrative practice and thanks to my father's popularity as advocate, I began my career on a note of success at the bar. Indeed, within a few years time, I acquired a leading standing with practice both on the civil and criminal sides. I was even recommended by the then District Judge Krishnaswamy for appointment as Public Prosecutor and Government Pleader. These were high offices in those days (the thirties and the forties). Moreover, there were outstanding senior lawyers at the Tellicherry Bar. Having made my mark as a young bright advocate not merely landlords and the well-to-do sections but also the workers and peasants sought my services in court. I became a public figure of sorts and was in the committees of government in that sub-district Tellicherry. Although my income largely came from the landed gentry, I was more known for my criminal practice. To appear for the working class, to defend the peasants in their struggles to fight for the accused in sensational cases was to become a favourite was a criminal lawyer, even if considerable civil practice also belonged to me. My human rights concerns were sensitised and I protested against the police torture, harassment of workers by industrialists and by the denial of fair demands of the organised peasantry by the feudal landlords. The fact that I was a non-official member in Government committees was, in the advisory committee of the Sub Jail, was the secretary of the S.P.C.A of which the Sub Collector was the President, did not remove the public impression that I was leftist and nationalist. True, I had appeared in a number of cases where leading communists were accused and where the vested interests of leading landlords and industrialists were at stake. To brand me as a fellow-traveller was a game of the vested interests.

Then came the Calcutta thesis of 1948 with B.T. Ranadive's militant call for seizing power. I was against violence and was a Gandhian. Indiscriminate arrests of communists were taking place and there was a rumour that I might be detained because I was vocal in my protest against irrational rashes of arrest of innocent cadres. Since I was critical of the B.T. Ranadive's strategy and was on friendly terms with Gandhians and officials since I was a successful lawyer with a standing in the district and my father was a leading lawyer and important public figure with big landlords as his clients there was no apprehension of my being arrested. No overt act or communist proclivity could be attributed to me and my life was transparent. It would be a baseless move and tactless treachery to detain me since government knew everything about me. (*Nevertheless, it did happen*). After nightfall, my wife and I were eating our dinner. She was weak since only five days had passed after the second baby Paramesh was born. As we were eating, the sound of a jeep driving up to my house was heard. What was it about? Some client? He could wait for the lawyer's convenience. But no. The circle inspector of Tellicherry whom I had cross-examined several times severely walked straight to the house impolitely. What brings you here Mr. Bhandare? I asked. To arrest you, he said, because Government has directed that you be detained under the preventive detention law. You may finish your meal and get into the jeep. I had no option but to obey. In the police station I was given a chair to sit which was the only privilege I enjoyed in the lock-up. My father was in

Quilandy, 30 miles away, in his country villa. My uncle, a lawyer of Tellicherry, came to see me but could not help me out of the lock-up. My father too, on getting tidings of my confinement in police custody, rushed to the place and gathered that only the Government could release me.

We have in our country Central Jails, sub-jails and police lock-ups where people are kept in custody. The worst of the three is the police lock-up where there is no sun, no entry of wind (a small aperture) nor any privacy whatever. The only company is that of the uniformed constables talking in rude diction which was part of their culture. I had to suffer it. There is no decent latrine and the dirty one we had was virtually open to public view because a constable stood watch near you as if every detainee was likely to escape from the toilet. The torture of the lock-up was over when I was taken to the nearby sub jail where conditions, from the standpoint of decency, were vulgar but far better than the police lock-up situation.

Before removing me to the detinue destination, the special ward in Central Jail, the Superintendent of Police (SP) took me home to make a routine ritual of search, with dubious potential for recovery of incriminating material. They found none but to their surprise my office room was stacked with records of civil litigation of rich clients. Where are the communist papers, the S.P. queried. None there were and they discovered that I had leading civil practice and less criminal work. But the notice served on me was that I was actively aiding in underground communist work and using the court for communist propaganda. Concocted lies and outrageous inventions were the charges served on me!

In the afternoon I was removed to the Central Jail in Cannanore and caged in a cell. I was all by myself. Iron bars and stone walls talked to me mutely. A warden would occasionally pass that way. There was no latrine with a sense of privacy and one had to make-do with the available facilities. In the loneliness of the prison cell time stood still. The minutes would not move and the hour slept with no duty to perform. The jail food what all that I had. The days, once in a long while, were punctuated by brief interviews once a week with close relatives. A low wall separated us and a warden stood hear as if some dangerous secret would be communicated. I had some plain paper with me and a pencil. I was drawing a rough blueprint of the house I had planned to build on a lovely plot I had bought before the police nabbed me. Somehow the jail staff misconceived my rough draft in pencil as a plan of escape; and so the paper was taken away. During daytime and night plenty of bugs spread under the bed and sucked the blood and at night, on top of the bug menace, came the mosquitoes winging, singing and stinging. So sleep was a feat and this ordeal went on for days.

I came to know that my father had rushed to Madras to meet Minister Madhava Menon. He was an important minister in the Madras Government but he was an advocate by profession and my father's friend and neighbour at Calicut. Madhava Menon had known me too. My father met him and gave the shocking news that the Madras Government had detained his son. "My son is a lawyer of standing and has a reputation in the District. Merely because he appeared for A.K. Gopalan and in some communist cases, he could not be kept in detention. Kindly have him released at once". This was my father's appeal made with feeling and impatient sense of justice. The minister responded and promised to help. He took my father to the Chief Minister Omandur Ramaswamy Reddiar who had directed the detention personally.

Why did the Chief Minister have to order detention when the District Collector had the power? Thereby hangs a tale. One day, a month before my detention, Arunachalam I.C.S, who was the District Collector of Malabar at Calicut, informed me at Tellicherry through his Secretary, to meet him the next day at 10 a.m. I was mystified as to why the Collector should summon me. Anyway, I promptly reported before Arunachalam at the appointed time. Are you a communist, he asked? I replied in the negative emphatically. Then he pursued the conversation with a stern intonation "but my government is determined to suppress the communists' violent movement hinting at the then notorious Calcutta thesis. Whoever is not our friend is our foe, he remarked. I told him that barring defending cases in court I had no art or part in any violent plots. I left the Collectorate and felt that he was satisfied with my stand. I learned later that leading congressmen who were industrialists of North Malabar had met and discussed my detention. They were, in a way, known to me well and had even engaged me in their civil cases, but they were hell-bent on liquidating the communist popularity. Vain hope! They thought this could be thwarted by my legal services which were available to the workers if arrested, being deprived Marx was too revolutionary for their small heads to understand. My detention was one measure they felt was necessary. They further felt that the Collector was not inclined to detain me. So they invited the Inspector General of Police, Vijayaraghavan O.I.P for a dinner discussion. They impressed on him the need to keep me out of the way. Mr. Vijayaraghavan, together with the Congress high-ups, cooked up a story that the Collector Arunachalam was a brahmin and was not willing to use his power to detain me, Krishna Iyer, another Brahmin. Therefore, the Government itself from Fort St.George, should detain the young leftist lawyer. The IGP met the Chief Minister, more or less gave this vicious version and pressed for his personal intervention because of the Collector's inaction. However, when my father explained my position at the bar, my standing in society and my co-operation in constructive work of government without any association in communist violence, Mr. Madhava Menon supported him. The Chief Minister directed my release at once. By the time the order trickled down to the prison Superintendent, I had endured thirty long days of insufferable incarceration. These thirty days burnt into me with acid fury. The hatred for unjust detention and love of personal liberty became my inalienable conviction. I knew jail life and resolved to undo, if some day I could, the slings and arrows of outrageous jail misfortune for every free Indian.

Please remember that political prisoners did not have to do hard labour and during day time enjoyed the freedom to sit in the verandah and meet fellow detainees. But at sunset you are back behind bars with bugs and mosquitoes abounding around and hardly any comfortable bed to sleep on. Long years later, in April 1957 I became minister for Prisons in Kerala and did all I could to transform prison atmosphere and reconcile it to the dignity that every prisoner is entitled to. My best constituency, because of the amenities I made available to prisoners during my term as minister, was the Kerala Prison Community. I allowed fresh air and brood sunlight to flow into cells, provided toilet facilities inside, permitted reasonably decent clothing and established canteens. Singing and playing were diversions for inmates and other freedoms and facilities made their life less than animal existence.

The anxiously awaited end of the month long imprisonment came to a close 30 days—count them in hours—later. They were the measure of my separation from my life's partner Sarada. The pangs of separation were mutual for me and my wife and I realised the poignancy of Shakespeare in Hamlet:

*Forty thousand brothers could not, with all their quantity of love, make up my sum. (Hamlet)*

The sorrow was shared by my affectionate mother. The family was re-united.

This was the end, but in the end is the beginning. This detention branded me a pro-Communist fellow-traveller which was a half-truth because I was Gandhian as well, and had some fundamental differences with Marxism. But the event was a turning point in my life. For, when in December 1951 candidates had to be chosen for the elections under the new Constitution. I became an obvious choice of the KMPP-CPI Alliance. Never would have been my inclination to fight an election. But with the detention my political complexion changed and I won the election. My public life and vision underwent a qualitative change.

Decades later, I became judge of the Supreme Court and wrote the Sunil Batra judgements dealing with prison conditions. It was humanism writ large. Sunil Batra jurisprudence, though delivered in the seventies in the Supreme Court as judgements, was inscribed in my soul in 1948 in the Cannanore Cenral Jail. He who has never lost his personal liberty does not know life in its entirety.

# 3

# Experiments in Law Making—as MLA, as Minister and as Judge

The rule of law is a basic feature of the constitution and as a lawyer by profession I was committed to the country's governance by jural command rather than by executive fiat. Where the rule of law is under eclipse tyranny, wearing democratic garb, dominates. When the judiciary, by hermeneutic inhumanity, lays down as law what is injustice, there springs the need for immediate rectification by amendatory legislation. Such a situation arose when I was a member of the Madras legislature. The High Court of Madras struck down as ultra vires a benign *'rule'* under the Malabar Tenancy Act whereby fair rent was ameliotorily fixed. The provision could be saved provided there was a substantive section in the Act empowering the Government to fix fair rent. So all that was needed to save the fair rent rule which operated to the benefit of a large number of agricultural tenants was to add in the Act a specific provision of empowerment. But, as usual, Government never bothered to know why the rule failed in Court, nor had it the creative sensitivity to salvage the invalidated rule by a remedial amendatory exercise. Indeed, there is a fundamental lacuna in our legal system which has been long ago pointed out by Benjamin N. Cardozo, pleading for an agency to moderate between the court and the legislature. More about it later. Regrettably, our legislatures do not care to play this corrective role and the court is not concerned with a communicative function.

Acutely sensitive to the cause of the Malabar tenantry I lifted the veil and discovered the simple solution of introducing a short new provision. Instead of educating the indifferent minister or bureaucrat for whom this was a matter of little concern. I drafted a small provision validating the rule and introduced it as *a private member's bill* in the Legislative Assembly. Rajaji was the Chief Minister and too tall for small me. Drawing by lot my bill got the turn and I moved it briefly explaining the purpose. Chief Minister Rajaji permitted the introduction but insisted on opposing the further passage until Government was satisfied about its need. Later, I met the Chief Minister and pleaded with him how the bill was meant to revive the rule framed by the Government to favour the tenants but was struck down by the court, mindless of the consequences. Rajaji then told me that he would consent to the later processing of the bill in the House only *if all the M.L.As from Malabar* signified their approval of my bill. I was a member in the Opposition. There were Congress members on the Treasury Bench, including the Law Minister Kuttikrishnan Nair. How could I make them agree? I was worried they would oppose, having regard to the political credit involved. However, I approached every member from Malabar, regardless of party, explained the implication and persuaded each one to consent. Thus the bill was passed in the Assembly; but there was a Legislative Council which had to pass the bill to make it a law. So I approached the Malabar members of the Madras Legislative Council and converted them to my cause, which was simple and non-controversial. Eventually, my private members bill became law, very much to the advantage of the large number of little tenants of Malabar.

My direct turn to initiate legislation came when I became a minister in the Kerala State way back in 1957 April. The ministry was headed by E.M.S. Namboodiripad and I held the portfolios of law, home, social welfare, et al. Almost the very first bills introduced into the House were manifest proof of my concern for *women*. One of them was designed to repeal the Travancore Christian Succession Act and the Cochin

Christian Succession Act. Both the feudal Acts contained provisions outrageously discriminatory to women depriving daughters of equal shares as heirs. Had my repeal bill been passed, gender justice would have come to stay, but Jesus notwithstanding the Christian church and community leaders adopted an aggressively masculine hostility to the measure and mounted a vehement campaign. Largely because of this unexpected male opposition the bill was referred for circulation for public opinion. I had to give in on account of the organised Church opposition. The bill was allowed to lapse. Gender history had to wait for more than two decades for the Supreme Court, by a different interpretation, to invalidate the Travancore and Cochin legislations in the *Mary Roy case*. Another bill, simultaneously introduced with the earlier one mentioned above, was the Kerala Dowry Prohibition Bill. The obnoxious dowry system spared no community or class and made women mere commodities. This bill was fiercely opposed by male communalists. Here again I lost the battle because of the colossal antagonism for the measure organised by the Church and other like-minded male chauvinists. I speak from memory which is amnesic, but the fact remains that I fought for the sisters and daughters of Kerala at the earliest opportunity, in vain though. A number of measures, people-oriented in essence, were moved and passed during my tenure including benevolent building rent control legislation. Security of tenure and compassionately fair rent were the highlights of the law. Two novel bills may be adverted to here. One of them was the Kerala Court Fees Act which contained exemption from Court fee for some weaker classes. A novel provision for promoting efficient legal service to the people by way of legal aid and to provide social security measures for the legal profession was incorporated by section 76 of the Act. Another democratic provision which had a benignant objective was introduced by way of amendment to the Kerala Civil Courts Act. The following provision speak for itself.

*20 B. Constitution and Functions of Committees*

(1) *The High Court may, constitute a committee for civil court subordinate to it or for two or more for such courts.*

(2) *The functions of the Committee may include, among other things:*

  (i) *the dissemination by means of publicity, advice and Instruction of legal knowledge to the general public;*

  (ii) *the making of recommendations to the High Court or to the Government, regarding the improvements to be made to court buildings, amenities to be provided for the litigant public and lawyers and other matters of a similar nature;*

  (iii) *the bringing to the notice of the High Court the activities of the staff of the court in the discharge of their duties with a view to stamp out corruption and reporting to the Government specific cases of corruption, if any, for appropriate action; and*

  (iv) *the provision of facilities for the closer association between the members of the Bar and the Bench in considering matters of common concern.*

(3) The committee shall discharge such other functions as are assigned to it from to time by the High Court.

A large number of bills had been introduced during my time with focus on the common people. The Kerala Agrarian Relations Bill, a draft measure I radically conceived and introduced as a member of the Madras legislature. But it did not make headway because of Chief Minister Rajaji's stiff opposition. What failed in Madras could win support in Kerala. Of course, the Kerala measure was moved by the Revenue Minister Smt. K.R. Gouri with all the erudite support I could lend. My Madras bill contained more exciting provisions like the Peasants Day. Anyway, despite the Supreme Court striking down the Kerala Agrarian Relations Bill, the Kerala legislature managed to secure a progressive legislation on land reforms. Perhaps the work on agrarian reforms carried out in these days was almost a pioneering work for which the country must be grateful.

Law-making is a creative art. To introduce a bill, to follow it up through the three readings in the House, to meet challenges and criticisms and yet to get through to the fulfillment of one's legislative objective is not merely a debating success but a spiritual solace. Ultimately, when I look back to my tempestuous days as Law Minister, I feel the battles were well fought and victory worthily won.

My career as a judge also was marked by law-making achievements. It is wrong to assume that the judicial function is exhausted by adjudicating disputes. The role of the judges in developing jurisprudence is at once exciting and creative. Let me quote Lord Denning:

*Many of the Judges of England have said that they do not make law. They only interpret it. This is an illusion which they have fostered. But it is a notion which is now being discarded everywhere. Every new decision—on every new situation—is a development of the law. Law does not stand still. It moves continually. Once this is recognised, then the task of the Judge is put on a higher plane. He must consciously seek to mould the law so as to serve the needs of the time. He must not be a mere mechanic, a mere working mason, laying brick on brick, without thought to the overall design. He must be an architect—thinking of the structure as a whole—building for society a system of law which is strong, durable and just. It is on his work that civilised society itself depends.*

U.S. President Theodore Roosevelt once observed about the judges that "Every time they (judges) interpret contract, property, vested right....they necessarily enact into laws parts of a system of social philosophy The decisions of the courts on economic and social questions depend on their economic and social philosophy". It is thus indubitable that judges bygenerate new law. My experience on the bench confirms it. I must frankly confess that through judicial interpretation, I too have innovated law. I shall give but one instance of such a creative operation. In Bangalore Water Suply and Sewerage Board Vs Rajappa, speaking for a majority of the court, I gave meaning and content to the concept of 'industry' under the Industrial Disputes Act. When Parliament, after long years of pending litigation about what is an industry, slumbered resulting in a plethora of cases accumulating in the courts, the Supreme Court, speaking for the majority through me, ruled imparting a dynamic meaning to the simple word 'industry'. The judgment, for its law and language, has elicited tributes from jurists. In several other cases, I have had to adventure into semantic exploration thereby making interstitial law. This is permissible, even according to the great Justice Holmes. Law-making from the Bench is no usurpation of the Legislative function. On the contrary, it is a judicial obligation in the process of interpretative adjudication.

I may wind up by saying that as minister and judge, as a legislator sitting in the Opposition, I have had the pleasure of serving the rule of law, incidentally making new law which I do not regard as a sin even if robed the brethren when the occasion necessitates it.

Before I conclude I must give expression to one thought and one incident vis-a-vis the court as an interpreting body vis a vis the House as a legislative body. There must be a live link between the Bench and the House so that what takes place in the higher courts may stimulate creative action in the legisative bodies. The great American Judge, Justice Cardozo, while he was Chief Justice of New York Supreme Court, made this point:

The Courts are not helped as they could and ought to be in the adaptation of law to justice. The reason they are not helped is because there is no one whose business it is to give warning that help is needed. We must have a courier who will carry the tidings of distress. Today courts and legislature work in separation and aloofness. The penalty is paid both in the wasted effort of production and in the lowered quality of the product. On the one side, the judges, left to fight against anachronism and injustice by the methods of judge-made law, are distracted by the conflicting promptings of justice and logic, of consistency and mercy, and the output of their labours bears the tokens of the strain. On the other side, the legislature, informed only casually and intermittently of the needs and problems of the courts, without expert or responsible or disinterested or systematic advice as to the workings of one rule or another, patches the fabric here and there and mars often when it would mend. Legislature and courts move on in proud and silent isolation. Some agency must be found to mediate between them.

Much of litigation and legislative frustrations can be obviated if there is a mechanism geared to the communication between the superior courts with their interpretative pronouncements and the Houses of Parliament and Assembly which represent the needs of the people. Absent such an agency, a vigilance organisation watching over the fate of its legislations in the court can act to set right error where, on technical grounds, the judges nullify socially beneficial laws. I shall give but one example. As Law Minister I moved and got passed the Kerala Agriculturists Debt Relief Act which provided for scaling down of debts. A decree debt is also a debt but the High Court of Kerala, taking a technical view, refused the re-opening of decree debts holding that there is no specific provision in the Act which relate to decrees as such. When I saw a report of this nugatory judgment reported in the press, I moved, within a week, for a provision which will nullify the judgement and make good the omission pointed out by the judge. Then the law was salvaged and the agriculturists were saved. My emphasis is on a functional mechanism which will be in perennial operation—a sentinel on the qui vive invigilating and thereby serving the useful purpose of avoiding legislative stultification.

# 4

# Mass Sramdan and E.M.S. Ministry

It has been my conviction that participative democracy has meaning only if people are involved in constructive programmes. This is a Gandhian thought and a Mao-ze-dung vision. Gandhiji was the Founding Father of the grand idea that the masses are the builders of the nation even though they may not be politicians or members of elite professions. Production by the masses is the source and signature of economic democracy, according to Gandhiji. The great Mao put this principle into practice and made the vast masses of the Chinese people work for reconstruction of the country in the shape of dams and canals, handicrafts and other skilled products, and eventually made China a great power, endowing every humble Chinese with dignity of labour, shelter and primary needs of life.

When I took over as Minister on the gracious summons of E.M.S Namboodiripad my portfolios included Law, Home, Prisons, Social Welfare, Irrigation and Electricity. My vision of development in the implementation of each portfolio was governed by the fundamental idea, as earlier explained, that the people in the towns and villages, whether they belonged to the masses or classes, were the real resource and operational power for Kerala of the future.

A people-oriented reflection of development convinced me that I could catalyse progress in every department under my charge provided I was able to harness the vast human energy and canalise it along creative direction and developmental dimension. There were people in large numbers who were idle though willing to work. There were natural resources waiting to be exploited which would employ the hands and minds of the common folk, given the opportunity of using the masses along productive lines. Though I hit on the idea of "sramdan" as the wonder drag whereby the pathology of want and misery could be corrected. I called it Operation Sramdan. By sramdan, I did not mean mere primitive manual work of the unskilled labourer fit for no specialised job. On the contrary, I envisaged mobilisation of people in various walks of life, skilled and unskilled labourers, engineers, doctors, lawyers and other professionals who could, if they would, add to the stock of value added assets which would go a long way in fulfilling the various needs of the Nation. In this perspective, I realised that there was large scope for bringing together nature's blessings, which were currently going waste, and people's capacity which remained untapped at present. Visionary statesmanship, therefore consisted in cutting across political divisions and class barriers and utilising, the human reservoir into fertilising, on a planned basis, the requirement of the people. This formula could be applied vis-à-vis, my ministerial tasks viz, to irrigation, electricity, prison reform, better policing, judicial reform and even legislation based on political consensus.

Let me begin with irrigation and its potential for bringing water to parched fields and awakening the people who had time to spare to donate their time and energy for the country's cause. One important step in this novel people's project was to make a study of the water resources of the State. The engineers, in the irrigation and electricity departments responded to my call and we produced a master plan of the water resources of Kerala. Thus we got a picture of the water wealth we possessed. But big projects were beyond our financial resources. *Small is beautiful*, is what Gandhiji taught us. Numerous minor irrigation projects and their feasibility (such as lift irrigation) became the concern of our irrigation engineers. And this was precisely what Prime Minister Nehru emphasised, when the master plan of the water resources of Kerala was presented to him ceremonially at the Kerala pavilion of a national exhibition held in Delhi in 1958. Everyone demands a big Bhakra-Nangal, a giant project, in every state, said Pandit Nehru. What we need is not mega projects but mini-schemes. Kerala, he argued, world do well to execute a large number of small and medium sized projects, which could be executed without huge cost and long delay. It struck me as a happy reconciliation between resources and manpower.

**A Divagation Relevant to Sramdan and Appropriate Technology Agreeable to the Indian Village**

Gandhi, all in all, was the true father of intermediate technology. His concept of development, of a model community, was through *volunteer* work and commitment to village regeneration. Schumacher once called Gandhi the greatest economist of the century because human worth, human dignity and, human hand were the key to the Gandhian concept of mass employment with no idle hands. It is important to remember the values implicit in this people-oriented development model coincides with the Cocoyoc Declaration adopted in October 1974 by a symposium convened by UNEP and UNCTAD on patterns of resource use, and development strategy. "Development must be designed, even at the humblest level, as a process of ensuring the advancement of man through his own endeavours". (says UNESCO). "Development must be aimed at the spiritual, moral and material advancement of the *whole* human being both as a member of society and from the point of view of individual fulfillment", repeats UNESCO. Thus, the primary aim was to meet the basic human needs of the average villager, giving full employment and self-realisation through work which implies the right not to be alienated by production processes that use human beings as mere tools or dispense with them as otiosity. This perspective inspired me in my approach to rural irrigation and electrification although I inhaled the idea from Vinoba Bhave and Mao's New China long before the UNESCO resolution.

Mobilise the people on constructive lines is the Mao Mantra whereby even mountains can be moved. But then, no project can win in the absence of a systematized plan of action wherein the concern of all elements are considered collectively and implemented according to plan. On this general foundation, I proceeded to frame my approach to galvanising the masses to donate labour for minor irrigation works. I had the hearty support to my philosophy and approach from the Secretary Irrigation, the Chief Engineer Kuttyamu and the substantial bulk of the engineers in the Irrigation Division. It is important to note that for success, a minister must be able to carry his administrative team with him. Kuttyamu was a brilliant officer with a people-conscious mind. Madhavan, his assistant, P.H. Vaidyanathan, the superb Superintending Engineer were highly co-operative in my visionary scheme. My idea was to call district conferences where representatives of the irrigation, revenue, block development and panchayat sectors were invited. All the political parties too were invited to participate in the district conferences. I must say that the Collectors entered into the spirit of my movement, even as political representatives, regardless of party consideration, attended each Conference. Each block was taken up for consideration of its (minor) irrigation potential. Panchayat Presidents came forward with ideas. So did the Block Development Officers (BDOs). The Irrigation and Revenue departments made available all the information at their disposal. I addressed the meeting with passion and conviction stating that we propose a people's transformation in the irrigation realities of each area. Interestingly, proposals, criticisms and other views about local projects were presented. The whole atmosphere was informal and informational. The mood was creative. I had made it clear that people's contribution by way of *fifty percent Sramdan* in the construction process should be forthcoming, as part of the people's contribution. Popular participation had patriotic value, I stressed. Panchayat after panchayat enthusiastically welcomed the offer. The Engineers and Revenue Officers were given specific dates to make blue prints of projects. Local vehicles were offered by the BDOs. The political parties took a positive stance and discarded negativity. Given opportunities and facilities, given the confidence that tangible results, not tantallising hopes, were the prospect, commoners would manifest talent, present realistic plans and display engineering skill.

I covered district after district and many new projects came up from discussions. *Sramdan* offers were readily made. In short, reconstruction programme in the irrigation dimension came to life and I could see how people generally were impressed with the new vision. India lives in her villages and villagers. Let me make it clear that we did not consider big projects but only mediumsized and mini projects. Studies were made and pamphlets were prepared explaining each project in Malayalam and the expected benefits if the projects were harvested as planned. Power to the people, guided and catalysed, is decentralised democracy—India's hope. Life is not logic, but experience. My experience was sometimes shared by my wife who, travelled with me, watched the proceedings and felt excited. I went from village to village, town to town and found large gatherings of people willing to pour their energy patriotically for executing projects. I would preside and explain briefly. My engineer would give the details in simple Malayalam and supportive speeches were forthcoming from various parties. Indeed, I inaugurated implementation of the whole State plan from a panchayat (Srikaryom), the President of which then belonged to the Opposition in the Legislative Assembly. However, he welcomed me at a huge gathering and announced that even though he, as party, opposed my government, he and his friends actively were supportive people-based schemes like this. A few thousand people had assembled to work free that day for the digging of a large village tank. The work was substantially completed in one day. The Promethean energy of the people at work is the creative creed of Brave New Bharat. This was constructive patriotism in action.

Another instance at Kottarakkara. A medium-sized irrigation project was to be inaugurated with mass participation as part of the package approved at the District Conference at Kollam. When I arrived, a leading congressman, with a large number of people, welcomed me into a public meeting. The Congress party was bitterly opposed to our Government at that time. The Congress President of the locality, presiding over the meeting described me as Lord Krishna bringing the blessings of water and so, though we are opposed to his Government, we warmly participate in the irrigation project. The local landlord gave us a feast in token of his appreciation of the advantage gained by the village. Quite a crowd, ready with tools, started digging the canal. At that time I noticed a lorry load of young men arriving and joining us. On enquiry I learned that they were the staff of the collectorate wanting to offer Sramdan. Why? I queried. Sir, we were inspired by your meeting at the Collectorate and felt that we should share by toil in the construction of the canal atleast as a token. I was deeply touched and felt convinced that by consensus we can rouse the masses into involvement in national reconstruction. The building of Bharat would be an exciting but realistic operation provided the millions threw themselves into the task. In yet another place, the Collector and the D.S.P accompanied me and were moved beyond expectation by people's *sramdan* operation. The M.L.A, Sri Govinda Pillai, of the party in power accompanied me throughout. Everyone was thrilled and the Collector told me that this phenomenal performance of the masses in action could not last a week after I left the ministry. Party spirit will spoil the game. There is a point in what he said. Party partisanship is the bane of politicisation of national reconstruction. People are inspired provided party considerations do not mar the undertaking meant for the people generally. I would call the whole movement as Operation Bhageeratha.

A variant of the Sramdan project involving semi-skilled workers may be a useful illustration of my thesis that local people, given inspirational incentives, will rise to levels of free labour, quantitatively more enthusiastic than contract labour. The project I have in mind is land reclamation at Kayamkulam from the shallow backwaters which could be utilised for large paddy cultivation. When the engineers and I arrived we were greeted by an adventurous mass of people prepared for reclamation work with boats and appliances. My recollection is that around 100 acres of land was dredged and the earth so recovered made part of the nearby fields. It was a rare feat which would have cost a large sum and long delay, had hired labour been employed. In my introductory remarks, I spoke with feeling that the gathered people were doing reclamation for their own children as common property. Once they were convinced, they tirelessly toiled to execute nationally useful reclamation. A few years later, an Irrigation Engineer came to me together with an Agricultural Officer. Meanwhile I had become a judge of the High Court. They told me that the people, all enthusiastic, were waiting for me to inaugurate the harvesting of the first paddy crop grown in the reclaimed land. You planned it; people executed it. We planted rice and it is ready for harvest. With creative joy you must take the sickle and cut the first crop although you may be a judge now. I was overcome with the spirit of the invitation. I went and did the job, sharing the joy of the people there. Long years later I gathered that the Revenue Department had taken over the land. What is stranger still, now the reclaimed land is where an electrical (thermal) plant has been constructed by the NEPC.

My grand vision of involving people in national construction did not stop with irrigation. I was minister for electricity. In those days, Malabar was starved of electricity in the villages, especially North Malabar. I extended the experience of Sramdan to the distribution of Electricity to villages. I held conferences for rural electrification, with political parties and panchayats participating. I offered electricity to any village which offered to me sramdan in the construction work like digging of deep pits for planting strong, tall 'treated' poles, drawing of electrical lines and the like. I even asked for teak poles to be supplied by the people if the area was rich in teakwood. I remember, with bewitching joy, how even political opponents and Trade Unionists joined this electricity extension scheme supplying *sramdan*. For the villages political antagonism is eclipsed where developmental perspectives animate implementation of schemes. I remember P.R.Kurup, then a fierce political opponent welcoming me gloriously when I visited his village for (shramdan sponsored) supply of electricity. He was a powerful president of the Panchayat there and mobilised the working class to sweat and toil for the people's sake. The electricity distribution work was completed to the joy of the people. The State Electricity Board first demurred on the ground that it was risky to entrust lay people with technical work. But they found to their surprise that people enthusiastically dug pits, drew lines and did what was skilled work beyond lay capacity. Given the will every person will do what may appear to be beyond him. The Electricity Board, in its Annual Report, welcomed the scheme and agreed that it was an achievement. What pleases me is that with popular co-operation villages of North Malabar saw light to their joy.

My success as minister, to the limited extent it was, could be traced to my politically impartial finger on the pulse of the people. Party governs, but governance must embrace the entire community without exploiting little achievements for party glorification. Politicization has ruined the country, divided and alienated the masses; but I still hope that if national inspiration, untainted by party considerations, summons people to the task, they will respond with service and sacrifice.

# 5

# My Creative Tenure as Minister for Prisons

Stone walls do not a prison make
Nor iron bars a cage;
Minds innocent and quiet take
That for an hermitage;
If I have freedom in my love,
And in my soul am free;
Angels alone, that soar above,
Enjoy such liberty.

I took over the portfolio of Jails and Social Welfare the day I became a minister, i.e., 5 of April 1957.

I have seen prisoners in Kerala Jails. I have been a prisoner myself as a detainee for 30 days in a Malabar Central Jail. I have been a visitor of a Sub Jail for several years. I have read about prison life and have known cases of under-trials languishing in prison for long years. I have come across cases of innocent persons convicted by court on perjured testimony. I have been shocked by humans swing on hangman's rope who were not guilty but convicted by court, on procured evidence and sentenced to life or death. I have come across, in my professional career as lawyer, instances of innocent young men being executed on hasty judicial verdict. In short, I have been horrified by prisoners being humiliated, tortured, deprived of privacy and denied primary human rights. I have seen a senior lawyer of the Tellicherry bar taken into custody and remanded to jail, having to carry even his faecal matter and his own urine. Mosquitoes and bugs sting and bite and bleed on humans in cells inside. These wretches have no cot nor bed but mere mattress and the bare floor to lie on. Sensitive souls are shocked as allegedly dangerous (but presumed innocent) under-trials are taken handcuffed and sometimes chained. This is the iron behind iron bars. These ghastly mibiux have been in my sight when I was in custody more comfortably as detainee. To cap it all, many prisoners, sentenced to rigorous imprisonment, had to wear a curious cap proclaiming that they were convicts and not patriots (as one might suppose from the Gandhi caps). Even as a detainee, every moment has been misery for me, every hour a horror and every day a never-ending ordeal. I had read Oscar Wilde in my college days. Let me recite:

> And the wild regrets, and the bloody sweats,
> None knew so well as I:
> For he who lives more lives than one
> More deaths than one must die
>
> I know not whether Laws be right,
> Or whether Laws be wrong;
> All that we know who lie in gaol
> Is that the wall is strong;
> And that each day is like a year.
> A year whose days are long.
>
> And yet, and yet,
> These Christs that die upon the barricades,
> God knows it I am with them, in some ways.

All this harrowing experience was imprinted on my soul on 5th of April 1957 when I took over ministerial control over conditions of incarceration in all the penitentiaries of Kerala. I took it as a solemn responsibility to humanise these hell holes and lend dignity and decency to these institutions and their inmates. This was a big challenge, because the prison department itself is a prisoner of iron conventions and hierarchical authorities. Prisoners, including even under-trials, were presumed to be criminals and harsh conditions of life in prison were regarded as obligatory justice. So that is what Hell is. Justice is the means by which established injustice is sustained. The Judge signs away a sentence and never bothers what infliction he awards. The police arrest and take a man to the lock up in the police station. He is nearly stripped and privacy is alien to him. Even answering calls of nature are done in the view of the policemen or the jail warder. This was state terrorism against which I protested morally, mentally and spiritually. It must be undone and sun and air, once banished from the lock-up and jail cell had to be given freedom to enter. When prisons came under my charge, I resolved to revolutionize the conditions and humanise the tormenting cells which had been hallowed by our national rebels sentenced for sedition during the British days. Harsh traditions and administrative praxis are difficult to overcome. Government has power, ministers can exercise it being pachydermic politicals, but the beaurocracy inhibits radicalism and burkes humanism, notwithstanding the Constitution and its progressive value marvels. However, I was determined to use the Kerala prison world as an experimental laboratory for constitutional parameters.

I endured prison life in 1948 for a month and knew its torments at first hand. That was the best education in prison reforms for me. Students interested in the transplantation and transformation of ideas from the Secretariat to the Judiciary may usefully read the two Sunil Batra cases of the Supreme Court rendered by me in 1978. Likewise, the abolition of hand cuffing by me in 1957 as minister reincarnated in a Supreme Court judgment in 1980. Ideas don't die and indeed are an incitement for change. As Minister in charge of Jail, I visited central jails and sub-jails, talked to prisoners and brought reforms based upon realities.

The first thing I did was to remove the insulting convict costume, replace it with the ordinary dress of a Malayalee, because I did not want a prisoner to feel, every time he looked at his clothes, that he was a sentencee and not a soul meant to be redeemed. I started a canteen inside every Central Prison. There were three in Kerala. Why did I do it? Corruption inside prison was ordinarily through bribing wardens to smuggle into jail beedies and other articles, freely available in the market but totally banned inside jails. I saw no reason why this ban should continue. If the jail canteen sells consumer items like outside, things could be purchased freely for payment. I introduced the wage system for prisoners, although the wages were low, being a first step in that direction in India. I liberalised interviews and parole system. I was convinced that de-humanisation is aggravated by solitude in prison and rehumanisation could be promoted by frequency in meeting one's family at home. Indeed, when I visited Stockholm in 1958, I visited a jail there and prisoners were allowed to live with their family a day every week. The tension built up by mentally wounding the prisoner, under-trials or convicts, does serious harm to his psyche. This is a cruel dimension of punishment which the law does not demand. I found the changed system worked well. A most interesting experiment which gave me soulful satisfaction may perhaps be narrated here. Of course, I used to allow prisoners to go and see exhibitions in the town. Of course, safety was taken care of. I gave sports facilities inside the jail as also opportunities for singing bhajans. But the special case I mentioned above is about a prisoner who, when I met him inside the jail, narrated his personal story in tears. Sir, in a quarrel between my wife and my mother I attacked my mother and she died. I was convicted to life term. I have no grievance against my sentence, but my wife and child who depended on me are starving. I am a professional musician with All India Radio accreditation. If you permit me to sing on the A.I.R. and see that the remuneration is sent to my wife direct, she would survive and I would sing and serve my sentence. I agreed, wrote to the A.I.R, assured them that he would be dressed like a Bhagavathar and the remuneration for singing may kindly be sent to the convict's wife. I wrote as a minister, received a favourable reply, organised periodical concerts by the prisoner and saved the family. Long years later, the prisoner was released (on remission) and returned home to normal life, I received a letter from him. By then I had become a judge of the Kerala High Court. The singer (former prisoner) wrote to me a letter: 'Sir, I was a homicide and you made me a human being. Now I am released and pray for you daily with your portrait in my prayer room'.

Liberal parole, though frowned upon by severe and oppressive traditions, is therapeutic, if rehabilitation is our prison policy. That being my conviction, rules for parole were progressively drawn up. I had occasion to grant parole to one Vasu Pillai who had been sentenced to life term. While on parole, he came to the visitor's gallery of the Assembly—an innocent democratic appetite! This was noticed by jinx eyed-opposition members who shouted at me for grant of parole for a life sentencee. I must caution here, with some trepidation, about amnesia affecting my narration. One convict, perhaps the same Vasu Pillai—had been sentenced to death and his mercy petition had been dismissed by the Governor, and by the President. This took place before I assumed charge as Minister. However, a writ petition in the High Court, on some ground affecting the validity of the sentence, resulted in a notice to the Government and Jail Superintendent. So the hanging was delayed and I came in as Minister with a humanitarian mission. The writ petition was dismissed but the man was alive. I am opposed to capital punishment, based on compassion and Gandhian philosophy. Death sentence is a barbarity even if the victim be a villain. I wrote to the Governor to grant commutation of sentence. I argued that one refusal is no bar to a humane reconsideration. However, the question arose whether after the President had rejected the representation it was open to the Governor to exercise his power. I took the view of a humanist jurisprudent that the Rashtrapati and the Rajpal had concurrent powers and therefore it was open to the Head of State to exercise clemency jurisdiction even after the President had declined. This ended in a controversial correspondence between me and the great Home Minister Sri G.B. Pant, the latter taking the view, supported by the Attorney General's opinion, that the President's refusal could not be re-opened by the Governor. I insisted, aided by my Advocate General's opinion, that the powers being concurrent and not hierarchical, there was no question of a superior authority vesting in the President, no reopening, no res judicata. Luckily for me, the noble Home Minister G.B. Pant, appreciating my compassionate stand, relented and found a solution. 'Kindly write to me with a request that I move the President to grant commutation; in that event I shall place the matter before the President for commutation. This was done by me readily because a life was at stake and salvation of a human soul was above legalism. Thus Vasu Pillai survived and later became a Tamil writer. Every stone has a sculpture within, if you know to carve it out. Inside every prisoner is a latent talent. The reformative theory is founded on the assumption that no man is born a criminal and every criminal can be redeemed into a good person. Every saint, I have maintained, has a past and every sinner a future. I described it in a lecture as Operation Valmiki.

In this context, it may be appropriate to mention about a successful correctional Conference I organised within a month or two of my taking office as Minister. The Central Law Minister A.K. Sen inaugurated it and judges from Kerala and Madras High Court participated. My welcome address was an erudite and luminous piece. Bernard Shaw had remarked: 'The object of punishment is to improve and nobody is improved by injuries'. This is the essence of correctional policy. The learned contributors to the conference concurred in this thesis and I was guided by this therapeutic perspective. While I was minister I experimented, and later as judge, my days in the Ministry educated me for my office as 'robed brother'. Be you monster or judge, excellence springs from the heart, cultured by compassionate imagination.

A few more matters may deserve specific mention. When I was a lawyer at Tellicherry, I was a visitor to the local sub jail. When I was an MLA in the Madras Legislative Assembly, I requested Government, through an interpellation, to make MLAs-ex-officio visitors of jails.

Rajaji, the astute and sardonic Chief Minister, repelled the idea, censuring the proposal as giving sinister access to politicians to pollute the prison ambience. I did not agree, because I thought that representatives of the people should know the conditions in jail and play a correctional role in improving the prison system. Anyway, my view did not get accepted with the suspicious person like Rajaji. But when I became a minister for jail I reversed and, as a good experiment in democratic access, I made all MLAs jail visitors. The Heavens did not fall nor was hell let loose. Politics did not sully the jails; very few MLAs visited correctional homes because prisoners had no vote and therefore did not form part of their concerned constituency. Nevertheless, I felt the gesture people-oriented, bringing jail life to the attention of people's representatives. Another move I made to bring jail image closer to public visage was to organise an annual day for every central jail. There would be a public meeting, speeches, and a play was put on the boards, the actors being prisoners. This gave the repressed inmates an opportunity to express their suppressed thoughts. Moreover the common people could know better what prison conditions were like. The right to know has a prison dimension.

Far more important was another step I had taken within a few days of the communist ministry taking over office. On April 9th or so (1957) I ordered that all the Central Jails would observe, as a festive occasion, two days each year relevant to each religion. Onam and Vishu (Hindus), the two Ids (Muslim), Christmas and Easter (Christians) were celebrated together by all the communities inside the prison; enjoyed a feast at the cost of the Government. This would promote, I thought, communal integration and a new camaraderie among the Hindus, Muslims and Christians within the prisons. The prison became a microcosm of communal amity through this process. Facilities for sports and games and for fine arts were provided to make life relaxed and less tense. Rehabilitation and reformation were the motivation behind the policy of transformation which prevailed during my brief tenure as jail Minister. Prison term, if continued too long, would make people hardened criminals, thus defeating the punitive humanism of modern penology. Therefore, a certain liberal approach to remission of sentences was adopted. Ordinarily, if the record of the prisoner was reasonably good, a lifer was released after eight years, so that the victim may still have time to turn a new page in life and be less hostile to society. I am aware that parliament, in its Legislative security, has since enacted a minimum of 14 years for life sentencees. But the clemency jurisdiction of Governors and President transcend this limitation.

Facilities for young prisoners to study and take examination were provided and I know of some young students making good at the examination. I must caution that persons of young age were never admitted into a prison. They were sent to a juvenile home, where special attention was paid to promote their conduct and capabilities. I still remember with joy an excellent juvenile home opened by me in Trivandrum. I had the enthusiastic help of a retired judge R. Sankaranayana Iyer (a correctional enthusiast) and a young specialist Dr. R. Prasannan (a fine man and later a Legislative Secretary) in Operation Juvenile Reformation. Alas! Both Sankara Narayana Iyer and Prasannan are no more. There were many social activists, including Sri, S.K. Kader (long later a judge of the High Court) who helped Government in the correctional project. Indeed, it used to be remarked in those days that jails were my constituency. Rescue homes for women had also been started during these days when I was in charge of Social Welfare. A big push was given to progressive policies to rescue women who had been forced into anti-social ways. Circumstances compel deviancies of young women and salvation is not by prison torture but by awakening the finer side of the person. Humanism has many dimensions. Prisons, rescue homes and juvenile homes are theaters where social retrieval will pay dividends.

A minister in charge of the police force must have a special concern for their welfare. So I was trying to find out their problems and practical difficulties and ready remedies possible. Accommodation was an important item. I found that the police quarters were so constructed that there was only one room which offered privacy. This was obviously inadequate for a policeman with wife and children. My finance minister was a fine man and close friend. But Achutha Menon was so parsimonious that he would never release funds unless circumstances compelled him. I found it difficult to get money from him to improve police quarters. So I managed to convert a verandah into a private room so that the police family could have two rooms at least to live and sleep separately. To augment the income of the constable, I decided to start welfare organisations where the members would be the wives of the police personnel. The Khadi and Village Industries Board helped me set up funds where the women could work. I also persuaded them to make envelope, pickles, pappad and other useful articles. The Special Armed Police and Malabar Special Police needed their domestic items of consumption and the Home Department could buy stationery so made. This provided a small but sufficient market and means of livelihood. Thus, I assured employment on a mini-scale for the wives of policemen and this came in hand for these poorly paid personnel. The Special Armed Police of Trivandrum had a talented wing who could give professional entertainment. They were allowed, subject to their duty and discipline and decorum, to perform at public functions and take 50 per cent for them and the other half for a common fund. I used to talk to the policemen personally about their condition. Some would require mutual transfers which could be easily arranged although in the routine course the procedure was dilatory and some unsympathetic note would end in the rejection of the application. On the whole, I felt that the police force, provided a compassionate approach were made, could be made humane. For instance, the rule 'shoot to kill' was changed by me and they were required to disable but not kill. This saved a number of lives even where firing was to be resorted to. The warm human being inside the cold Khaki is good, provided the spirit is kindled. My IGP once complained, Sir you call us whenever a lathi charge or firing is necessary but never put us as members in a milk distribution committee or socially useful body, the result is that people look upon us not as gentlemen with difficult duties but as violent flagellants. I could understand this and did my best to remove the grievances. Once I suggested to the Health Minister that people who underwent vasectomy be given monetary incentive since the population problems deserved to be tacked by novel means. When he declined I drew on the resources of police establishment and gave ten days extra leave and some money for every policeman who underwent vasectomy. Many did turn up for the operation. I had persuaded Circle Inspectors to offer *shramadan* for my small irrigation works where I had given a call for people's shramadan. Believe it or not, several police stations did offer some sharamdan; it may perhaps be dismissed as token. But symbolic identification with the masses in constructive work by disciplined policemen has a value and wins people's goodwill.

By way of aside, I may mention a single instance where a plantation strike was going on and in a tense situation the police opened fire and a worker was killed. When I came to know about it as Home Minister, I felt unhappy and hurried up the hill to meet the widow of the plautation worker who died. I told her that I was the Home Minister and the bullet that took her husband's life, alas, came from the state police. I sat near her, shared her grief and pleaded that I was feeling contrition. I am of the view that any life lost diminishes humanity. I solaced her and sought her forgiveness. Later I relieved the trigger-happy District Police Officer of strike management responsibilities. He belonged to the traditional police culture and so I put a young man in his place, with a plea for humanism even while handling tense situations not uncommon in strike-bound areas. This was my general approach of compassion although I do not rule out stray police excesses even during my time. The Khaki does not change its colour merely because the Minister is a soft soul.

The Inspector General of Prisons Sri John and the Home Secretary Sri Krishnamoorthy were of the same humanitarian and penological wave-length with me and as a team worked with zeal for the success of jail reform in Kerala. Together we made Kerala's custodial centres a paradigm of redemption.

Here let me go into a divagation. Maybe, anecdotage is a sign of dotage. Even so, some anecdotes are too telling to be omitted. When cases of commutation came to Government they had to reach the Governor whose signature set the seal on the fate of the plea. While the pen of the Rajpal disposes, the mind of the minister decides. Save in the rare cases explained in Shamsher Singh's case, the minister considers and concludes and the Governor sets his approval as a matter of course. Once, in a clemency case during my tenure, the Governor sent for the whole file with the evidence in the case for him to judge whether the recommended death sentence reprieve should be rejected. I sent the file but made a note that the Home Minister (me) had already examined the merits and decided in favour of commutation and so the Governor may be spared the toil of reading voluminous pages of testimony of witnesses. The case ended that way.

Long years later, when I was a sitting judge on the Supreme Court Bench I visited Trivandrum. Srimati Jyoti Venkitachalam was the Governor of Kerala. She and I were in the Madras Legislature in the fifties together and so, as a gesture of courtesy, she invited me for lunch and we met at the Raj Bhavan. After lunch, we sat spending time going over old times. There was a heavy pile of files on the table and looking at that heap of papers, Governor Venkatachalam explained to me how she was paging through those papers which represented criminal case files. Her lament was that she had to go through them all to decide on commutation and reduction of sentences. The ministry had recommended early release or reprieve, but she was not satisfied about that concession to hardened criminals until she perused the files and herself satisfied about the merits of the applicants' conscientious but constitutionally untenable. I recollected my old days as minister recommending to the Governor not to be bothered about the file since, as minister, had taken the decision on commutation. However, I did not make any comments to the Governor about her position vis-a-vis that of the minister regarding the process of decision in the light of

Cabinet Government principle. The minister decides, the Governor signs.

I have heard it said that when Dr. S. Radhakrishnan was President, he often delayed and declined to sign death sentences even if the Home Ministry had rejected the plea for mercy. Delay you may, but decide the minister does.

Sometime later, a batch of writ petitions challenging the Parliamentary amendment obligating *fourteen years as minimum prison terms* for life sentences. Incidentally the power of clemency also became as issue in the course of arguments. I wrote the judgment for the larger bench and clarified the constitutional position. In the cabinet system of government (Westminster pattern) the Cabinet rules, the President reigns, the minister makes the decision, the President or Governor, by obligation, approves it except for a second consideration if necessary. Anyway Vasu Pillai, referred to earlier in this paper, saved his life because the Minister exercised his compassionate jurisdiction. He might have lost his life in all probability, had the last word belonged to the Governor.

By way of diversion, I may mention that in the case argued in the Supreme Court, a document was produced relating to some North Indian State where a remission of a few years sentence was granted only on the irrelevant ground that the minister was making his first visit to the prison. The court held that remission and commutation should be on rational considerations, not in the vanity, humour or fancy or other circumstance which had no relation to the incarceration or the prisoner's condition.

The reader now has before him some recollections of mine about the days when I was a Minister in charge of the Police Department. I add here, as a supplement, a long ago speech I delivered in the Legislative Assembly in support of the police budget. It reads fresh even today and the points made by me there are relevant to police management even after half a century.

Minister for Law (Shri V.R. Krishna Iyer) : Sir, I move for a grant of Rs. 2,03,43,200 under Demand XV—Police:

Sir, I think I should make a few remarks in support of

this Demand in the face of the criticisms that have very often levelled against this Department. I submit that in India to-day and in this State also a reorientation of the police policy is urgently necessary because we have got to transmute the Police State of the British period into a welfare State. The British Administration and our new Constitution are effective symbols of what the purpose of the Police State was and the objectives and glowing aims of a Welfare State and a socialistic pattern of Society should be. It follows that the Police which is the coercive arm of the Government should undergo a fundamental change in quality. Attempts have been made in various States to put this into effect. For instance, in Bihar, I believe a Committee has been constituted for the purpose. In Kerala, in a much bigger way and with more inspiring aims and objectives, a High Power Committee has been constituted for bringing about this transformation; and with a view to making the Police man a friend and a guide to the people instead of one who is there to harass, to tease and to frighten, I believe the House will lend its unstinted co-operation to the working of this Committee in a successful manner, so that we in Kerala may well take pride that we have led the way in making a new police policy suited to the changed circumstances in the country.

There may be criticisms about the police. I admit they are imperfect; they have their own traditions. We cannot overnight make angels of men. But we know which way the wind is blowing. We are aware of the changes that have to be brought about in the police in a Welfare State. I hope hon. Members of this House will give their valuable suggestions so as to quicken the pace of the change, and see to it that the criticisms do not injure the qualitative transformation that is sought to be attempted. I hope it will be appreciated that this is not a matter of politics at all. In a democracy one day one party may be in office and another day another party may be in office; but who ever rules, the set up, the orientation, the very fabric of the police administration has only to conform to the change in the Indian life which has been brought about with independence. This change has come in the social, political, and economic structure of the society and it must affect the police man and naturally the function of the Police in the new set up has to be different from the one which it was in the past. I would like to crave of the House to give this help to us to forge ahead this change. I do not say that suggestions coming from that side will be motivated. Let us look at these things in an impartial way. Let us have help from every side of the House; that will help the State as a whole. That is all about the High Power Committee.

I would like to mention again that the Police has a very difficult job to do. The laws made by the State have to be enforced by the Police. But then the Police by themselves may not to able to achieve this objective. You know that Parliament can do anything short of making man a woman but it would be fatuous to imagine that a piece of legislation can be enforced successfully by the Police alone. The prohibition policy is a notable example as to how without the fervent and imaginative support of the people, a law can be a tragic failure. I would therefore appeal to all the sections of the House to give their help in enforcing the changes because it is only through popular support and zeal that a law can be effectively enforced.

I may just inform the House of two or three social pieces of legislation which will be shortly moved here. The Suppression of Immoral Traffic in regard to which a new campaign is started is nothing new so far as this Government is concerned; but it is an All-India move. It indicates the signs of the social consciousness of the people having been awakened against this unsocial evil. Now we have to enforce the law dealing with immoral traffic in women which is a blot and a stain on our society. This evil should be removed. This task which is now entrusted to the Police, I request, may not be left entirely to the Police; the people must support this peoples' movement for the suppression of immoral traffic and they should be on the side of the Police, to guide them, to alert them and to make their endeavour successful.

Now I wish to say something in regard to prevention of begging. In this State there are certain pieces of legislation here and there in this matter; their enforcement in certain cities and towns has been attempted with the help of the Police, but, generally speaking, these matters are to have the dynamic support of the people as a whole even to achieve some amount of success. I, therefore, entreat the Members of this House without reference to which side they belong, to go to the rescue of the Police force in making our society cleaner by eradicating all these evils. Our people should become the vanguard in the enforcement of this legislation, and the Police on their part will be helpful.

One other thing about which I wish to make mention is this. In this Budget, there is provision for developmental activities by the Police. Here there was a question regarding wastage of time by this able bodied Armed Reserve Police. I do not think that time is being wasted by them doing nothing; for one thing, they have to undergo certain drills and physical exercises to keep themselves always physically and mentally fit; so that they can act readily when there is a call. Nevertheless, there is the important point that our Police force must mix with the common people and share their difficulties and happiness and also participate in their developmental activities, because a patriotic police force cannot separate itself from people's aspirations and from their magnificent endeavours. We are building in India a great socialistic State and in this vast endeavour we want the active participation of our Police. It has two distinct advantages; and secondly we are able to get as much contribution, manual and otherwise from all our people including the Police and other white collared people. Here the Police should lead the way; the Police in the State should be with the people in developmental enterprises. So, a sum is allotted for the Police for shramdan in the Budget; perhaps it is a unique feature here. I remember to have read our Prime Minister saying that the Police in some other State having built up a building all by themselves. The shramdan activities of the Police should be encouraged, because it is a right lead they are giving to the rest of the governmental services in the State. This is a distinctive feature to which I wish to draw your attention for your eventual acceptance.

Now, there is the complaint that our Police is having very little pay and that their job is arduous. There is some merit in it; they are really the underdogs and they are being paid inadequately. But, then you have to remember various factors when dealing with such a number of people. The Police force is a large force and even a little increase in their remuneration would swell into a huge sum which we will not be able to bear all of a sudden. But there are other ways in which their emoluments could be effectively increased. By helping them and their family members, by giving them opportunities to contribute to the society by producing more and also by having institutions where they can spend some time joyously in recreational activities, we can improve their lot. With this object in view, which 25 families of policemen are living, we are giving them Rs. 1,000 for starting these kshemakendras in various places. We are also starting Amber Parishramalayas and also giving some facilities for the children to enjoy themselves—children's park and such rudiments of pleasant life are being made available to the families of the Police. Government have taken a lead to help them by going half way by giving nucleus grant of Rs.1,000. The Khadi and Village Industries Board is also giving considerable help to them in this direction. I hope that the House will agree that these are really some aspects which bring sunshine to the otherwise monotonous and hard life of the police men.

I would like to mention just one other aspect by way of preliminary submission to this House and that is regarding the traffic accidents in the State. Of late, there has been an alarming increase in traffic accidents.

That is something that must cause a good deal of anxiety in the minds of all thinking people in the State. How could we put an end to this? Our State is highly populous; there are over 1,000 people living per square mile area which is an incredible number. Our roads are narrow and they cannot be widened because of the people living on either side. The only way we can eliminate the deaths of numberless children, men and women on our roads, is by making our people understand the rules of the road. Every now and then we hear stories of some lorry driven into a tea shop or house on the roadside or such other accidents happening—strange things unheard of in other places. How can we put an end to this menace on the roads? Young children are going to the schools not knowing whether they would return to their homes. I therefore suggest that we should evolve a sense of traffic consciousness among all sections of the people using the roads—the cyclists, the motorists, the pedestrians, the children, etc. The motorists should be made to stick to the rules of the road. The motorists should feel the agony of a family who is deprived of a child in a road accident. Every driver should feel it while he drives his vehicle. If it is done, these accidents could be minimised; it is not by prosecutions and fines imposed by courts that the road accidents could be prevented.

We must have a new consciousness, a new feeling and a thought of sympathy for those who frequent the roads. A driver, when he is called to order by a police man; should not feel that he is being harrassed; he should feel that it is a wholesome guidance that is given to him by a fraternal correctors and not merely as cumbersome engines of repression. Then regarding corruption, I do believe that there is some amount of corruption among the Police. Every effort is being made to eradicate the evil. Something will be done in future also to do away with this evil. Sometimes we find two or three people on one cycle and the whole family on one motor bike going along our roads. Such things are happening. These mean accidents. When a cyclist is being prosecuted or warned by the police or when a pedestrian Jay-walking on the road is asked to walk along the sides, he must not misunderstand the position. I hope a lead will be given by the House and they will also offer their valuable help in changing the public mind and make them really road conscious so that these road accidents could be minimised. I would also like to mention in this connection that the Armed Reserve Police act in the matter of enforcement of traffic rules and to regulate traffic and also to request the people to observe the rules of the road. I request the House that they should welcome this move and also encourage this move by the Police in the near future.

One other point to which I would like to draw the attention of the House is the terrific nuisance which is being caused by the din of microphones day in and day out in our residential localities, in the country-side, and everywhere. A man can be assaulted not only by physical force, but by the noise created by microphones—aerial attacks on his sleep. If there is marriage somewhere, the whole locality will not be able to sleep for days. Then you find every teashop keeper having a loud speaker using it in such a way as to attract people from a radius of one mile. For that he will play the Columbo radio or some other gramaphone record; that distracts the attention of the pedestrians and other road users causing accidents. In public interest, we have to regulate the use of microphones. I request the House that there should not be any political consideration in condemning the use of microphones in this manner. A Judge of the Madras High Court long ago said—there was a case before him that some pious dance and singing which was going on in the night until 2 a.m. or 3 p.m. should be restrained, as it was disturbing the sleep of the people all around which was not permissible—"Society's peace at night cannot be disturbed because of a few pious fanatics who want to jump and sing. That sort of anti-social piety is not permissible". Therefore from the nuisance aspect, from the point of regulation of social life in a calmer atmosphere, we have to regulate the use of these microphones, particularly near hospitals. We have our hospitals mostly located in busy areas. Suppose there is a public meeting held some 50 yards away with microphones and all kinds of noisy processions going on with loud-speakers. Suppose there is a patient who is operated upon that day in the neighbouring hospital; just imagine what would be his condition if his rest and sleep are to be disturbed by the din of all these activities. We want the stillness of the night guaranteed to every citizen of the State. From that view severe regulations have to be imposed. When those things come, Police will have to do their duty in enforcing those regulations and you should not then misunderstand them. These are certain particular things which I want to mention to you.

There are other points in regard to the Police, and I hope there would be some criticisms which I shall try to explain as far as possible. But one thing I wish to mention here. Whenever any complaint has been brought to my notice, prompt action was taken; every effort was made to see that impartial and effective police action is made available in the State to all parties irrespective of party affiliations. If there are still imperfections and drawbacks, that can be set right, if pointed out; but then, it is another thing to impute motives. So, I request this House to look at things in a generous spirit and offer constructive criticisms which will be listened to with great reverence, and as far as possible the state of things would be rectified without assumption of an air of infallibility.

With these words, I move this demand for the acceptance of the House.

Another supplement which I would like to add is excerpts from Sunil Batra vs. Delhi Administration (1978) where in a long and separate judgment I have expressed sentiments, thoughts and juristic views which are law today thanks to the ruling of the Supreme Court but finds expression even in my early Recollections. Ideas don't die. They bloom afresh and promote the human rights of those for whom the bells of the Constitution toll—the prisoners of India. The excerpts from Sunil Batra cases stress the consistency of my views and constancy of my commitment.

> The province of prison justice, the conceptualization of freedom behind bars and the role of judicial power as constitutional sentinel in a prison setting, are of the gravest moment in a world of escalating torture by the minions of State, and in India, where this virgin area of jurisprudence is becoming painfully relevant. Therefore, explicative length has been the result and so it is that, with all my reverence for and concurrence with my learned brethren on the jurisdictional and jurisprudential basics they have indicated, I have preferred to plough a lonely furrow.
>
> In the later case of Charles Wolf, the court made emphatic statements driving home the same point.
>
> Mr. Justice Marshall expressed himself explicitly "I have previously stated my view that a prisoner does not shed his basic constitutional rights at the prison gate, and I fully support the court's holding that the interest of inmates in freedom from imposition of serious discipline is a 'liberty' entitled to due process protection".
>
> Mr. Justice Douglas, again a dissenter, asserted: "Every prisoner's liberty is, of course, circumscribed by the very fact of his confinement, but his interest in the limited liberty left to him is then only the more substantial. *Conviction of a crime does not render one a non person whose rights are subject to the whim of the prison administration, and therefore, the imposition of any serious punishment within the prison system requires procedural safeguards.* Of course, a hearing need not be held before a prisoner is subjected to some minor deprivation, such as an evening's loss of television privileges. *Placement in solitary confinement, however, is not* in that category".
>
> If judicial realism is not to be jettisoned, judicial activism must censor the argument of unaccountable prison autonomy.
>
> 'Dangerousness' as a cover for police and prison atrocities is not unusual, as a recent judicial enquiry

by Mr. Justice Ismail in a Tamil Nadu prison indicates: "The black hole of Calcutta is not a historical past but a present reality".

Mr. Justice Douglas stressed this aspect in Wolf. V. Mcdonnel, (1974) 41 L ed 2d 935 at 976:

"We have made progress since then but the old tradition still lingers. Just recently an entire prison system of one State was held as inhumane. The lesson to be learned *is that courts cannot blithely defer to the supposed expertise of prison officials when it comes to the constitutional rights of inmates.*

"Prisoners often have their privilege revoked, are denied the right of access to counsel, sit in solitary or maximum security or less accrued 'good time' on the basis of a single, unreviewed report of a guard. When the Courts defer to administrative discretion, it is this guard to whom they delegate the final word on reasonable prison practices. This is the central evil in prison....... the unreviewed discretion granted to the poorly trained personnel who deal directly with prisoners.

"The benign purpose behind deprivation of freedom of locomotion and expression is habilitation of the criminal into good behaviour, *ensuring social defence on his release into the community*. This rationale is subverted by torturesome treatment, antagoism and bitterness which soil the correctional process. 'Fair treatment ..... will enhance the chance of rehabilitation by reactions to arbitrariness' (1972) 33 L Ed 2d 484).

Rehabilitation effort as a necessary component of incarceration is part of the Indian criminal justice system as also of the United States. For instance, this correctional attitude has been incorporated as a standard by the National Advisory Commission on Criminal Justice Standards and Goals (1)

".....A rehabilitative purpose is or ought to be implicit in every sentence of an offender unless ordered otherwise by the sentencing court".

In Mohammed Guasyddub v, State if A.P. (1977) 2 SCC 287 : AIR 1977 SC 1926) this Court strongly endorsed the importance of the hospital setting and the therapeutic goal of imprisonment:

"Progressive criminologists across the world will agree that the Gandhian diagnosis of offenders as patients and his conception of prisons as hospitals—mental and moral—is the key to the pathology of delinquency and the therapeutic role of 'punishment'. The whole man is a healthy man and every man is born good. Criminality is a curable deviance........ Our prisons should be correctional houses, not cruel iron aching the soul .... This nation cannot—and, if it remembers its incarcerated leaders and freedom fighters—will not but revolutionize the conditions inside that grim little world. We make these persistent observations only to drive home the imperative of freedom—that its deprivation, by the State, is validated only by a plan to make the sentencee more worthy of that birthright. There is a spiritual dimension to the first page of our Constitution which projects into penology."

All this adds up to the important proposition that it is a crime of punishment to further torture a person undergoing imprisonment, as the remedy aggravates the malady and thus ceases to be reasonable justification for confiscation of personal freedom and is arbitrary because it is blind action not geared to the goal of social defence, which is one of the primary ends of imprisonment. It reverses the process by manufacturing worse animals when they are released into the mainstream of society. Roger G. Lanphear, in a recent study, has quoted a telling letter from a prisoner which makes the poignant point:

(IA) Dear Mrs. Stender:

"You cannot rehabilitate a man through brutality and disrespect. Regardless of the crime a man may commit, he still is a human being and has feelings. And the main reason most inmates in prison today disrespect their keepers is because they themselves (the inmates) are disrespected and are not treated like human beings. I myself have witnessed brutal attacks upon inmates and have suffered a few myself, uncalled for, I can understand a guard or guards restraining an inmate if he becomes violent. But many a time this restraining has turned into a brutal beating. Does this type of treatment bring about respect and rehabilitation? No. It only instills hostility and causes alienation toward the prison officials from the inmate or inmates involved.

If you treat a man like an animal, then you must expect him to act like one. For every action, there is a reaction. This is only human nature. And in order for an inmate to act like a human being you must trust him as such. Treating him like an animal will only get negative results from him. You can't spit in his face and expect him to smile and say thank you. I have seen this happen also. There is a large gap between the inmate and prison officials. And it will continue to grow until the prison officials learn that an inmate is no different than them, only in the sense that he has broken a law. He still has feelings, and he's still a human being. And until the big wheels in Sacramento and the personnel inside the prisons start practicing rehabilitation and stop practising zoology, then they can expect continuous chaos and trouble between inmates and officials. Lewis Moore."

We must heed the wholesome counsel of the British Royal Commission.

"If the suggestion were that, because of enormity of the crime, murderers ought to be subjected to special rigorous treatment, this would run counter to the *accepted principle of modern prison administration that imprisonment is itself the penalty and that it is not the function of the prison authorities to add further penalties day by day by punitive conditions of discipline, labour, diet and general treatment*".

The Tihar Jail is the scene and a glimpse of it is good. Law is not a brooding omnipresence in the sky but a behavioural omnipotence on the earth, a do-don't calculus of principled pragmatism. So, any discussion of prison law problems must be preceded by a feel of the cell and surroundings. For this reason we now set out the inspection notes left by Chief Justice Beg, who visited the 'condemned cell' along with his two brothers on the bench:

"We inspected the cell in which the prisoner was confined. We were relieved to find that conditions there did not correspond to the picture which eloquent arguments of his counsel before us conjured up in our minds. We had been led to believe that the prisoner was kept in some kind of a dungeon with only a small hole through which light could penetrate only when there was enough sunshine. *It was true that the prisoner was living in a room with a cemented floor and with no bed, furniture, or windows in it. The light came from a ventilator with iron bars on the wall at the back of the room and the wide gate of iron bars in front. The light was, however, enough. It is also true that there was no separate room for the petitioner to take a bath in or to answer calls of nature. But, in this very room, the site of which given on a diagram furnished by the jail authorities, water and sanitary fittings were installed in one corner of the room. In front of the room there was a small verandah with pakka walls and iron gates separating each side of it from a similar verandah in front of an adjoining cell.* The entrance into this verandah was also through a similar iron gate. *The inner room in which the prisoner was confined had also a gate of two bars.* All gates were with iron bars in frames so that one could see across them through the spaces between the bars. All these gates were locked. *We learned that the petitioner was able to come into the verandah at certain times of the day. At that time only he could communicate with other similarly kept prisoners whom he could see and talk for all practical purposes, it was a kind of solitary confinement.*

"We did not see a separate guard for each prisoner in the row of cells for prisoners sentenced to death. All these prisoners were certainly segregated and kept apart. But it is difficult to determine, without going into the meaning of 'solitary confinement', as a term of law whether the conditions in which the petitioner was kept amounted to 'solitary confinement'. Probably, *if small windows with iron bars were provided between one cell and another, the prisoners could talk to each other also so that the confinement would no longer be solitary despite the fact that they are kept in separate adjoining cells.*

"The petitioner did not complain of any discomfort other than being kept in 'solitary confinement' and being made to sleep on the floor. He asked us to see another part of the prison where under-trials were kept. When we visited that part, we found dormitories provided there for under-trial prisoners who had beds there and their own bedding and clothing. They also had, in that part of the prison, radio sets, some of which belonged to the prisoners and others to the jail. The under-trials were allowed to mix with other, play games, or do what they wanted within a compound.(emphasis added)".

True, our Constitution has no 'due process' clause or the VIII Amendment; but in this branch of law, after Cooper (1971) 1 SCR 512: (AIR 1970 SC 1318) and Maneka Gandhi (1978) 1 SCC 248 : (AIR 1978 SC 597) the consequences is the same. For what is punitively outrageous, scandalizingly unusual or cruel and rehabilitatively counter-productive, is un-arguably unreasonable and arbitrary and is shot down by Arts. 14 and 19 and if inflicted with procedural unfairness, falls foul of Art. 21. Part III of the Constitution does not part company with the prisoner at the gates, and judicial oversight protects the prisoner's shrunken fundamental rights, if flouted, frowned upon or frozen by the prison authority. *Is a person under death sentence or under-trial unilaterally dubbed dangerous liable to suffer extra torment too deep for tears?* Emphatically no, lest social justice, dignity of the individual, equality before the law, procedure established by law and the seven lamps of freedom (Art. 19) become chimerical constitutional claptrap. Judges, even within a prison setting, are the real, though restricted, ombudsmen empowered to proscribe and prescribe, humanize and civilize the life-style within the carcers. The operation of Arts. 14, 19 and 21 may be pared down for a prisoner but not puffed out altogether. For example, public addresses by prisoners may be put down but talking to fellow prisoners cannot. Vows of silence or taboos on writing poetry or drawing cartoons are violative of Art. 19. So also, locomotion may be limited by the needs of imprisonment but binding hand and foot, with hoops of steel, every man or woman sentenced for a term is doing violence to Part III. So Batra pleads that until de-capitation he is human and so should not be scotched in mind by draconian cellular insulation nor stripped of the basic fellowship which keeps the spirit flickering before being extinguished by the swinging rope.

The manacled numberd of the Tihar Jail community appear to be alarmingly large and fluctuating, if we go by the averments in the affidavit of the petitioner and the counter affidavit by the State. In January 1978 according to Sobraj, there were *207 under-trial prisoners* with bar fetters in Tihar Jail and all of them, exception Sobraj, were Indian citizens, all of them belonging to the 'C' class, which is a poverty sign, and *many of them minors!* We are reminded of what Douglas, J. observed in Hicks (1966) 33 US 252:

"The wanderer, the pauper, the unemployed—all were deemed to be potential criminals.........

"I do not see how economic or social status can be made a crime any more than being a drug addict can be."

Even the intervener, Citizens for Democracy, has, with passion but without partisanship, complained that 'over a hundred other prisoners in *Tihar Jail* are subjected to these inhuman conditiond. The State has controverted the arithmatic but has not refuted the thrust of the submission that a substantial number of under-trial prisoners has suffered aching irons over their anatomy. As against 207 the State admits 'a total of 93 prisoners ........in bar fetters'. There is no dispute that all but the petitioner were of the 'C' class category, that is, men whose socio-economic lot was weak. The Superintendent of the Central Jail has a case that on Jan. 20, 1978, 'the bar fetters of 41 prisoners were removed'. Likewise, on Feb. 6, 1978, bar fetters of 26 prisoners were removed. The trend of the counter-affidavit is that this Superintendent has taken some ameliorative measures to normalise conditions in the Jail. The discrepancies between the competing statements do not demolish the gravamen of the charge that the 'iron' methodology of keeping discipline has had a somewhat dangerous access into the prison Superintendent's mental kit. If irons must rule the jail community there is jejune justice in our prison campuses. The abolition of irons altogether in some States without calamitous sequelae, e.g., Kerala and Tamil Nadu, is worth mention.

The winds of change must blow into our *carcers* and self-expression and self-respect and self-realization creatively substituted for the dehumanising remedies and 'wild life' techniques still current in the jail armoury. A few prison villains—they exist—shall not make martyrs of the humane many; and even from these few. Trust slowly begets trust, Sarvodaya and antyodaya have criminological dimensions which our social justice *awareness* must apprehend and actualize. I justify this observation by reference to the noble ut inchoate experiment (or unnoticed epic) whereby Shri Jai Prakash Narain redemptively brought murderously dangerous dacoits of Chambal Valley into prison to turn a responsible page in their life in and out of jail. The rehabilitative follow-up was, perhaps, a flop.

In short, the technology of raising the level of awareness, not generating hatred by repression, shows the way to making prison atmosphere safe and social defence secure. Criminology and consciousness are partners in community protection.

# 6
# Some Random Reminiscences of Days as a Kerala Minister

When I recollect my past and take my pen to set down my thoughts and memories Cowley's admonition comes as a caveat:

> It is a hard and nice subject for a man to write of himself: it grates his own heart to say anything of disparagement, and the reader's ears to hear anything of praise for him.

More forbidding is the fact that at age 88, memory is not a wholly dependable witness even if there be the will to be objectively truthful. Anecdotal accuracy allows no alibi for dotage and old age and that lends trepidation to my narration. Even so, substantial authenticity is within my command and so I yield to the pressure of disinterested friends who would like to know history at first hand from one who has been a non-communist participant in the raging events of the first Communist Kerala Ministry of 1957-59.

I was a young lawyer with a flourishing practice and promising professional future in a district centre called Tellicherry with a lucrative bar and an old tradition. Lawyering has many allurements and opportunities to be in public life. And if you have 'progressive' inclinations, Leftist movements throw a bait. In any case, no *pronounced* socialist agitation activised me in my college days although Gandhian and Nehruvian influence with crimson penchant did mould my outlook. Gandhiji's *My Experiments with Truth* and Nehru's *Autobiography* did impact on me a great deal. And in North Malabar, the theatre of my legal activities, peasant struggles, working class agitations and satyagraha movements were demonstratively manifest in the forties of the last century. I got involved in these operations *not* in the political sense but largely in the professional dimension. Compartmentalisation is not possible in human affairs and litigation means clients' grievances, sympathy for causes and opposition to oppression. Impalpably but indelibly, one's mentality is shaped, one's reputation is coloured, one's cold neutrality ceases to be a reality. This process did not spare me and I was looked upon as a reliable leftist lawyer, eventually an acceptable Leftist candidate for the first general elections in 1952 from my constituency, under the fresh Constitution. A successful young advocate, popular with all sections of society and socially active through various public organizations, is a covetable candidate and good catch, if he has a left slant and the constituency is not dominated by a single community or party. I filled the bill and a KMPP—Communist Alliance, recently formed, pressured me into the fray. I ran for the Assembly seat and won, although the battle was hard, the constituency multi-communal and the victory margin was of a few thousand votes only. I was an *Independent* candidate and even the Muslim League supported me since they opposed the Congress and had no strength to set up a League candidate. It is sweat and toil to campaign, to canvass, to put out a manifesto, hold numerous meetings, challenge the invincible Congress with Nehru himself addressing a mass rally. Those were virgin days of adult franchise, of scarce resources and public appeals where the standing and quality of the candidate mattered. I realised the truth of Winston Churchill's noble words:

> At the bottom of all tributes paid to democracy is the little man, walking into a little booth, with a little pencil, making a little cross on a little bit of paper—no amount of rhetoric or voluminous discussion can possibly diminish the overwhelming importance of the point.

Malabar was then a part of Madras State and I spent four thrilling years of debates, repartees and oral struggles for people's causes in the Madras Legislature. The great Rajaji with sharp intellect, Kamaraj the common man with uncommon commonsense, C. Subramaniam, later Bharat Ratna, who flourished in any office under any leader (except Narasimha Rao) were the commanding greats on the Treasury Benches while Andhra Kesari Prakasam, the able parliamentarian Tennethi Viswanthan, G. Nagi Reddy, later turned Naxalite, P. Ramamurti, a powerful communist intellectual and forceful speaker in English, Tamil and Hindi, were ranged in the Opposition benches. I was an Opposition activist notable for my role in the question hour and other legislative business in the House. Those raging debates are 'old, unhappy, far-off things and battles long ago' but to remember the confidence gained, the repartees exchanged, the youthful gush of eloquence with a 'left' thrust but without communist jargon—these were my preparatory days in public life and fearless combat. And we had Sivashanmugham Pillai as Speaker of the House, rich with Westminster scholarship, May's parliamentary practice and rules and rulings on his fingertips, assisted by R.V. Krishna Iyer as Legislative Secretary then whom none higher sat as master of parliamentary procedure and culture.

An advocate by profession specializes in oral presentation clear and convincing. The legislator—not the walk-out antic and jump into the well of the house circus brand, which is abundant in our time,—the legislator who argues passionately, patriotically and sharply has a functional satisfaction when orality is used to interrogate the minister through interpellations or intervention in debate as bills are taken up for the second reading. My Madras term during 1952-56 gave me plenty of opportunity for cultivating the power of the spoken word and instant retort unfazed by titans sitting opposite. A lashing speech, pungent or cynical or packed with harsh humour, gives soulful satisfaction, especially when you carry a point in the House or expose the faux pas of a midget minister. I had occasions to enjoy such perorative spells. Of course, the inspiration came from that parliamentarian wonder, and sharp-as-a-blade brain of Rajaji and the great, though sometimes halting, sublime eloquence of Jawaharlal Nehru.

After all, a mere Independent, without even the gift of the gab, would be but a minnow among the titans of the Madras legislature.

In 1956 end, the Malabar MLAs were packed off to Kerala consequent on the reorganization of the States. The first election to the Kerala Assembly came and I became a natural choice as a candidate and won the seat in Tellicherry, the Communist Party having substantially supported me. The party, along with the few Independents whom it supported, gained a narrow majority and became the obvious choice to form the Government. Thus, the first election to the Kerala Assembly became notable in history because it was the first time that in a bourgeois ballot the Communist Party secured a majority against the Congress with the great Nehru at the Centre who had attained the acme of his noble stature as a world Statesman. E.M.S. Namboodiripad, the outstanding leader of the Communist Party, was the unquestionable leader of his party and set about forming a ministry after due democratic consultation. We met at a large public meeting in Ernakulam and there Namboodiripad, the leader, explained the party stand and announced the proletarian fundamentals of his proposed Government *within the framework of the Indian Constitution.* The same evening he requested me to serve as a minister in his Cabinet and overruled my reluctance. My professional practice, although only at the regional level, was high incomewise and reputationwise and naturally a minister's salary being small (it was Rs. 500 per month in those days); I had to make professional and financial sacrifices and give up the princely residence of a lovely Bungalow I had built by the side of the Arabian Sea with a vast expanse of coconut grove and a hillock which gave me a beautiful private beach. To abandon the very good things of life and have to move down to Thiruvananthapuram as a Minister of a small State was a serious choice and had to be a family decision. After consultations and overcoming remonstrances I judged in favour of acceptance of ministership.

Between Travancore-Cochin and Malabar there was political iron curtain before the formation of Kerala State so much so I was an ignoramus in relation to the political realities and unknown to the leading personalities of Travancore-Cochin. Probably the people of Travancore-Cochin, speaking generally, were not familiar with the happenings, political personages and developments in Malabar. Nevertheless, the movement for a united Kerala State, gained rapid momentum and possessed passionate appeal. It was in this scenario that I was ushered into Kerala electoral politics culminating in my becoming a Cabinet Minister. Indeed, the politicians of Travancore-Cochin treated me as a person of inconsequence—perhaps not having heard of me save vaguely, but tolerated me because E.M.S. had brought me in. At this point, I must pay grateful tribute to Chief Minister Namboodiripad for having reposed in me considerable confidence without hesitation. I was made minister for Law, Prisons, Social Welfare, Power, Irrigation and Inland Navigation. He had in his mind the idea that I should also handle the Home and Justice portfolios, which are important in any Government. When the Governor raised a point as to why files relating to courts were being disposed of by Krishna Iyer, E.M.S. formally made over the portfolio of Home and Justice to me. This was a great administrative challenge and all the dynamism and creative innovation I was capable of, had an opportunity for expression. Being fresh in the field and an idealist by temperament, I tried innovative experiments in every department entrusted to me. In the fullest sense, I threw myself into the job, hoping that a transformation could be produced in every sphere, coming within my entrustment. To dynamise a static instrument, to activise a fossil apparatus is, a soulful operation.

I do not propose to deal in detail with the functional fury which drove me into doing unprecedented things since that will be too vast a canvas and too taxing a claim on my failing memory. Inevitably, I am selective and propose to turn the focus only on certain aspects of my multidimensional commitments as Minister.

While functioning as a minister in Kerala, I had occasion to meet Prime Minister Nehru, to write to him on various subjects and seek his guidance in confronting obdurate reactionary opposition from the Congress

Opposition in the State. This brought me close to him. I had great admiration for the noble statesman in Nehru, the uninhibited expression of views by him, even when they were critical of his Party within my state. His vision inspired me, his grace fascinated me, his sneaking affection for me endeared me, his value system made me his ideological adorer. Chronologically speaking, I should be dealing with my dynamic days as a minister, especially in the field of irrigation and electricity, law, police and the court, but I deem it fit to deal with the last chapter of my life as minister, because of its historical importance. It may not be out of place to emphasize that I was fired by enthusiasm in all that I did because of a happy partnership at home, I mean the spiritual, emotional, conjugal dimensions. It was my good fortune that my wife (Sarada Krishna Iyer) played an invisible role, an intangible part sans which my efficiency, such as it was, my daring and dynamism, such as it was, would have diminished into humdrum political conventionalism and Secretariat files syndrome. Her lively presence and tacit participation in all that I did gave me an electrifying disposition which words cannot describe adequately. Wherever I went, whichever public meetings I addressed, whatever projects I tried to execute, there was her felicitous stimulus—certainly no officious influence. Life is more than one's faculty. There is a facility deeper than pomp of office which is the enzyme that catalyses one's capacity. There is a companionship which in its vibrancy, imparts verve and vision. That power was Sarada for me.

I take up for a close up last phase of the E.M.S. Ministry in its first span—1957-59. A Communist ministry's victory through the ballot was a performance difficult to digest for the Congress bourgeoisie. This extraordinary and unexpected phenomenon generated mistrust and hostility among the traditional politicians, the business community and in the Kerala context, the Church which in those days had been a pervasive negative force in public affairs. Right from the start, the impression was created by leading Congressmen that the Constitution was in danger in Kerala because, in their publicised perception, the Communists, according to their dogmatic formula, were no believers in the rule of law and democracy. The Church was the antagonist of Marxists. I distinctly remember the Chief Minister Namboodiripad, the protagonist of the Party, explaining the fundamental stance of his Government to be the implementation of the progressive policies and programmes of the Congress party which remained as unimplemented resolutions. Not the Communist Manifesto, but the Congress agenda of Land Reforms, protection of workers rights, social justice and the like were to be the immediate agenda of action. Obviously, to this agenda of governance neither the Congress nor the Church could take exception. This radical strategy, which was the bedrock of the Constitution, disabled the Opposition in its anti-communist tirade. But the duty of the Opposition—in this case the Congress plus—is to oppose and capture Power. Debarji, the then President of the Indian National Congress, came to Kerala and was critical of the police policy of non-intervention in labour disputes and peasant struggles as a Party stratagem to boost the proletariat. I met him as Home Minister and explained with lucent lucidity, the stand of the Government of sure intervention when a law and order situation compelled such a move. But this was contrary to the traditional role of using the police for supporting the employer and the landlord to the detriment of the *kisan* and the worker in their legitimate demands. He seemed satisfied.

In 1958 there was an international conference of jurists in New Delhi organised by the International Commission of Jurists (ICJ) and inaugurated by Prime Minister Nehru, where an impression was sought to be created that with the Communists in power the Constitution was in peril. The Secretary General of the I.C.J came all the way to Trivandrum to investigate into the charge of constitutional breakdown. I took the initiative of inviting for lunch this leading jurist (I forget his name) so that he could discuss with me, one to one, his apprehensions and evidence and his specific criticism, if any, of the doings of the Government, vis-a-vis Operation Police Neutrality. After lunch, we spent a few hours in a thorough-going analysis of facts and events, of policies and programmes, of jural philosophy and constitutional dialectics. In the perspective of the Indian Constitution and its value constellation enshrined in the Preamble we discussed without inhibitions and obsessions. My total frankness in exchange of views impressed him and his doubts were cleared by me according to my understanding of the law and human rights. The language I used did not have any cosmetics of professional communists nor 'comrade' jargon but was simple legal diction. Both of us enjoyed the opportunity of the meeting. Later he left for Madras and there he addressed the Cosmopolitan Club, a prestigious body, invariably presided by a sitting judge of the High Court. Justice A.S.P. Iyer was at that time the President of the Club. The Secretary General of the I.C.J, in the course of his address, referred to his fruitful meeting with me. In a fine stroke of humour and felicitous paradox he seems to have said: 'either I am a communist and I do not know that or the law minister Iyer is not a communist and he does not know that; so compact was our mutual understanding of the issues and agreement on the policy of the Government'. This was conveyed to me in a letter the next day by A.S.P. Iyer. I mention this to drive home the point that as the Minister in charge of Police Administration, I was abiding by constitutional norms and the rule of law, never allowing the police to play into the hands of the party minions or even bosses. I may categorically assert that even in the matter of transfer of police officials, I did not admit party interference, but heard them, made my own investigation and acted on my findings. My Home Secretary Krishnamoorthy and my two Inspectors General of Police had faith in my respect for their views and this confidence went a long way in the integrity of the department. The police did policing, never played 'call girl' role of politicians, tycoons and local landed bosses. As the Communist governance gained acceptance, the Church was restive and Opposition Parties provocative. Land reforms, welfare measures, educational liberation from the stranglehold of private managements and all-round progressive policies in agriculture, irrigation and electricity generated weathering hostile political storm, the Opposition losing ground. I skip that hostility and mini-terrorist confrontation tactics.

Then came the *Vimochana Samaram* organised by a combination of forces and opportunist gang-up of political malcontents, desperately driven to unconstitutional operations with the tacit approval of the Indian National Congress headed by Smt Indira Gandhi and of other leaders like Sucheta Kripalani, the active quasi-terrorism of the Church and other communal bodies. At that time, the Nair Service Society Leader and distinguished public figure Sri Mannath Padmanabhan played the role of freshner leading a militant agitation with mini-terrorist mission. It had the massive and muscular support of the Church and indoctrination against communism. The Muslim league, other communal bodies and the doyen of Kerala politics Pattom Thanu Pillai, were arrayed against the Government. It was a terrible strain for me to preserve law and order and maintain peace in the State. Of course, E.M.S., the principal performer backed me. *Vimochana Samaram* literally means liberation struggle. The *declared* object of these semi-militarily marshalled gang-ups against us was to overthrow the Government by *sheer violence*. The Congress, to begin with, was covertly behind this plot but finding the initial successes gained by the unholy axis, came into the open to lend the struggle a colour of political respectability. Indeed, the Central Government and the Congress leadership at the top—not perhaps Nehru—were aware of this anti-constitutional monstrosity. Rabid threats were made by the leaders that they would physically overthrow the ministry. With regal pomp the furor was carried in a procession by palanquin bearers. Violent demonstrations escalated. Para-military training in church compounds were given. To adapt Winston Churchill in a different context, the pernicious project with plural participants were like 'a gigantic quilt of incongruous crochet work, a monstrous moment of shame built by pigmies'! I kept my cool, the Communist Party, under restraint, did not retaliate. This experiment in non-co-operation with evil was for me a sublime experience. To think Gandhian and to talk Gandhian, were commonplace. But to *act* Gandhian for a Government was a high-risk operation and unique gamble. The Home Department had the duty to keep the peace but was challenged at every turn by unruly processions, stone-throwing at buses and vulgar slogans, with a leader carried in a palanquin on triumphant marches. The State Police could have resisted and dismantled the zoological display but would not. The State had the gun, but if fired against determined gangs and goons would result in bloodshed, which was precisely the object of the engineers of the melodrama and malice, namely overthrow of the Government by forced resignation or Presidential Proclamation. The ministers agreed with my perspective of passive police non-resistance, a historic process which succeeded in large measure under grave provocation and theatrical tantrums. Considerable casualities would have been the result if the police had used force to quell the unruly mob, often under fluid intoxication. The police force, though well equipped, did not hit back. True, there were one or two fixings in uncontrollable situations, which claimed a young woman's life which I regret. I must pay a tribute to the police of those days for having demonstrated that the strong could be non-violent even under insult or infuriation. To be meek is not to be weak.

I was not willing to oblige the mini-terrorist hordes in the political outfit of Operation Overthrow, alive though I was to the responsibilities of keeping the peace and equipped though the Police Force was to overpower the rude crowd. Since the attempt was to create some violent contexts and provoke police action I too was careful to deny them the opportunism. They tried to jump in front of my car so that if the car hit anyone a scene could be created and agitation against police violence ignited. To avoid collisions I used to walk from the Secretariat instead of driving in car. True, a young woman Florey died of police firing but if the traditional police praxis had not been abandoned, hundreds would have been killed or injured violence breeds violence. Police non-violence is a difficult, delicate but divine methodology which could be practised if only the Mahatma message has entered the soul of the Home Minister down to the last constable. I vainly tried the great experiment. How easy to trigger, how hard to resist the temptation when the gun goes off in an instant and the wild bullets fly in different directions but dear Indian life dies of shot. No, there is a joy in non-cooperation with evil. And I rejoiced in the great opportunity to experiment with truth when challenged by menacing untruth.

It is not out of place to mention, in fairness to the Congress Party that several outstanding congressmen like Damodara Menon and V.K. Krishna Menon kept out of the ugly operation. However R. Shankar, the leader, later lent full support to the movement. Quite a few young congressmen, including students, involved themselves in this intoxicating adventure unconcerned with its unconstitutionality. The frenzy was of such a high pitch that many of the Congress youth were drawn into the fray unthinkingly and in the desperate expectation that the Communist Government must fall and the Congress would step in. The grand propaganda against the Communist regime, baseless when tested on facts and law, so infuriated the adolescent elements that they never bothered about the right and wrong of the movement. What is a more, the process was punctuated by arrivals from Delhi representing the Congress at the national level to instigate the 'overthrow adventurists'. The whole operation was rank communalism with the Church giving the lead and the NSS magnetic leader lending (palanquin) lustre. Nehru's Congress should have abhorred with contempt the vulgar, violent, vicious project. However, even so gracious a lady as Sucheta Kripalani came all the way to give moral boost to the flagging movement. She thundered about the violation of the Constitution and alleged the freedom of movement had been blocked. I gently telephoned her, invited her for tea as Home Minister and requested her to tell me where there was obstruction to freedom of movement. My police, I told her, would facilitate her visit to any place she wanted. Thereafter, she raised no voice of protest but quietly left. The general impression was given that the ruling Congress party being active participant, the fall of the State Government was imminent. In short, it was assumed that horrendous hooliganism organised with Congress support would buy Central sympathy and end up in President's Rule and so, the days of the Communist ministry were numbered. This was a false expectation and myopic illusion because the constitutional process was made of saner stuff and illegal atrocities, with the connivance of the party in power at the Centre, could not be a ground for the Central Government to intervene in favour of the operators of the grave contra-constitutional strategem. Article 356 is a solemn Constitutional trust, not an unscrupulous political tool for opportunist misuse.

Police pacifism has limits when charged with the task of controlling mobs run berserk. Arrests in number and remand to jails had to be resorted to having regard to large-scale breaches of law and order aggravated by the feeling that police weapons would hang limp. We had to take over buildings and declare them ad hoc prisons. But life inside for the detainees was comfortable thanks to my jail reform policy with fair freedom behind bars. At the height of the bedlam agitation when the jail population, for short spells, ballooned, I remember (the late) Sri Ram Subhag Singh, a Central Minister, visiting Tellicherry, where I was camping as Home Minister, to know the lot of the jail inmates. He went into the jails to see the treatment meted out—horrible, he expected, to Congress prisoners. To his incredulous relief, the jail inmates were having a happy time. Straight he came to me and asked me why this policy of *comfortable* confinement. I told him that humanization of prisons was everywhere in the State as a new reform. He was thrilled and remarked I was inviting more "satyagrahis" by offering happy, though restrained, holiday.

An anecdotal deviation takes me to an unusual incident. The noble Nehru, I presume, was innocent of the black-guardly ballyhoo and berserk breaches of the peace pursuant to the conspiratorial Project Subversion of an elected government. Why did those of power in Delhi blinks at the dubious game with unconscionable ease. My Home Secretary received a communication from the I.G. of Police in charge of Railway Protection that there was serious apprehension that in view of the uncontrolled commotion in the State, railway tracks were in danger. He demanded absolute safety of railway property. The Congress Party within Kerala is in the Opposition but in Power at the Centre. It joins the unconstitutional Operation Overthrow and threatens safety of life and property and sitting in the Railway Ministry, seeks protection against their own Congress miscreants within Kerala! What a comic contradiction! So, in reply to the Railway Ministry's communication the Kerala Home Secretary told the Railway I.G that all the protection the State gives to its own property, will in full measure be given to the Railways. The whole idea was to embarrass the State Government, the threat to Railways being a mere pretext. Had we responded expressing inadequacy of police force to line up all over the Railway track, breakdown of the constitutional responsibility would be the inference! Crafty gambit!

Another canny move adopted by the Central Home Minister may be reluctantly referred to. I used to meet the Chief Justice periodically to clear administrative matters pending between Government and the High Court. Many administrative issues were sorted out this way with promptitude. On one occasion Chief Justice Koshy (of the Kerala State) confidentially told me that there was a reference to him from the Home Minister to let him know whether the communists of Kerala were interfering in the investigation of cases which would be a grave matter of the party thwarting investigative justice. The Chief Justice told me that, after an enquiry, he was satisfied that there was no such party interference in investigations. His reply to the Home Minister was confidential but sufficient to nail the propaganda that the party in power was meddling in police investigations. Here again I suspect a sly attempt of the Home Minister to trap the State Government into a finding that it was guilty of unconstitutional use of power through party comrades. If the Chief Justice had said 'yes' that would have been a ground for Presidential Proclamation.

Considerable prejudice existed against the communists among conservative sections and the Establishment when the first ministry was formed as an extraordinary novelty and expression of popular upsurge. The proprietarial hated communists in power and were apprehensive that all their wealth would be seized by Government—an impossibility so long as the Government was run *under* the Constitution and there was a Central Power which had no truck with the communists. The impression was spread that the State Government would lay hands upon all lands probably imagining some Leninist coup. In 1957 or 1958, Vinobha Bhave had held a National Sarvodaya Conference in Kalady, Kerala. There was talk of land reforms in the communist party which was really an implementation of the Congress partys pious resolutions. Congress rhetoric was sought to be made Leftist reality. Anyway, when Vinobhaji was coming to Kalady I was thrilled because of his Bhoodan Movement and decided to attend the conference, fascinated as I was by the land distribution policy of Vinobhaji. When I told E.M.S., the Chief Minister, that I had decided to attend the Kalady conference he graciously told me that I could as well represent the Government, particularly because I could supervise the facilities needed for such a vast conference. I did go and was persuaded by Jaya Prakash Narayan to sit on the dais. As the conference began, Vinobhaji addressed the large concourse and advocated Bhoodan as a great cause. When he finished his speech Jayaprakash Narayan, quietly proposed that I, as Minister of the Government, should address next. This was an unexpected summons but I fell in with the suggestion and delivered a long speech in the course of which I emphasized the importance of land reforms. I stressed the spiritual value of Vinobhaji's movement in softening the resistance of latifundists to agrarian reform. So I pleaded that Vinobhaji's movement would diminish resistance and promote a moral pressure in favour of land reforms. Once this softening was done, the State would take over the same movement by agrarian legislation providing for ceiling on land, taking over the excess and distribute the surplus to the landless. Thus, there was a harmonization of processes between Vinobhaji and the Kerala Government's proposed land legislation. There was wide applause and the great JP, who sat next to me, wondered whether that was the policy of the Communist Government. I replied to say that I, as Law Minister, represented the Government at the conference and therefore my voice should be treated as authentic. JP was happy.

Land for the tiller was no more a slogan but a pending legislation. This did antagonise landlords but did not deter agrarian reforms. The Kerala Agrarian Relations Act was passed. Then came the Kerala Education Bill which was a daring stroke to free education at the lesser levels from the commercial stranglehold of vested interests, including the Church and the NSS. The school industry, pervasively and profitably spread over the State, was an uncontrolled source of income and influence for the Church and other communal bodies, financed by the State but with no voice in the healthy management of the institutions. Private enterprise may be permissible in the educational field but arbitrary privatisation enjoying public financial support in a field where State and society have vital concern is a grave contradiction. This compelling logic was the raison d'etre of the Kerala Education Bill. It had nothing to do with communism but much to do with people's interest. This measure of social control was just and necessary. The circumstance that the Communist Government takes the initiative is no justification to see *red* in the project. Prof. Mundassery, a leftist Independent, was the Education Minister who knew his business, a reasonably radical and courageously committed to the cause. The Party agreed, the Cabinet concurred, the Bill was drafted, moved, debated and passed. Then ensued an uproar as if the October Revolution had happened. The Church, the largest beneficiary of the lawless (but governmentally fully financed) system was hurt and rose in revolt and let loose an avalanche of agitation. Macro and micro communal interests running private educational business were tempted to rebel. An anti-Education Bill movement was mounted. A lawless battle was brewing. The call to use physical (!) force to force the Communists from office was raised. American interest in unseating the Communists from the saddle was obvious and the Church, under religious disguise, was the conduit pipe for flow of funds, according to secret police reports I received as Home Minister. Thus emerged a contra-constitutional, anti-Communist, chaotic agglomeration of forces spear-headed by the Church, funded covertly by U.S. sources and formally headed by the popular, otherwise socially respected, Sri Mannath Padmanabhan— a great gain and bargain for the Direct Action terrorism united under the banner of Vimochana Samaram (Liberation Struggle). Every element, with some grouse against Government or Communist influence, threw its weight to spread chaos in the cosmos. Public bus transport, public offices and public functions attended by ministers became targets of violent demonstrations and victims of mob fury fabricated with suspect resources.

The police were under general instructions to make their presence minimal and weapons dormant. The entry of the Congress Party, with its colour of Central Power, created great confusion and many misapprehensions about the legitimacy and prospects of victory. Nehru's great name and a reactionary struggle with his Party's participation looked incongruous.

Alone the Communist Government, with a few Leftist independents, resisted this unrighteous onslaught. The common people were dazed. Gentlemen of goodwill were shocked. People, by and large, remained stunned. This scene of tumult and lawless outrage could not be tolerated. There was pressure from Communist friends on me to use the detention process. I refused although circumstances were anarchical. I had too much democracy in me to resort to preventive detention. Governmental violence, even if amply warranted, would be an appetizer and catalyst for the Overthrow plot which would otherwise peter out. Every preventive detention would have provoked the cry of Communist dictatorship while blinking at the Opposition's sound and fury signifying nothing except a negative demand for removal of Government, which would have died a slow natural death. Barbarous noises, bereft of the driving force of just demand have a short run like epileptic fits. Indeed, there were signs of the *Vimochana Samaram* wasting its lusty lungs. However, the reality for those who had to rule, was grim because day to day life in the State was disturbed by convulsive outbursts, especially in the Travancore-

Cochin area.

During this unrelenting crisis came the news that the All India Congress Committee was meeting in Ooty to consider the Five Year Plan. That would be an occasion for all Congress men to assemble and for Nehru and Indira Gandhi to be dominantly present. Ooty was in a different State and was a remote health resort. The meeting was to take place in the huge accommodation of Arranmore Palace. It occurred to E.M.S. Namboothiripad, who had to bear the burden of a Government under siege to suggest to me to apprise Prime Minister Nehru about the violent violation of the Constitution, activated by the Congress in Kerala and operating under the vicarious guidance of the President of the Congress. E.M.S. knew that I had easy access to Nehru. He knew that I could present the facts at first hand, being the Home Minister myself. He further knew that if the Congress in power at the Centre frowned on the Congress-led upsurge in the State, the imbroglio would be cleared. However, there was no bright optimism because the dark forces which played the desperate game were deeper than Nehru and the red rose that he wore could control.

**Pilgrimage to Ooty**

I was residing in Cantoment House which was my official quarters. I agreed to travel to Ooty on a mission of convincing Nehru that a raging crazy mobbish movement dominated by babel and brute force, had gripped the State, the political leadership of which was taken over by the State Congress leadership in association with a rabble group of communal organizations the leadership of which belonged to Sri Mannath Padmanabhan and muscle power was supplied by the Church in general. After all, Nehru was a man of vision, a statesmen and one who ruled the country *under* the Constitution. Therefore it was my expectation (illusion) that he would listen and call to order the misbehaving politicians. Whenever I undertook journeys, personal or political, my wife used to accompany me. She was a public-spirited woman, shared my views on most matters and was, in many dimensions, a progressive partner. Inevitably, her company reinforced my confidence in the pilgrimage I undertook. Indeed, it was a pilgrimage, temporal, humanist and patriotic. To defend the Constitution was my duty; to restore peace in the State was my function, to create conditions for a socially just governance within the Kerala State was my passion. So we drove together, reached the hill station of Ooty and settled down for a three days sojourn hoping to meet and explain and gain my objective. I met Sri Damodara Menon, leading Congressman and Sri V.K. Krishna Menon whose stature was high and clarity of thought beyond being mired by parochial politics. Both the Menons were keenly sensitive to the tragedy taking place in Kerala and advised me that the only solution to the problem was to place the entire matter, in its raw reality, before Panditji. So I was on the right track and sought an appointment with the Prime Minister on the very first day. My wife too accompanied me. Nehru was full of grace and received us at lunch break. It was sheer delight to sit and eat with him. He cut a mango and explained to my wife from where it came and what special taste it had and how it has to be sliced. There was affection in his conversation but I had gone with a sombre purpose which I broached with him with persuasive advocacy. Panditji listened and was prima face impressed. He called Indira Gandhi and told her: 'Indu, Krishna Iyer has come from Kerala to discuss some political problems of the State. Give him a hearing and understand the issues'. 'Yes', she said and I waited for an opportunity to meet her and unfold my case in its provincial ferocity.

A credible rumour was afloat in Kerala that Smt Indira Gandhi, President of the Indian National Congress, was aware of the Kerala convulsive conspiracy and, in a sense, connived at the shocking doings. But that apprehension did not deter me from talking to her about the organised attempt at a contra-constitutional coup. She did not give me an early interview until her father mildly rebuked her for the delay. Eventually I presented to her what struck me as outrageous in the Kerala scenario. She did listen, made no comment and absorbed what I said. The third day I met Panditji again and explained to him the need for his action to call off the indefensible political outburst with the cute co-operation of his party. He was angry and obviously displeased with the cataclysmic upheavel. He assured me that he would condemn it, which he did in a press interview at Coimbatore. The prejudiced media in Kerala did not publicise it. I had pressed Panditji to come to Kerala and behold for himself the savagery. My meeting with Panditji was in June. He promised to come to Kerala, see things for himself and take suitable steps. He did come in July and stayed for 3 days to acquaint himself with the macabre maneuver. I returned with that promise and hoped he would call the bluff beholding the organized chaos. I felt Nehru would get into a raging mood and deplore the Operation Overthrow. As expected, the Prime Minister arrived in Kerala with the avowed purpose of solving the political mess. He stayed for three days and met the Kerala Cabinet twice. E.M.S., the Chief Minister, received him with warmth and hope and briefed him about the tragicomic turn of events with the suspicious backing of the top echelons in the Congress.

Meanwhile, in the chronicle of events, one matter of relevance deserves mention. Mr Ashok Mehta, astute politician, had, a few months earlier, presented to Parliament thirty two charges against the Kerala State Government. I have not been able to understand that such a resolution can be moved in Parliament against a State. Political allergy cannot torture parliamentary propriety. The Constitution does not provide for that and the procedure is not permissible even if the accused be a Communist Government, but the motion levelling charges against the state was moved and the Home Minister forwarded those charges to the State Home Minister giving an opportunity to furnish a reply. The Central Home Minister's functional amplitude does not extend to asking the State Government about charges as if he is prosecutor and the State ministry the accused. Anyway, I took elaborate pains to meet every charge and present our case and forwarded it to the Speaker (or the Home Minister, I do not recollect). The next time we heard about the charges was from Panditji at his meeting with the Kerala ministers.

At the meeting with the E.M.S. Cabinet, the Prime

Minister raised three issues and desired us to respond. Firstly, he wanted the thirty two charges raised by Ashok Mehta to be enquired into, meaning that we should submit to such an enquiry. Secondly, he insisted that a judicial enquiry should be held into the police firing which resulted in the death of Florey. Thirdly, he demanded to know whether the Kerala Government would agree to suspend section 11 of the Kerala Education Act which hurt the private managements of educational institutions. We took a day's time to reply and E.M.S. convened a meeting of the MLAs and leading members of the party to discuss all the three points raised by the Prime Minister. The situation was critical, the Prime Minister's presence climaxed the crisis; the Communist Ministry's destiny was on trial. Inevitably, the discussion at the meeting assumed a seriousness and involvement, called for the closest exchange of views, wisdom and judgment. The leader, E.M.S., explained to the gathering the purpose of the meeting and then began a discussion which was frank and fair with every viewpoint presented.

The Prime Minister had raised the issue of Ashok Mehta's thirty two charges against the Kerala Government and I had dealt with them in detail in the preparation of a reply to the Home Minister. I assured the comrades gathered that there was no merit in any of the charges and we could come out creditably if they were enquired into. So it was informally agreed that Panditji be told that we would abide by his verdict on the charges and were willing to treat him as arbitrator. On the next issue of suspension of Section 11 of the Kerala Education Act, for the time being we agreed to the suggestion if that would mean an end to the anarchy and imbroglio. There was some difference of opinion on the question of judicial enquiry into the police firing resulting in the loss of life. There a firm stand was taken by some members, including Sri Achutha Menon, an outstanding comrade of integrity and conviction, that we should not consent to such an enquiry. His reasons were sound. In the Statewide bedlam created by the Opposition forces, the police had a trying time and had done the job admirably with the least violence, given the circumstances of bully and ballyhoo. Therefore anything which would affect their morale should not be agreed to. A judicial enquiry would demoralize the police, argued Achutha Menon, a man of few words but firm stand. I took a diametrically contrary view. My submission was that it was part of the democratic movement of the country that whenever there was a police firing resulting, in casualties a judicial enquiry was demanded. Merely because we were in power, there was no case of *our* police being demoralized. We must agree to the judicial enquiry. In the heated discussion my insistence was equally firm. I went to the extent of saying that if the Government did not agree to the judicial enquiry I would quit rather than submit to the rejection of the suggestion for an enquiry. Naturally, my unexpected and inflexible stand had its impact. The parting of ways had come I thought, especially in the background of the general feeling against me that I was not stern enough to use the police or to detain leaders who were mischief-makers. The charge was that I was *too* legalistic and constitutionalist. I owned the accusation that I would act only according to the liberal values of the Constitution and would not mind losing my office forsaking my conscience. This turned the scales and there was agreement about a judicial enquiry.

It may be mentioned here that I was relieved of the Home Portfolio and Sri Achutha Menon was made the Home Minister in the last days of the Government. I was given instead portfolios of Agriculture and Co-operation. It is fair to mention that Achutha Menon also did not or could not use the power of preventive detention.

The next day we met the Prime Minister and to his surprise apprised him of our decision to accept all the three points he had proposed, namely his enquiring into the thirty two Ashok Mehta charges and our abiding by *his* decision, the suspension of Section 11 of the Kerala Education Act and the judicial enquiry into the police firing. I guess the Prime Minister must have been inwardly stunned at our offering no resistance to his three proposals. He left us promising to consider our reasonable response.

I presume that he met the Congress leaders and told them about what had happened. I presume that the hungry oppositionists were after our flesh, not fair play. They were not for Nehru's good offices but for dismissal of the Ministry. Nehru did not communicate his conclusion that day although he was scheduled to leave for Delhi the next day. He had come and studied the chaotic situation and grossly untenable position taken by his party at the State level. He had found the Communist Ministry submitting to his formula. What else remained except for him as Prime Minister and party leader to tell the Overthrow Adenturists that they would not be allowed to carry on the unlawful struggle. But Nehru had ceased to be made of sterner stuff by 1959 July. He could not summon the rage and courage and will to command that the absurd *Operation Overthrow be jettisoned.*

The third day, the day he was leaving, I went to the Raj Bhavan in the morning to greet him and gather his ruling. As I approached his suite, the great Nehru dressed in impeccable white and with the red rose on the lapel, was coming out. His usual grace had vanished from his face as I turned to greet the great man. Panditji, you are leaving today the cataclysmic problem remains unresolved. We have agreed to all that you wanted. What then is your solution? First, he stared at me and then his face drooped, his hands holding on to the rope, almost fainting. I have two historic photographs with me hanging on my wall which depict Nehru's pathetic posture and Nehru fainting face. He recovered his presence and talked to me about the mass upsurge but offered no solution. Later, at the airport he told the press about the wall of separation between the people and the Government and the mass upsurge was uncontrollable except by fresh election. What constitutional doctrine this? I do not agree with his diagnosis nor his recipe but the Prime Minister decided, perhaps in consultation with his party men, that there was no way of getting rid of the Communists from office by reasonable process and therefore resorted to the curious theory of a wall of separation between the Government and the people. This doctrine would mean that any organized group indulging in large scale violence and attracting mob following could justify a coup and claim that the Government must quit and a fresh election should be held. Too dangerous a doctrine, too unconstitutional a theory, too incongruous a jurisprudence, too outrageous a grammar of anarchy.

**Back to the People**

Jawaharlalji came, saw and did not conquer. Why? Probably because he was overpowered by the reactionary elements hell bent upon displacement of the ministry—nothing short of it. Panditji presented a pathetic appearance on the third day because I guess there was an inner struggle. His constitutional sense and integrity would have directed him to continue the ministry unhurt because all his three desiderations had been unconditionally accepted by the E.M.S. Ministry. I could see in his face a contradiction writ large. Was he striving to extricate his conscience by proposing a fresh election giving his solution a seeming democratic touch! Actually, it was an abetment of a constitutional anathema, so I felt but I could sympathize with the inner Nehru protesting against the pernicious prescription. The real Nehru was on the decline. Anyway, he left and the rest is conjecture so far as I am concerned. It is reported that the Congress Party, under Indiraji, passed a resolution asking for a dissolution of the Assembly and the dismissal of the ministry through a presidential proclamation. Anyway, the truth is hidden as a riddle wrapped in a mystery inside an enigma. Sri Mannath Padmanabhan and Company in their slowly waning upsurge had declared, as a morale booster, that they would triumphantly march into the Secretariat and take over power *by force.* The Congress Government, at the Centre obliged them with a President's rule. A monumental blunder! Democracy in danger!

I was returning from Mysore after attending a ministers' conference on Co-operation. On the way I addressed the Bar Association in Hyderabad and later arrived in Madras. Vice President Radhakrishnan, whom I had known briefly, was in the city. I called on him and narrated to him the vicious course of events and the threat of dismissal. He assured me that as soon as he reached Delhi he would talk to the Prime Minister, obviously to dissuade him from the drastic measure. Whether he would have succeeded is very doubtful. Anyway, by the time he reached Delhi, the Home Secretary(Sankar) had left for Trivandrum with an order (of execution constitutionals) under Article 356. We travelled together from Madras to Trivandrum and I guessed that he was carrying our death sentence. That evening, the Governor Sri B. Ramakrishna Rao, in quick despatch, summoned us all. He gave us tea at the Raj Bhawan and told us politely that our ministry would cease to be. We left him and the next day there was a send off and farewell function by the Secretariat officials to E.M.S. and the Cabinet comrades. Namboodiripad, in a fine firm but furious speech, wound up by saying that we were going. He added we are going to the people and will return from the people into the ministerial office. Back to the people we went who voted at the next election in substantial numbers although falling a wee-bit short of a majority of seats to form a Government. I lost at the hustings by 7 votes or so but I challenged the election with specific invalid votes of my adversary. I challenged the verdict in court. The court upheld me, I won the seat and returned to remain in the Opposition a role which was a patriotic experience to challenge corruption and expose dubious legislation.

> 'History is not a web woven with innocent hands. Among all the causes which degrade and demoralise men, power is the most constant and the most active.' (Lord Acton)

A concluding caveat: to have ratified and glorified a grammar of anarchy in Kerala 1959 by Central surrender syndrome was the beginning of the end of the Indian Constitutional Order.

**Post Script**

The facts stated in this Recollection are half-century vintage and therefore I may have faltered here and there, amnesia admitting of no exception to old age. Therefore, readers must forgive minor errors which might have crept in when tested with strict historicity. Most reluctantly I observe that the abbreviation of time and the browner shade of the evening of life may have pathologically but unwittingly led to some departure from facts.

My quasi-gubernotorial journey ends here. Back to the bar I came and picked up a lucrative practice combining it with a social justice dimension and involvement in public activities. Then came the pressure from the Chief Justice of my State, (M.S.Menon) a celebrity and luminary in his own right, to accept judgeship. I was reluctant and large circles of friends in the State took opposite views on my elevation to the Bench. Many held that they would lose a statesmen who could play a role in public life detached from party politics. My own former colleague and Chief Minister E.M.S. persuaded me, with a Marxian touch, that I should not decline Power when there was the offer since high office (a branch of the State), could be used for the liberation of the people, a contrast to a process of elite justice. With due regard to professional propriety, I consented to be on the Bench-viewed in retrospect I have no regret. That event was a great portent, a radical functional change from minister to judge. My crimson sole remained the same. My operational passion to serve the people according to the Constitution remained the same. My judicial career however, is a refreshing chapter giving me a great opportunity to perform my oath-bound duty under a Secular, Socialist Democratic Republic.

# 7

# Kuttiyadi Project—An Odd Serendipity

Long years ago, indeed more than half a century back, I was a busy practicing lawyer at the Tellicherry District Centre. By good luck I had a lucrative practice on the civil and criminal side although I was quite young and therefore impetuous and enthusiastic in fine fighting mettle and searching for discovery to win cases even when pitted against doyens. It so happened that in the early fifties of the last century I was briefed by a large landlord who laid claim to extensive forests in a mountain area near Perambra. My client was Marakkar, a rich Muslim. His ambition was countered by his Christian friend, Pothen by name, who, in turn, was a sort of latifundist. There was dispute between the two over a mountain tract, which ended in an interminable criminal litigation. Tired of paying fees to lawyers and finding no end in sight in court both sides agreed that they would abide by the verdict of the two lawyers appearing in the case rather than carry on with the forensic battle. I was one of the two lawyers and the other was the late P.Govinda Menon, a good criminal lawyer who was elevated to the bench of the Kerala High Court a few years later. Menon had such faith in my integrity that he expressed his willingness to abide by my judgment if I made an on-the-spot study of the high hill assisted by expert land surveyors to locate a tri-junctional point. It was a tough job to climb, but an adventure to ascend the mountain. Assested by a group of mountaineers familiar with the region, I did an 'Everest' expedition, as it were. The scenic beauty of the land around was enchanting. Mountains and oceans are always a great visual happiness if one has a love of the infinite and I had. Reaching the very top I heard the sound of a torrent. I turned and enquired of my friend what the great noise was about. Poised in the middle of the myriad universe I beheld a foamy marvel. A colossal waterfall leapt from the high range in full fury down to the bottom of the mountain beyond my sight. It was a glorious vision of Nature challenging Man offering vast energy and waking up with thunderous loudness what my aesthetic consciousness could ever comprehend. It seemed to me like a dream. The terrific truth dazed me. There was a whisper within me. Nature's voice. Wake up, young man, here am I with boundless energy flowing into a terrain starved of even an erg of electricity. All around me, the people looked at my amazement and told me about the majestic Kuttiyadi water fall, which could, if tapped, produce a titanic wonder. No government, no engineer listened to Nature's call till then. Creative curiosity with humanist propensity unveils hidden light. I was thrilled and came back to my client. We settled the land dispute but the mighty Kuttiyadi stream danced down in vain with none to embrace or exploit. But in my mind was born the embryo of a Power Project, which could generate enormous power and irrigate tracts of cultivable land.

This dynamic developmental idea slumbered in my mind until I remembered it a couple of years later when I became an elected member of the Madras Legislature sitting in the Opposition and interrogating, by interppellations, the possibility of bringing into reality the Kuttiyadi project, useful for irrigation and electricity generation.

The Madras government had been frequently charged by the people of Malabar—Malabar was part of Madras State in those days—with gross neglect of its developmental potential. My repeated interpellation in the House elicited the same negative reply that there was no prospect of any Kuttiyadi project and the hon'ble member's proposal was nothing more than a chimera. Years rolled by. The Kerala State was formed. The location of the Kuttiyadi project formed part of Malabar in the Kerala State. I became a member of the Kerala Legislature and was entrusted, as Minister, with the portfolios of Irrigation and Power. One of the first things I did was to go to the site of the Kuttiyadi Project accompanied by a brilliant Engineer, the late K.P.S. Nair who was the Chairman of the Kerala Electricity Board. The great Engineer in K.P.S. Nair was astonished at the grand prospect of a Power Generation Plant in his vivid imagination. Yes, the project took shape, the divinity of the Kuttiyadi torrent transformed itself into a blessing for the Perambra population. Water is a divine gift but humanity must be worthy of it.

In due course, the Kerala Engineers completed the Kuttiyadi Project which was ready for switching on ceremony. Who should do the ceremonial task? The Minister Mr. M.N. Govindan Nair, a good friend of mine and loved by the people? No. The people said no. Not because they loved M.N. less but because they wanted to honour the man who discovered the Kuttiyadi plan. Thus they came to me. Meanwhile I had became a judge of the Kerala High Court. At the affectionate insistence of the Perambra people I put my robes aside, hurried to the hallowed spot, switched on the power project and made the people of that region happy about some assured power. This was serendipity incarnate.

# 8

# My Vintage Response to Compassion for Living Creatures

My mother, gentle by nature, was soft to all of us and fed the two cows we had with affection. She milked the innocent animals herself—Gandhiji called cows poems of pity. She left enough milk for the calves which waited impatiently for the opportunity to reach the udder of the dam. She wept when the hungry begged and gave away what little food was left over at once. Her commiserative disposition did mould our character. Years later, in college days when I read William Blake I thought of my mother and how moved she was by human suffering and by animals in distress. Here is a moving piece from Blake:

> A dig starv'd at his master's gate  
> Predicts the ruin of the State,  
> A horse misus'd upon the road  
> Calls to Heaven for human blood.  
> Each outcry of the hunted hare  
> A fibre from the brain does tear,  
> A skylark wounded in the wing,  
> A cherubim does cease to sing.

Now let me tell you how I did an unwitting act of killing a poor dog. My father, a successful moffusal lawyer, had a licensed rifle; and thereby hangs a contradiction. The gun was not meant to be used but was a status symbol. Even so, a pellet in the barrel and an accidental trigger may wound or kill. Violence has no innocence, as I learnt to my consternation. One day, out of foolish curiosity, without my father's knowledge, I, a young boy, handled the heavy fire power, pulled the trigger and aimed it clumsily at a stray dog in the distance. Alas, although I was not even in my teens and had never known the terrorism of the barrel, the bullet hit, the dog died in agony and I felt the guilt of murder. Blake again:

> The caterpillar on the leaf
> Repeats to thee thy mother's grief
> Kill not the moth nor butterfly,
> For the Last Judgement draweth nigh

I naively violated reverence for life and this repentance was the beginning of my compassion.

Years rolled by and as a young lawyer I developed humanist sympathies. Tellicherry (Malabar), where I enjoyed good practice and had a public life beyond the Bar, drew me into various fields including the SPCA (Society for the Prevention of Cruelty to Animals). One Jayarajan ICS was our Sub-Collector and ex-officio President. At his instance I became the SPCA Secretary. My wife, Sarada Krishna Iyer, had a public image, loved public activities and was an elected member of the Executive Committee of the SPCA. There were active, committed inspectors. Jayaraj—I speak of the 1940s—was the finest officer I had seen and a terror against the corrupt, the racketeers and the anti-social elements but unsparing against violators of animal welfare. So the SPCA became a powerful instrument and I went all out to detect and prosecute cruelty cases.

I acquired, by experience, an expertise in locating kinds of cruel practices on domestic animals and was harsh on the offenders. I used to raid the houses of illicit butchers in the wee hours of dawn to catch them while in the process of killing young calves in the kitchen. I used to spot limping ponies and bullocks on the roads as I was going to various courts in my car, stop them, release the animals from the torture and remand the wounded creatures to the custody of veterinary hospitals. Indeed, bullock cart drivers and jutka drivers by instinct knew my car and their fate, if caught. I surprised slaughter houses to catch butchers who used cruel methods of bleeding cattle to death as a favourite process. There are painless method of killing but the bleeding method is preferred by the butchers on the alleged score that the meat would taste better and the holy Islamic practice sanctioned this mode. I launched numberless prosecutions in cases of cruelty although in the long run, I found them mere exercises in futility. One such instance needs mention. Late at night one day, my wife and I heard a lamb cry. We jumped out of our bed and went down to our neighbour's gate. There, to our horror, we discovered a humble lamb which had squeezed through the gate into the compound of the landlord being bitten by a ferocious watchdog. The kid was bleeding and bleating. We shouted to the landlady of the house, got her to open the gate, extricated the innocent animal and took it in my car to the veterinary hospital. Its life was saved and our heartbeat became normal. To save a life, a little life, is a sacred duty and spiritual solace.

Years later, I persuaded the Kerala Government to pay, out of its exchequer, the salaries of SPCA inspectors. This is the only instance of a State in the country paying the salary of a voluntary body like the SPCA. I love elephants and enjoy the great festivals which provide the glorious spectacle of giant tuskers, bedecked and majestic and patiently halting for hours at night. Is it not piteous crime to tame a pachyderm into motionless posture for the pious pleasure of insensitive devotees? It was a joy to visit Thekkady where wild elephants used to roam in forests mindless of the spectators in the boats floating in the nearby lakes. Once, in the United States, I had the rare occasion to hold two very young lion cubs and get photographed. This was in a sanctuary off Los Angeles.

How exciting it is for a lion to lie contented after its morning fill of a zebra or deer or wildebeest! I have seen them resting in the National Park in the outskirts of Nairobi and in the volcanic crater of Ngorongoro. It was a thrill to see the kangaroos in Australia and the wildebeests, giraffes and zebras in East Africa. But there is nothing to beat the rhino retreat in Assam and the camel trail in the Arab deserts.

It is strange but true that Rukmini Devi, one of the most

humane and gracious ladies associated with Kalakshethra, Madras and President of the Animal Welfare Board insisted on my becoming Vice President of the Animal Welfare Board of India. I was a judge of the Supreme Court (?) but did agree to be on the Board even as I was a Minister in Kerala while continuing notionally to be associated with the SPCA Tellicherry. The universe of animals is the glory of God and humanity belongs to the larger fraternity of Creation. Long years after my retirement, when I settled down in Kochi (Kerala) I took steps to set up the SPCA (Karuna) in the small city in the hope of reducing cruelty to animals. But I have failed because the SPCA does not have crusaders for the cause of animal welfare. The best of institutions in the world wins or loses depending on its great leaders and cadres.

Ngorogoro Crater is a world heritage centre in Tanzania. Its rim is at an altitude of around 7000 feet and its floor 2000 feet below. This awesome hundred square miles of canyon-like hollow holds the richest assemblage of wild life, the most celestial wonder of Creation to behold which is Nature in its abundance, diversity and divine delight. I had travelled from Nairobi to Kilmanjaro to attend a Tri-continental Conference and I was taken by friendly Indian settlers for sight-seeing; and as our jeep in slow locomotion, at each remove revealed, there came into our excited view the rarest of the rare wild species in repose and chase—beasts and birds, lions, leopards, ostriches, rhinos, elephants, giraffes wildebeests and other varieties of animals which baffle description, thrill the eye and fill the heart with Nature's beauty unadorned which is adorned most. What a volcanic glory extinct but exquisite!

What about Kilimanjaro itself at the foothills of which I stayed in the felicitous company of a snow-clad mountain, right on the Equator! It was a lovely peak nearly 20000 feet in height rising right to the top blessing my eyes as each morning I opened the windows to get a glimpse of the ice-capped Infinite.

Nairobi, where I stayed for a couple of days, as a Conference guest of the then President of Kenya, Mr. Kenyatta, is a lovely city and in its outskirts is a national park a drive through which threw me into ecstasy. Roaring lions, after their breakfast of deer, gently lay in the jungle ignoring tourists driving close by. Wild game, with none to hunt on the sly, were a feast for the eye, harmless once hunger is met, provocation absent and man does not threaten. The real wild animal is man perhaps!

While in Australia I went to a park where kangaroos frolicked with the young ones in the pouch of the mother's womb, with long hind legs and long tails hopping without attacking visitors. A joy to keep looking at the pranks of these novel creatures!

Have we in India anything similar to offer to dazzle the visitor? Yes, the unique rhino in the Assam sanctuary with tough skin, long head, small eyes and nose with single horn, has no parallel. And the wild elephants, with long tusks of precious ivory and pachydermic majesty are a rare pleasure. Thekkady (Kerala), Mudumalai (Tamil Nadu) have fascinated me. We have lions too. And tigers and boars, wild pigs and a miscellany of species of monkeys apart from beautiful species of birds which are a rare miracle of Nature.

A delectable anecdote may not be out of place here. We have in the Gir forests a lion game sanctuary. My visit was arranged by the Tourist Department. I was a sitting judge of the Supreme Court then. So wish is followed by fulfillment and facilities flow with ease. I got into a well-protected vehicle, drove into the woods and at a given signal the van stopped and we alighted at the spot where tied to a tree was a hefty bull calf. Why this trembling creature here? I asked, apprehending grave animal injustice. *That* is to tempt the lions to pounce on the prey, said the tourist officer. I had the shock of my life. To kill that pathetic calf to please my curiosity shall never happen, I resolved. Let us free the victim animal and return to the guesthouse, I ordered emphatically with the authority of a judge. Yes sir, the bull calf shall not be touched. We guarantee its safety, the officer assured me. Three gunmen with weapons ready to shoot, stood by the beast. Meanwhile, by smell and sight a few lions appeared with appetite for the meat. They ferociously moved towards the calf. I thought the game was up. Bovine casualty was but a minute away. Three leonine killers moved with eyes zeroing-in the bovine target. Then the three riflemen stepped forward. Wild beasts love their life. And so, the lions looked at the guns in fury but stopped out of fear. The awesome manes frightened me. But the gunmen around me insulated me from peril. The lions shifted their focus to the projected weapons and stopped. When the guns moved forward the kings of the forest slipped away. I had a full view of the lions and their retreat in the face of firepower. There are no suicide squads among wild beasts. Bovine sacrifice was aborted because the guns did the trick. But how did these savage beasts, roaring as rulers, know when to withdraw? Power comes through the barrel of a gun, our political leaders know from Mao Tse Tung. Lions too seem to know! The shaken bovine lived to see another day. I drove back with a guilty conscience.

Another avian experience. Dream of a million parrots taking off at dawn, making the sky glorious green, flying in countless platoons to some invisible blue distance! This million dollar show is what my wife and I witnessed in the island off Jodhpur! The lake below and the sky above daily testify to these parrot troops winging their way back to their island home at dusk. Perched on trees, they flutter and sleep to wake again the morrow morn with a message of green peace! This celestial sight is a unique avian splendour which nowhere else have I come across—the bewitching beauty of birds in spectacular numbers innocently journeying in search of food, not for war in the air carrying ghastly bombs to drop in enemy territory!

But in Kochi I have come across places where parrots, trapped in Karnataka forests, with a wing clipped to make them powerless to fly, being sold to be kept in decorative cages for guilty entertainment.

Having regarded the Buddha and Gandhi as my cultural heritage, having delivered powerful lectures on compassion for living creatures and persuaded, in Rugmini Devi's gracious company, the tough Prime Minister Morarji Desai to ban export of monkeys for cruel experiments and frogs for culpable delight of meat why did I, a vegetarian from birth, take delight in lions with piercing eyes, making ferocious glances at a helpless heifer? Darwin was right:

> We must, however, acknowledge, as it seems to me,
> that man with all his noble qualities...still bears in his
> bodily frame the indelible stamp of his lowly origin.

In India serpents are worshiped and killed. But no lover of animal who visits a snake park can miss the marvellous colours of these creeping reptiles and their peaceful co-existence even though some of them, if hurt bite with deadly poison. I have seen in Madras and in Pappinissery (Kerala) large snake parks with bewildering varieties of some snakes with eerie and some with exquisite skins and creeping habits. Some of them are small, some large, but pythons and boas which construct and kill are twenty seven species and huge in size. I was scared to go near them even in their violent cages. King Cobras, vipers and a wide variety of these vicious wonders, once confined to the farm, do not do harm if fed properly and never hurt wantonly. Of course, we are, by instinct, frightened by snakes, but many people play with them. It is a joy to watch them, because God has made them *ordinarily* non-poisonous. I have been enthralled by the glorious varieties and beauty of these creeping creatures looking for prey but caged away from visitors. Once you take care not to be bitten by them, most snakes are not poisonous but a few hundred species carry venom in their fangs. A few months after I had visited that unique collection of snakes at Pappinisseri, some political malefics with vendetta against the organization which was maintaining the rare collection of reptile marvels destroyed them by fire—a cruelty which is more than barbarity because snakes have no politics and are a charming creation. Why kill them in captivity? One thought occurred to me. Some of the king cobras have stripes and stars on their skin, loveliest at sight. But sometimes stars and stripes on flags carried by armed forces into other countries are far more wicked and venomous because they kill, not individuals, but whole humanity, not by fangs, but by bombs-us!.

A circus with roaring lions is an entertainment for viewers but torture for the frightened, unfree rulers of the wilds. It is drugged, threatened and made to roar to order and perform on the intimidatory command of the commanding coward who holds the whiplash and a revolver. What a savage delight when it obeys and plays its part! What a humiliating trauma for the terrified beast ordered to act contrary to instinct. And yet, the most cruel deal is the cribbed cage where it is kept and fed. Even captive lions have rights against circus terror. Have'nt they? Once, when invited as a special guest for a circus show, I insisted on first seeing the animal cages. A huge lion crouching in a cramped space with half-closed eyes and subdued, the fury lay there in helpless pity. Shock and awe humbled the royal beast into slave submission. I directed the manager, with moral authority, to change the narrow cage and the manager agreed. A menagerie with man acted wild beasts is no good exhibition but savagery to take delight in distress. I agree with that extremist animal lover Maneka Gandhi that wild animal games as circus attraction should stop. Man is perhaps the wildest beast on earth, the Buddha, Mahavira and the Mahatma notwithstanding. Our world has produced Hitler and Mussolini and permitted barbarous bombing of Baghdad by President Bush and Premier Blair killing countless mothers and children and tearing up Mesopotamian Civilization!

While young, I have beheld with fright and delight the snake charmer, discreet with a coiled cobra in his covered receptacle, fascinating a curious crowd. He would sit, take out his pipe, play a tune and out came the cobra with its kingly hood unfurled. As if it enjoyed a music concert, it would sway and dance to the tune of the snake charmer without biting him. How did he transform this venomous reptile into a venial, venom less snake? The magic is easy to guess. Its fangs were removed and the toothless wonder became a harmless creature offering pleasure to the street crowd which contributed coins for the charmer's upkeep. This was innocent joy for boys to look on, the cobra's felonious fangs having been robbed. But what about the serpent itself? Nature violates to scaly body with no limbs and eyelids coils quietly until prodded into poignant performance. Here is Maneka Gandhi's sensitivity about animal cruelty. Compassion is an animal right. Anyway, it is better to play with these rare reptiles than to kill them when most of the species, even according to Gandhi, are non-poisonous. The victim is at least alive. What about kindness to terrible, venomous ones? It is a moral issue.

The most cruel animal, of course, is man although, in his arrogance he acts in the name of right and justice which is a euphemism for exercise of cruel power. Sigmund Freud, in his letter to Albert Einstein, wrote what strikes me as truth: "we may define 'right' (i.e. law) as might of a community. Yet it too is nothing else than violence. It is the communal, not individual, violence that has its way".

Could we transform our violent earth into a glorious planet where everyone will share what Walt Whitman in his 'Leaves of Grass' put in poetry a vision of an ideal world:

> I think I could turn and live with animals, they are so
> Placid and self-contain'd,
> I stand and look at them long and long.
> They do not sweat and whine about their condition,
> They do not lie awake in the dark and weep for their sins,
> They do not make me sick discussing their duty to God,
> Nor one is dissatisfied, not one is demented with the
> mania of owning things,
> Not one kneels to another, nor to his kind that lived
> thousands of years ago,
> Not one is respectable or unhappy over the whole earth.

Pleasant is that sweet bird pheasant flies low, is brightly coloured with long tails, is a picture of innocence and is easily scared into the bushes for fear of being killed for sport. When I was in Mentmore Towers as a guest of Maharshi Mahesh Yogi decades back I used to wake up, open the window, wonder at the artless pheasants which flew into the yard with none to hurt them since all the inmates were in deep meditation and I was of kindly disposition. What a delight at dawn to see these beautiful beaks picking its feed from the ground and, on the slightest sound, winging away lest it be shot for sport! My morning meditation was idly watching 'the glossy, varying dyes, his purple crest, and scarlet-circled eyes, the vivid green his shining plumes unfold, his painted wings and breast that flames with gold' (Pope). I have never seen a lovely pheasant after I left Mentmore Towers where I was wholly immersed in tranquility. But beating the pheasant in splendour and belonging to the same species I guess, is the Indian Peacock. Every time I go to Jaipur I avidly look for these magnificent birds which love to rest on tree tops, come down in majestic gait, ground-feed harmlessly and when the mood excites the male at sight of a peahen, it struts and dances with large plumes spread out and displays, with dazzling beauty, how God is the world's greatest bio-painter. Fleet-footed, fine-feathered, with sharp eyes and beaks, in rapid locomotion, enemy of snakes and celestial vehicle of Lord Subramanya, this Indian bird is a triumph of Creation.

Even rats can be holy and harmless as I discovered when I visited the *rat temple* in a North Indian State where, on the floor, in the rooms, on the ceiling, everywhere, in fearless numbers, why in the sanctum sanctorum itself rats, crowds of them run round. Friendly and free inside the temple, but outwardly they are killed, vivisected and used for experiments as if what works on rats work on humans. Of course, many men are rats, though!

Slaughter of goats as temple sacrifice never propitiates God but the practice still persists (We, of the SPCA totally arrested this unholy unlawful praxis. Even cattle are killed in Assam and Bengal as sacrifice and compassion for all living creatures, a fundamental duty, is flouted!

In China, I found the most terrible culinary cruelty. Even dog's meat is delicacy in some parts of China (and neighbouring States) is a delicacy. Most creatures are eaten in that great country. I saw large transparent receptacles of glass in Chinese hotels, which display many snakes leaving it to the consumer to choose what he fancies. That would be cooked and served. In the Soviet Union, which my wife and I visited more than once horse's milk and meat, were favourites. In one city, at a dinner when I was a chief guest I was struck with horror and embarrassment when a goat head was circulated for me as Chief Guest, to touch it as a custom ceremonial before the dinner began. I refused on principle but the rest consumed the mutton as glutton. There is no arguing about vegetarianism before a people for whom a barbecue meal, grilled on an open fire, is delicious. American's love to eat the legs of frogs *live*, with an easy conscience, is their culture. I wonder what Lord Buddha would do in such a milieu.

Our Maharajas were traditionally hunters for pleasure and killed for sport. It was a cruel game which violated wild life conservation. Times have changed. Our Raj Bhavans preserve parks where harmless wild beasts flourish. In Chennai (Madras) it is a delight to watch the abundance of deer of divergent species rapidly running around fearless of molestation and innocent in their habitat. Whenever I have stayed in the Raj Bhavan, I have enjoyed the Deer Park around. In Hyderabad, a similar feast for the eye awaits the guest. I have often walked up to watch the fenced area where relatively friendly wild animals prowl and even rabbits can be spotted in the bushes in beautiful frisks. Of course, our Zoos are rich in varieties of beasts, birds, snakes, crocodiles and apes. While a minister in Thiruvananthapuram (Kerala), my official bungalow was proximate to the Zoo. The lions there used to roar at sunrise, may be in search of prey. I used to wake up listening to the roar of the lion and still recollect the remarkable alarm. When a captive lion roars, there is no panic but pleasure.

It shall be the duty of every citizen of India to have compassion for living creatures (Art. 51A (g)).

> Man, biologically considered,...is the most formidable of all the beasts of prey, and, indeed, the only one who preys systematically on its own species. (W. James : Memories and Studies).

# 9
# Back to the Bar

The end of July 1959 was also the end of the E.M.S. ministry of which I was a leading member. As the next day dawned I was powerless as a minister—a rare experience of survival shorn of minister's apparel. I was not made for a political career (Bernard Shaw's definition of a political career is biting cynicism. *He knows nothing.* He thinks he knows everything. (That clearly points to a political career). I had retained my own old car without which my mobility would have been a problem. Before joining the ministry I was a lucrative lawyer in Malabar with a flourishing practice and prosperous prospects. However, I had taken a decision not to return professionally to the moffusal bar after my tenure as Law Minister since I was confident and ambitious enough to join the High Court Bar hoping to command a reasonably good practice. I was altogether new to the Travancore Cochin part of Kerala or full time High Court practice. I had disposed of my beautiful beachside mansion at Tellicherry and so, on the fall of the ministry, I was technically homeless. Nevertheless, my wife was my strength and we two drove down to Cochin, the seat of the High Court. I stayed for a few days with my brother-in-law who was also an advocate. I applied to become a member of the Bar Association. The Secretary received from me the fee for life membership and put up my application for acceptance by the Executive Committee of the Bar Association. I was not a communist and my career as a Minister had demonstrated my functional independence and ideological freedom from the Communist Party. My convictions were those of a socialist in the bourgeois sense. However, the Board of the Bar Association considered my application with an inclination to reject it. Why? Because a Minister of a Communist party was a danger to the bar; so they felt, perhaps? The President of the Bar Association was a fine gentleman, K.V. Suryanarayana Iyer, whom I had appointed as Advocate General, (a former Dewan Bahadur). He advised me to withdraw my application which I thought was cowardly. I rejected the pusillanimous proposal and mentioned to him that I had already paid my membership fee which had been duly accepted by the Secretary and therefore, rejection of my membership without good ground was challengeable. I scraped through and became a member of the High Court Bar. I encountered a similar difficulty in securing a residential house on rent. The same untouchability syndrome. Those who were landlords with vacant houses were unwilling to let in a former communist minister. My fellow-traveller antecedent was undesirable enough to disqualify me from tenancy. Here again, after some persuasion, I managed to secure a reasonably good house from a good gentleman, Nandana Menon, who was free from bias. He himself was once a judge of the Cochin Chief Court but was screened out when the Travancore Cochin High Court was formed. He was a fine man with a sympathetic disposition and I offered to pay the rent he demanded. Thus, I settled down to practise by about the end of August 1959. The prejudices of the Bar Association notwithstanding, briefs did come to my chambers because I had established a reputation in the whole State as a successful minister for Law and Justice. People had faith in me, judges were impartial and I could pick up practice rapidly. Soon I rose to a leading position and judging by income, was a success in the profession. Clients from all over Kerala sought my services despite my leftist slant. Gradually, I emerged as one of the top lawyers of the High Court Bar. Years rolled by and by about six years at the Bar, I had to face another encounter.

The General Assembly elections came in 1965 and the constituency where I was a favourite from where I had won the seat two or three times, was naturally to find me as a candidate backed by the Marxist party. But this was not to be.

What was the contretemps? Everything looked rosy. I was popular in the constituency. The Marxist party's strong support would have made my success at the polls an easy achievement. The Marxist party with E.M.S. as its head discussed the matter with me and agreed to support me wholeheartedly. Everything was going the way I desired. But a hitch at the last moment upset the whole process. The party Secretary desired I should adopt the electoral symbol of the Party for my candidature. I demurred. Why? Because I had always, on prior occasions, chosen the symbol of an Independent which was different from the Party symbol. This was in accord with my conviction that while I agreed broadly with the communist theory on dialectical materialism and with the Party on peaceful transformation. I had basic differences on certain fundamentals. So I insisted on my choice of a separate symbol. The party had a point too and would not yield; and so the rupture came. I left, breaking my relations with the Marxists on the electoral front, contested as an Independent from Tellicherry and lost colosally. Of course, I had no discomfiture since politics was not my career. Back at the Bar, I captured my position at the top with ease. Then came another embarrassing episode in my life. Had I won the election the most that could have happened was the opportunity of becoming a Kerala minister. In long retrospect, such a possibility would have been a calamity. Politics is fickle and not my cup of tea. It reminds me of Shakespeare's Measure for Measure:

> Drest in a little brief authority,
> Most ignorant of what he's most assur'd,
> His glassy essence, like an angry ape,
> Plays such fantastic tricks before high heaven,
> As make the angels weep.

I lost the election and won a future at the Bar. I made friends with all. The judicial fraternity was also friendly to me. They were not altogether new to me. While I was Minister for Justice I had occasion frequently to meet the then Chief Justice at his office to sort out administrative problems concerning the Court and Government. Sometimes the Chief Justice would call to his aid one or two other judges.

I remember, a particular occasion when he persuaded most of his colleagues to come for the meeting at his residence where I was suppose to discuss some important issues including the number of working days on which the judges would sit and hear cases. The All India Law Ministers Conference (with me as a member) held in 1957-58 had resolved that the judges of the High Courts be gently persuaded to sit for 210 days, an addition of ten to them practice of *200 days*. I flew to Cochin from Delhi to meet the Chief Justice and the companion judges at his official residence and requested them in all humility to accept the proposal of 210 working days. To my surprise some judges reacted sharply against the suggestion. Are we workers for whom you prescribe the number of working days? asked the indignant brethren. I was mild but firm. But the judges did not agree. Then I told them plainly that the resolution of the All India Law Ministers' Conference was not a trifling affair but a serious proposal in the context of colossal arrears of dockets in courts. They would not yield and I told them that my only alternative was to amend the Kerala High Court Act which prescribed the number of working days of judges and make it obligatory by raising the number to 210, a minimal increase but a judicial gesture that the judges were mindful of the problem of more disposals. We separated on that note. Although I told Hon'ble Chief Justice that I would wait for two weeks more to know whether Judge & Co. would fall in line with my simple proposal. I wrote to the Central Home Minister G.B. Pant about the negative attitude of the Kerala judges. He wrote in turn to the Chief Justice of India about this unfortunate attitude and then came a letter, so I guess, from Chief Justice S.R. Das to Chief Justice Koshy admonishing the judges of the Kerala High Court. Meanwhile, I had introduced a bill to amend the Kerala High Court Act providing for 210 working days. When the bill was pending came a letter from Chief Justice Koshy agreeing to the increased number of days and there the matter ended happily. I mention this episode only to make the point that the judges on the bench were not new awesome figures for me but friendly personalities with whom I had occasion to meet briefly and rarely in my capacity as Minister for Justice.

The defeat in the election in 1965 brought me fully into practice. My political background had brought me close to the people at large and to the various public figures of the State, regardless of partisanship. This was a great asset for me not in my professional income but in my role as a public figure in the political life of the State. I was also involved in a number of organizations with a Leftist slant, and on the whole was more than a moneymaking lawyer. My lawyerly practice did not diminish and my popularity suffered no reduced mileage.

One day the then Chief Justice M.S. Menon asked me to meet him in his chambers. He was a brilliant judge, full of wit and humour, brief in his judgements, racy in his style and profound in his grasp of jurisprudence. His court was a treat to watch and a joy to argue cases. To appear before him and escape unscathed was an experience and I had several occasions to appear, win and lose. I was mystified when I was summoned to meet him, which I duly did. He enquired whether I had given up election politics once for all or intended to pursue political fortunes. I replied firmly and clearly that I had no intention whatever to fight elections any more and that candidacy in elections was out of agenda and was a closed chapter of my life. Even at that moment I had no idea why Menon wanted to meet me—a riddle, wrappe in a mystery inside an enigma. When my answer was unmincing, Menon sprang a surprise. The Chief Justice, with quiet courtesy, told me that I should consent to be a judge of his Court. He gave me no option and his attitude was peremptory. I hesitated and wanted time to consider. He was in a mood to overrule any dissent from me. I had my problems and so took leave of him promising to meet him later. I had not known Chief Justice Menon intimately at a personal level. But I cannot understand the election latent in his present request. Frequently Menon sent for me to know my positive response. I was evasive but then the Chief Justice knew how to get things his way. Apparently because of a hint from him (which I came to know later) the Chief Minister E.M.S. Nampoothiripad sent his cabinet colleague Gouriamma to persuade me to accept the offer. State power, she pleaded, was a necessary tool for transformation of India into a socialist republic. She pressed this point and left. On the contrary, my close friend and former colleague (and for a time a most respected Chief Minister) came to me to dissuade me. If you become a judge it may be good but then as a public figure accessible to people on public issues we will miss you. Therefore, please consider seriously before you walk into an office of aloofness. Anyway, after considerable cogitation, consultation and vacillation, I surrendered. After the due ceremonial process, I was sworn in at an impressive, crowded full court sitting as a judge of the High Court of Kerala. In my reply to the pleasing references from the Bar, which was a rich formality in Kerala when a new judge was sworn in, I replied, as was the custom. There are excerpts from what I said from the bench addressed to the Bar and the people of India. My judicial manifesto was articualted, unfolding my vision and mission and spelling out my solemn agenda in diction which reads fresh even now, in ideology a forecast of what I performed on the Bench in the Supreme Court. My words were charged with conviction and I spoke with feeling. I reproduce it in extenso as it is authentic autobiography and flash of futurology.

> My Lord the Chief Justice, Brother Judges, Brothers and Sisters at the Bar.
>
> 1. At long last, the tantalising process of choosing Judges for the Kerala High Court has worked itself out and the swearing in – has taken place. During these mystifying months it has occurred to me that the many facets of the problem of choice of Judges need a fresh national look, in the light of experience gained during the last nearly two decades. But that is by the way.
>
> 2. Let me, first of all, express my profound gratitude to my Lord the Chief Justice for his great consideration for me and his persuasive role in transforming a para-political, poly-chromatic, free-lance lawyer into a sequestered, strait-jacketed judicial personage. I am deeply thankful to my warm and venerable and oft-spoken friend, Shri Kuruvilla, for his generous words of pleasing sentiment and hyperbolic encomium. Shri. Suryanarayana Iyer, of course, represents the Bar Association and is a revered, towering doyen of the Kerala

Bar. But he brings to my mind intimate associations of a few decades in different spheres of life. I can, therefore, understand his being partial and emotional on this occasion and I am moved by his touching references to my indirect Guru, my father, who, to my deep regret, is too invalid to share in this ceremonial episode. Sensitive awareness of my serious limitations and short-comings forbids my regarding even a fragment of the nice and complimentary things spoken here as true of me. Rather these are words of warning to me as to what I should strive to be and I shall endeavour my utmost to live up to the upright standards and exacting expectations of my brothers at the Bar and of the public at large. I must confess that I am overwhelmed—and indeed heartened—by the avalanche of felicitations and flood of goodwill from the legal fraternity and the broad community on what is descried as my elevation to the High Court Bench.

3. When my metamorphosis from lawyer to Judge or its probability became known, many of my friends and well-wishers were puzzled and some were even tantalised. I was asked: Why did you? Did you, really? I did not give any clear reply. The truth was that the Hamletian dilemma of to-be-or-not-to-be afflicted me too when I gave hesitant consent. Life is a rugged journey with its sharp and strange turns; it is an odd adventure where the exciting forenoons are followed by the mellow afternoons. Sound and fury are succeeded by the still, small voice. Even so, In my career thirty hectic years after I was called to the Bar, an unusual change has occurred to-day. May be, there is a divinity that shapes our ends, and may be 'I have promises to keep and miles to go before I sleep'. But, speaking for myself, life becomes meaningful and finds fulfillment, whatever be the department of activity, if the larger cause of humanity is served, if the tryst with destiny that our nation made long years ago is redeemed and I have had some patriotic role, some small contribution to make in that behalf, be it as an administrator, promoter of public causes, advocate or Judge. Viewed in the humanist, nationalist perspective, there is no inconsistency or discontinuity in my wearing

the judicial robes. And after all, I am convinced that supreme national service can be rendered as Judge of the High Court also. But in this great task of administering justice, the Bar and the Bench are complementary and interdependent and share the common mission of securing justice to every citizen in the country and of creating a just society amidst us. The advocate pleads for right and against injustice. The Judge fulfills himself in the quest for truth and justice. Together, the divine duet of doing justice is played. To me it is, perhaps, a soul-satisfying experience.

4. In India to-day, Judges have not merely to adjudicate on rights and wrongs, but have to be sentinels on the qui vive. They face newer challenges, shoulder a vaster range of responsibilities in upholding the Constitution and the Laws. For, Justice is an ampler, truer concept and the Rule of Law a more positive and dynamic idea, with socio-economic content and political overtones not implied in them by orthodox jurists. The social goals enshrined in the Preamble to our Constitution, the Fundamental Rights Chapter and the Directive Principles of State Policy broadly and vaguely project our current legal philosophy. The judicial organ, being part of the State, shares the national objective and perspective of political and economic democracy, and spells out from the Articles of the Constitution and the corpus juris of India, the legal framework of a secular society with egalitarian urges, thus departing from the old order and sense, themselves on trial. The forensic institutions and the legal system itself need a new orientation, a modern grammar and vocabulary and simpler techniques of social engineering, if they are not to be accused of humble measure, to be a judicial activist and treat my career ahead as a fresh call to service in the cause of the rule of law, which not merely keeps the executive in leash, but insists upon the basic and equal right of every individual to a really free and good life. It is my humble prayer that I be given courage and vision to live up to the sacred trust of the high office, for, I am keenly sensitive to the demanding nature of the judicial process, which strikes

at social evils, legislative transgressions and quasi-judicial injustices. The magnitude of the danger to the Rule of Law is great in these days of self-righteous violence and mass violation of law where rioting is confused with revolution and organised disregard of law is considered the route to a higher form of democracy. An-eye-for-an-eye as a means of justice leaes justice and everyone else blind in the end. This is inhuman. If law runs counter to life, you had better change the law, not challenge it. If the Constitution hampers progress, you must amend it, not defy it nor deny it. That is the discipline of democratic legality, which I shall try to uphold and enforce, strictly in tune with the Constitution and the Laws. In this exciting endeavour, I crave the goodwill and guidance of my Lord, the Chief Justice and the Brother Judges; I seek the co-operation and sympathy of the legal fraternity and hope that the people as a whole desire a peaceful and orderly life, maintained and upheld by the noblest and most pivotal national institution in the Indian Constitution, an upright progressive and fearless judiciary. I, once again, pledge to keep faith with the great traditions of this Court and to serve the community in my new capacity, in the cause of a just order—a new dedication to an old cause. Let us do the task, together as a team.

Decades have rolled by but if I were asked to rewrite the same speech today I would not change a word of it because it reflects my thoughts as of then and now.

# 10

# My Judicial Career—How it Began

Long years ago I made my judicial tryst with destiny when in July 1968 I was elevated to the bench of the Kerala High Court. The usual ceremony of swearing in a new judge is by the whole court assembling in a large hall, followed by 'references' from the bar and appropriate response from the judge who is newly elevated. This customary procedure in the hallowed hall took place in my case also. From the bar to the bench is a leap forward with a sublime obligation to do right and justice without fear or favour, affection or illwill. When the speeches from the bar concluded I responded in all conscience in an address which is reproduce below:-

Reply by the Honourable Mr. Justice V.R. Krishna Iyer

My Lord, the Chief Justice, Brother Judges,
Brothers and Sisters at the Bar,

1. At long last, the tantalising process of choosing Judges for the Kerala High Court has worked itself out and the swearing-in has taken place. During these mystifying months it has occurred to me that the many facets of the problem of choice of Judges need a fresh national look, in the light of experience gained during the last nearly two decades. But that is by the way.

2. Let me, first of all, express my profound gratitude to my Lord, the Chief Justice for his great consideration for me and his persuasive role in transforming a para-political, poly-chromatic, free-lance lawyer into a sequestered, strait-jacketed judicial personage. I am

deeply thankful to my warm and venerable and soft-spoken friend, Shri Kuruvila, for his generous words of pleasing sentiment and hyperbolic encomium. Shri Suryanarayana Iyer, of course, represents the Bar Association and is a revered, towering doyen of the Kerala Bar. But he brings to my mind intimate associations of a few decades, in different spheres of life. I can, therefore, understand his being partial and emotional on this occasion and I am moved by his touching references to my indirect Guru, my father who, to my deep regret, is too invalid to share in this ceremonial episode. Sensitive awareness of my serious limitation and shortcomings forbids my regarding even a fragment of the nice and complimentary things spoken here as true of me. Rather, those are words of warning to me as to what I should strive to be and I shall endeavour my utmost to live up to the upright standards and exacting expectations of my brothers at the Bar and of the public at large. I must confess that I am overwhelmed—and indeed heartened—by the avalanche of felicitation and flood of good will from legal fraternity and the broad community on what is described as my elevation to the High Court Bench.

3. When my metamorphosis from lawyer to Judge or its probability became known, many of my friends and well-wishers were puzzled and some were even scandalised. I was asked: Why did you? Did you, really? I did not give any clear reply. The truth was that the Hamletial dilemma of to-be-or-not-to-be afflicted me too when I gave hesitant consent. Life is a rigged journey with its sharp and strange turns; it is an odd adventure where the exciting forenoons are followed by mellow after-noons. Sound and fury are succeeded by the still, small voice. Even so, in my career thirty hectic years, after I was called to the Bar, an unusual change has occurred to-day. May be, there is a divinity that shapes our ends, and may be afflicted me too when I gave hesitant consent. Life is a rugged journey with its sharp and strange turns; it is an odd

adventure where the exciting forenoons are followed by mellow after-noons. Sound and fury are succeeded by the still, small voice. Even so, in my career thirty hectic years, after I was called to the Bar, an unusual change has occurred to-day. May be, there is a divinity that shapes our ends, and may be 'I have promises to keep and miles to go is redeemed and I have had some patriotic role, some small contribution to make in that behalf, be it as an administrator, promoter of public causes, advocate or judge. Viewed in the humanist, nationalist perspective, there is no inconsistency or discontinuity in my wearing the judicial robes. And after all, I am convinced that supreme national service can be rendered as Judge of the High Court also. But in this great task of administering justice, the Bar and the Bench are complementary and inter-dependent and share the common mission of securing justice to every citizen in the country and of injustice. The Judge fulfills himself in the quest for truth and justice. Together the divine duet of doing justice is played. To me it is, perhaps, a soul-satisfying experience.

4. In India to-day, Judges have not merely to adjudicate on rights and wrongs, but have to be sentinels on the qui vive. They face newer challenges, shoulder a vaster range of responsibilities in upholding the Constitution and the laws. For, Justice is am ampler, triune concept and the Rule of Law a more positive and dynamic idea, with socio-economic content and political overtones not implied in them by orthodox jurists. The social goals enshrined in the Preamble to our Constitution, the Fundamental Rights Chapter and the Directive Principles of State Policy broadly and vaguely project our current legal philosophy. The judicial organ being part of the State, shares the national objective and perspective of political and economic democracy, and spells out from the Articles of the Constitution and the corpus juris of India, the legal framework of a secular, society with egalitarian urges, thus departing from the old order and conservative common law concepts. The

Judges and the Courts are, in a sense, themselves on trial. The forensic institutions and the legal system itself need a new orientation, a modern grammar and vocabulary and simpler techniques of social engineering, if they are not to be accused of exotic, expensive obsolescent and tardy features. I shall endeavour, in a humble measure, to be a judicial activist and treat my career ahead as a fresh call to service in the cause of the rule of law, which not merely keeps the executive in leash but insists upon the basic and equal right of every individual to a really free and good life. It is my humble prayer that I be given courage and vision to live up to the sacred trust of the high office, for, I am keenly sensitive to the demanding nature of the judicial process, which strikes at social evils, legislative transgressions and quasi-judicial injustices. The magnitude of the danger to the Rule of Law is great in these days of self-righteous violence and mass violation of law where rioting is confused with revolution and organised disregard of law is considered the route to a higher form of democracy. An-eye-for-an-eye as a means of justice leaves justice and everyone else blind in the end. This is inhuman. If law runs counter to life, you had better change the law, not challenge it. If the Constitution hampers progress, you must amend it, not defy it nor deny it. That is the discipline of democratic legality, which I shall try to uphold and enforce, strictly in tune with the Constitution and the Laws. In this exacting endeavour, I crave the goodwill and guidance of my Lord, the Chief Justice and the Brother Judges; I seek the co-operation and sympathy of the legal fraternity and hope that the people as a whole desire a peaceful and orderly life, maintained and upheld by the noblest and most pivotal national institution in the Indian Constitution, an upright, progressive and fearless judiciary. I, once again, pledge to keep faith with the great traditions of this Court and to serve the community, in my new capacity, in the cause of a just order – a new dedication to an old cause. Let us to the task, together as a team.

Not merely because it is unconventional and solemn but also because it unfolds a creative career, a profound promise and a transformation in my life I regard it a turning point in my Kismet. By gaining access to a notice opportunity to perform what I deem was a dynamic dimension of service to Indian humanity I have striven to promote social justice with spiritual satisfaction.

# 11

# A Meeting with Indira Gandhi during the Emergency

V.K. Krishna Menon was close to Indira Gandhi from her younger days. She had told me once that Menon used to coax, cajole and compel every Indian student in London, including herself, to work for the India League and they had to sit late in the night to finish the job assigned to them. But they liked the work as it was part of the patriotic struggle from Britain for Indian liberation. When Krishna Menon died a Memorial Society was set up and I happened to the founding President. Lalit Sen, a princely young man, a fine person of charming manners, now no more, was the Secretary. He had served under Nehru when the latter was the Prime Minister and had known Indiraji intimately. The first death anniversary of Menon was observed with a memorial lecture by Jennie Lee, an outstanding Labour personality in London and a friend of Indiraji. The committee of the society resolved to invite Indira Gandhi to preside over the function. And so, Lalit Sen fixed up an appointment for both of us to meet her and make the request to preside over the function.

The Emergency was then in full fury. Jai Prakash Narain and many distinguished persons, who opposed this authoritarian aggression on people's rights, were kept in detention. The nation was in tension and people all over the country raised their voice of protest and many were duly detained, including several innocents from Kerala. I was then a sitting judge of the Supreme Court, but went to meet the Prime Minister in her office for making the formal invitation to preside. Lalit Sen and I entered her chamber in with Block as per appointment and I mentioned the purpose of our visit. But she expressed her reluctance to preside over the meeting. However, out of regard for Menon's memory and her friendship with Ms Lee she agreed to sit next to me at the meeting over which, according to her, I was the appropriate person to preside. I found that pressing her further would not change her mind. So it was decided that I would preside and she would be present next to me. O.K. Once that was settled, I asked Lalit Sen to leave and wait outside. Indiraji and myself were the only two persons in the South Block office.

That morning, the news of the arguments of the Attorney General Niren De in the case challenging the Emergency had been carried which hurt me deeply. The constitutional consequence of the Declaration of Emergency was, urged the Attorney General, the Court was helpless even in cases of police men shooting innocent men. The Court's power to try or punish was under eclipse so long as Emergency lasted. This argument, by democratic standards, was unconscionably outrageous. Yes, but the judges were not outraged, save Khanna, the great dissenter. They merely listened, the prospect of unperturbed by the monstrous mayhem on human rights and fundamental freedoms; and eventually upheld this shocking proposition in pronouncements at learned length. Alas, the darkest hour of forensic downfall, except for the historic dissent of Justice Khanna, was when this disastrous jurisprudence marred our law reports.

When I met the Prime Minister this atrocious argument of the Attorney that the police could shoot but the court, supreme in name, was a powerless power was troubling my soul. So I put it to the great lady, Madam Prime Minister. Is our democracy so dead that when a police bullet brazenly hits a simple human there is no remedy during the Emergency? Great Prime Minister, groomed by sublime Nehru, could your government terrorise the nation with such a dangerous submission in the Supreme Court? Indiraji was taken aback by my accusatory poser. "No, judge," she was apologetic. "I agree that democratic values must be respected. I do not know what the Law Ministry is instructing the Attorney General to argue. I am no lawyer. Will you advise me when such egregious blunder happens"? "I am a sitting judge and cannot and will not counsel the highest Executive without forfeiting my judicial office, as happened to an American Judge who tendered advice to President Lyndon Johnson".

Then ensued a brief but solemn conversation. In the tone of a caveat, but in all humility, I apprised her of the grave national tension prevailing in the country and the urgent need to bring down the explosive heat. In Bangladesh the great Mujibur Rahman, by declaring himself President, became the victim of assassination. Kindly take measures to tone down and tranquillise the national situation. Indiscriminate detentions of harmless people was aggravating the hostility. I know of such harsh incarcerations. I spoke with feeling. She calmly heard me. She has a finer side. 'Bangladesh is a small state and things that happen there cannot occur in our large country of vast diversity. Her reference was to the terrible tragedy of the Mujibur assassination. (The pity of it? Later history had a different tale of Indira assassination to tell). She admitted that from Kerala Dr. K.N. Raj had sent a telegram complaining of wrongful detention and the Home Minister had not yet replied to an enquiry by the Centre about the circumstances of the custody. Emergency, some States think, gives totalitarian power, she complained. Anyway, I left her with the satisfaction in my soul that I had done my admonitory duty and she had known my mind.

That very evening Sri Om Mehta, Home Minister (of State) suddenly called on me. The Prime Minister had asked him to meet me and get the names of those unpardonable detainees about whom I had mentioned to her at my afternoon meeting. I gave four or five names of such persons who, to my best belief, were guiltless but were in preventive detention. Later I learnt that they were all released—perhaps on enquiry through the I.B.

## CODA

A few days after the *ADM Jabbalpur* judgment (Emergency

Case) was delivered there was a dinner where judges were the guests. Sri Niren De, the Attorney General, was also there. He came upto me—I was sitting in a corner and sat to tell me something deeply sombre and pathetically confidential which he wanted to unburden and reveal to me to relieve his conscience. "What was it about? You are a socially sensitive judge and can appreciate my profound anguish, he said. 'What was the agony in my soul, which gave me sleepless nights? It was about my defense of the Emergency. I did not want a ghastly law which would banish judicial jurisdiction in the face of subjective executive violence. I thought of the strategy of shocking the judges into sanity, into rousing their revulsion into reading down the deadly law into claiming space for judicial invigilation as haven of human rights. So I urged the damned extreme position hoping that humanist jurisprudence would be the indignant robed reaction. So I pressed, against my heart but with the expectation of awakening the aghast protest of the Bench. If the police abused power the court would not sit and watch with cauterised conscience but would act in fiat justicia spirit—so, I thought, would be their response. I wanted the robes to rage against that violent view I propounded and come down on such Emergency inhumanity. But, to my surprise, barring Khanna, the other justices heard but did not furiously resist. I felt sad as a jurist but found success as Counsel. Sir, frankly I passed through mental stress which I now confide in you because your conscience would have rebelled". The narration ended, the dinner was over. And Niren De passed away not long after. Nariman, the admirable and conscionable advocate resigned his post as Solicitor General. But I believed the Attorney General's confessional version. Then why did he not give up his office? Good men, gripped by grave crises, sometimes cave in, maybe. Niren De was a serious, sound advocate who argued later for democracy and against gross misuse of Presidential Power of supersession of State autonomy, *but failed*. Anyway, the *A.D.M. Jabbalpur* ruling ranks in disgrace with the Dred Scott case where the American Supreme Court pronounced that Negroes were slaves to be owned, not humans who could own. Lord Atkin has the last word in Liversidge v. Sir John Anderson:

> I view with apprehension the attitude of judges who on a mere question of construction when fact to face with claims involving the liberty of the subject show themselves more executive minded than the executive. Their function is to give words their natural meaning, not, perhaps, in war time leaning towards liberty, but following the dictum of Pollock C.B. in Bowditch v. Balchin (I), cited with approval by my noble and learned friend Lord Wright in Barnard V. Gorman (2): "In a case in which the liberty of the subject is concerned, we cannot go beyond the natural construction of the statue." In this country, amid the clash of arms, the laws are not silent. They may be changed, but they speak the same language in war as in peace. It has always been one of the pillars of freedom, one of the principles of liberty for which on recent authority we are now fighting, that the judges are no respecters of persons and stand between the subject and any attempted encroachments on his liberty by the executive, alert to see that any coercive action is justified in law. In this case I have listened to arguments which might have been addressed acceptably to the Court of King's Bench in the time of Charles I.

Our freedoms are in peril if our courts suffer pusillanimity or arrogance.

# 12
# Thou Shall not Kill

Young at the bar at the Tellicherry District Centre, I had the good fortune to acquire soon a lucrative practice which I attribute more to a lucky concatenation of circumstances than to better legal acumen or daring advocacy. My mentality? A socialistic perspective, compassionate disposition and litigation as a challenging opportunity to convince the court of the truth of your cause. Idealism is elan and every brief is a battle for right and justice. In the miscellany of my professional life many murder cases sought my services. Macaulay's colonial justice perception rated Indian life as of such scarce value that death sentence was the rule for murder and life imprisonment an exception. His penological pharmacopoeia presented hanging as a routine nostrum for homicide. This harsh nosology, in British and ICS judges' hands, made the Indian in the dock, with Sec. 302 IPC labelled in the charge, a victim's life written off. They *swing*, save in the rarer cases of lucky *kismet*. There was a revolt in my soul when I found pachydermic judges sentenced innocent persons to capital penalty since our grave doubts never struck the 'robed terror on the bench' 'reasonable' enough to earn the benefit of 'British' doubt.

With burning conviction I assert that I have come across cases where the evidence clearly warranted a verdict of 'not guilty' but the sentence visited was one of death penalty. I was conditioned by this experience against death sentence, apart from the cultural heritage which was in my blood against taking a human life even if there was proof of murder. Indeed, I have known of cases in the High Courts hearing death sentence cases being disposed off in a few sentences of dismissal of the appeal. While England has abolished death sentence, Gandhi country believes in judicial homicide as a retributive corrective. Of course, there have been exceptional judges with commitment to values although the ghastly instances have been far more. I speak so firmly because, after examining the materials on record, I have been thoroughly convinced of the innocence of the accused but the ICS judge has had no compunction in his conscience in rejecting every plea. Way back in 1937, when I was but an apprentice at law, a strange case occurred. One accused, tried by the Sessions Court of Calicut, was cursorily sentenced to death. But when the matter reached the Madras High Court for conformation of death sentence the judges found that some young immature cross-examiner had hardly done justice to the case. So the case was sent back to the same Sessions Judge for retrial. Judge Happell (who later became a judge of the High Court) appointed a Sr Advocate to handle the case for the accused. My father, V.V. Rama Ayyar, an excellent cross-examiner and leading criminal lawyer, appeared for the accused, presented the case in a different way and the same judge Happel acquitted the accused, reversing his prior death sentence. Imagine the tragedy, had this reversal not taken place.

I know of a murder case where I appeared for the accused. The evidence was clearly in his favour but the police investigator terrorised the father of the accused to give evidence against his own son and that tilted the scales. The father the same evening came to me, wept that his son be saved and convinced me that he swore against him under violent intimidation by the investigator. The law has no heart and the young boy was executed.

## ANOTHER MACABRE EPISODE

There was a sensational case of murder in broad daylight in Payyoli, Malabar, where five persons chased the victim, but two withdrew after a while. The remaining three overtook the deceased and stabbed him to death. The F.I.R contained the names of all the five although two of them had given up the culpable pursuit. During the investigation the Inspector of Police was satisfied that two were innocent of the murder, but he manipulated evidence against all the five on the same lethal lines lest the court should take the view that if the F.I.R was concocted in regard to two the other three might also be given the benefit of doubt. If the case ended in an acquittal the police officer's career would be in peril, he apprehended. So he fabricated evidence against all the five, and in merciless equality, all were executed for the crime. When I asked the Inspector about the matter he admitted that two were falsely implicated but, to secure the conviction of the other three, he had to sustain the guilt of every name in the F.I.R. Otherwise, in the event of acquittal, a judicial censure might jeopardize his career. On independent enquiry I gathered that the two innocents became martyrs of factitious judicial probability. I was deeply hurt in my bosom when I gathered the truth while dealing with a connected civil case. I have other examples from my own professional career of the guiltless being sent to the gallows by judicial warrant.

An extraordinary instance recorded by Justice A.S.P. Iyer, dramatising a grave case of an innocent man going to the hangman's halter, in his book "25 years a Civilian" is a tragic tale. Let me extract a page from my book titled 'Death and After' where I have reproduced Justice A.S.P.Iyer (P-63/64).

> The Sub-Collector's bungalow was a big and spacious one, but had no compound walls and was situated in the same compound as the District Judge's Bungalow and the District Medical Officer's Bungalow. One room in the even bigger District Judge's bungalow was not used, the reason assigned being that a previous District Judge had committed suicide there, He had sentenced a man to death for murder, though the man had protested that he was at Chicacole, miles away from the scene of murder, at the time he was alleged to have committed the murder and thus could never have committed the murder. The sentence was confirmed by the High Court and the man duly hanged. Some time after that, the man's spirit is said to have appeared before the District Judge in his sleep at 2 a.m. at night and told him, "It is you who have committed the murder and not I. If you go and look up the records in the Chicacole Sub-Collector's office, you would find that in a mahagar I have been noted as having been present

there that day. The conscientious District Judge, an Englishman, took his car and went to Chicacole and found that the statement was true. The man had not been able to mention it when alive as he did not know that his presence was noted in the mathagar. The District judge is then said to have taken his own life on the principle enunciated in Hammarabi's law, "A life for a life". His example is reminiscent of the ancient Tamil King Nedunchezhiyan who died of shock on realising that he had wrongly sentenced Kovalan to death for a crime he did not commit.

When I became a judge of the Supreme Court death sentence cases came before my bench for adjudication. When there were concurrent findings by the Sessions Court and the High Court, the recorded evidence left no room for departure from the conclusion. The question of confirmation of the death sentence became a serious problem of humanism and compassion and of the adoption of the reformatory theory of penology as against the savage, sadist deterrent and retributive alternatives. In Ediga Annamma's case (1974 SC 799), a young woman had been sentenced to death for foul murder under gruesome circumstances. By British Indian standards this infliction of lethal ferocity could not be faulted but the compassionate vision of the Constitution and the ethos of non-violence of Gandhi country did make a difference in interpretation of the Code. Hermeneutics varies with cultural perceptions and in my view, death sentence has suffered obsolescence, and even the United Nations in their relevant International Covenants advocates abolition. The Supreme Court of the United States struck down death sentence as unconstitutional since it was unguided power vested in the judge. Adopting a humane perspective, myself and Justice Sarkaria held that, even if technically death sentence did not suffer from unconstitutionality in India as held earlier by a larger harsher bench, there was still scope for evolving parameters whereby death sentence would be as good as dead. I wrote a long judgement exhaustively travelling through various countries to reach the conclusion that the world was veering round to abolition of death sentence. We reduced the death sentence to life imprisonment, although on the facts it was a case of horror. Judicial clemency, operating on the wings of creative compassion, touches heights of sublimity and that is what *Ediga Annamma* did. The pronouncement became a sensation because the brutality of death sentence was negated to the alarm of Draconian judges.. The same day, during lunch recess, Chief Justice Ray telephoned me and we met in his chambers. Have you held death sentence unconstitutional asked the disturbed Chief Justice in astonishment. Don't you know that a Constitution Bench has upheld the *vires* of death sentence? Chief, I am aware of the Constitution Bench ruling but within the provisions of 302 IPC it is perfectly open, indeed obligatory for the court to weave guidelines to make the harsher penalty a rarer option and life sentence for murder being made the rule rather than the exception. Although his spiritual philosophy is profoundly rooted in Swami Vivekananda, his pragmatic perceptions reveal judicial severity. We cannot have two philosophies, one for personal and other for professional consumption. *Life is dear* and cannot be taken even by the judicial brethren except under compelling circumstances. I had relied on the British abolition of death sentence and strengthened my conclusion with a wealth of value based material. In more than one case I had affirmed the same conclusion although brother Justice A.P.Sen for whose friendship I have affectionate esteem did differ from me in those rulings. I was in a majority and so won the day for *Life*. In yet another case, I disagreed with Justice Kailasam who insisted that since three persons had been murdered by the accused, death sentence was the only condign punishment. Luckily, Justice Untwalia supported me and I held that counting the dead bodies is not decisive of the severity of sentence but a totality of circumstances, with weightage for Life as against Death, should form the conspectus of the judicial. The Life versus Death eventually ended in a five-judge bench decision where the court seemed to stand by my view holding that death sentence should be awarded *only* in the rarest of rare cases. Victory for the case of human life was still elusive for me but a great march ahead had been achieved.

One day shortly after my retirement, I received a lovely letter from Lord Scarman, one of the greatest judges of the

Common Wealth. He wrote to me thus:

> Dear Judge,
>
> I am sending you a copy of the Privy Council Appeal Judgement from Jamaica. The case is Riley Vs. the Attorney General. You will see that Lord Brightman and myself in our dissenting opinion made very great use of some observations of yours in the Supreme Court.
>
> Yours sincerely,
>
> Leslie Scarman

I take the view that the reformatory process is a vote against death sentence. Let me give extracts from one of my judgements, largely to emphasize my social philosophy tuned to spiritual values and constitutional vision. These humanist imperatives relevant to death and death sentence moulded my judicial values. They make odd bit unique reading for a court pronouncement.

> "But 'murder most foul' is not the test, speaking scientifically. The doer may be a patriot, a revolutionary, a weak victim of an overpowering passion who, given better environment, may be a good citizen, a good administrator, a good husband, a great saint. What was Valmiki once? And that sublime spiritual star, Shri Aurobindo, tried once for murder but by history's fortune acquitted.
>
> "The dignity of the individual shall not be desecrated by infliction of atrocious death sentence merely because there is a murder proved although crying circumstances demand the lesser penalty. To exemplify, supposing a boy of fifteen incited by his elder brothers, chases with them a murderer of their father and after hours of search confronts the villain and vivisects him in blood-thirsty beastiality. Do you hang the boy, blind to his dignity and tenderness intertwined?
>
> "Our culture is at stake, our Karuna is threatened, our Constitution is brought into contempt by a cavalier indifference to the deep reverence for life and a superstitious offering of human sacrifice to propitiate the Goddess of justice.
>
> "We must always have the brooding thought that there is a divinity in every man and that none is beyond redemption. But death penalty, still on our code, is the

last step in a narrow category where, within a responsible spell, the murderer is not likely to be cured and tends to murder others, even within the prison or immediately on release, if left alive—a king cobra which, by chronic habit, knows only to sting to death unless defanged if possible. The patience of society must be tempered by the prudence of social security and that is the limited justification for deprivation of fundamental rights by extinguishment of the whole human being. The extreme penalty can be invoked only in extreme situations".

Western winds against Death Sentence give hope for Life. The International Court of Justice at the Hague recently ordered the U.S. to stay the execution of three Mexicans and reserved the right to intervene in dozens of other cases (Feb 6-2003 Houston Reuters). I have plenty of material strongly suggestive of illegal execution of innocent people held wrongly guilty. Just a few I am extracting below to confirm my assertion that death sentence on death sentence is overdue:

> "U.S. Senator John Kerry (D-Mass), who is likely to seek the 2004 Democratic nomination for President, recently voiced his opposition to the death penalty during an interview on "Meet the Press".
>
> I don't think it is right to have a criminal justice system that kills innocent people. Over 100 people have been released from death row in America in the last year with DNA evidence and other evidence showing they didn't commit the crime for which they had been (convicted), some of them in jail for 10, 15 years for a crime they didn't commit.
>
> (Meet the Press – transcript, December 1, 2002).
>
> Former Federal Chief Judge Calls Death Penalty "Legalized Murder".

While I had established an abolitionist reputation for compassionate punishment, there came an invitation from the Amnesty International for me to inaugurate a world conference against death sentence to be held in Stockholm, Sweden. The Prime Minister Olaf Palme was, of course, to inaugurate the conference first and I was to come next. But a little anecdote is of some interest in this connection.

Morarji Desai was Prime Minister of the country and Atal Bihari Vajpayee, the Foreign Minister. Having accepted the Amnesty International invitation I had no problem about finance since the entire cost would be happily taken care of by the host institution. Nevertheless, since I was leaving the country as a sitting judge, although I did not require the permission of the Central Government, I still felt it fair to inform the foreign minister about the matter. So I telephoned Vajpayeeji, appraised him of the invitation for the International Conference and sought his good wishes. I made it clear that the State had no financial commitment since the Amnesty International was my host. But the gracious Vajpayjee immediately told me that his ministry would meet all the expenses of my trip to Stockholm and that I need not rely on Amnesty for this purpose. I was pleased with the proposition but knowing austere Morarji Bhai and his incorrigible parsimony I was sure that he would not allow his public resources to be diminished even though it might be a matter of prestige that an Indian judge was to inaugurate an International Conference. So I cautioned Vajpayeeji that the Prime Minister would not release the public purse and the foreign ministry may not be able to foot my bill. The optimistic External Affairs Minister told me that he would meet the Prime Minister himself and get financial clearance. But the next day he called me so ruefully to express his disappointment at the Prime Minister's attitude. For Morarji Bhai the public treasury was more important than my inauguration of the International Conference. But I did go to Stockholm, did passionately present my humanist opposition to death penalty but travel cost was handsomely met by Amnesty, the globally committed organisation for human rights.

Before I wind up, I must quote extensively from Shiv Mohan Singh (1977 SC 949).

> **1. *KRISHNA IYER, J.*** :- If 'survival after death' may aptly describe any litigative phenomenon, the present review proceeding may well equality for that quaint claim. The relief of review relates to the death penalty imposed upon the petitioner by the trial Court, confirmed in appeal, and dismissed even at the stage

of special leave by this Court. In the ordinary course, judicial finality has thus been affixed on the capital sentence so awarded although Presidential clemency, which has been sought and negatived, may still be open under Article 72 of the Constitution. Mercy, like divinity, is amenable to unending exercise but in this mundane matter it is for the Head of State to act and not for the apex Court.

2. Sombre sentencing is the Fifth Act in the tragedy of a murder trial and, for the Judges of the Supreme Court, assumes a grim seriousness and poignant gravity since the petitioner's final appeal for judicial commutation, if rejected, may perhaps prove imminently fatal to his life. Even so, when we chronicle the events connected with the judicial proceedings in this Court it will be realised that our review power has repeatedly been invoked in vain and naturally a further exercise of the same power must be justified by the compelling pressure of fresh circumstances with the limits of the law. The nature of the judicial process, even at the tallest tower, is such that, to use Cardozo's elegant expressions, 'a judge even when he is free, is still not wholly free; he is not to innovate at pleasure; he is not a knight-errant, roaming at will in pursuit of his own ideal of beauty or of goodness; he is to draw inspiration from consecrated principles.' Where the judge's values and those prevailing in society clash, the Judge must, in theory, give way to the 'objective right.'

3. The focus, therefore, must turn on the existence of grounds of manifest miscarriage of justice unavailable on the earlier occasions. Before that, a brief reference may be made to the 'criminal' facts.

4. A treacherous murder of a tender school-body the petitioner, the circumstances of which were so heartless and heinous, terminated condignly at the trial Court and the High Court, the extreme penalty having been visited on the offender for his horrendous killing. This Court refused special leave to appeal, drawing the dark curtain on the criminal proceedings. The petitioner struggled to extricate himself from the executioner by a

sequence of desperate steps. On his behalf, a motion for re-hearing the special leave petition was fruitlessly made to this Court. A review petition was made again to this Court in vain. Yet another, out of same motive but with modified reliefs, was made and dismissed. Then followed an application for directions regarding remand of the case of the Court of Session for reconsideration of the sentence in the light of Section 235 (2) of the Code of Criminal Procedure, 1973. Dismissal of this proceeding did not deter the petitioner from persisting in moving this Court. That is how the present review petition has been put in on his behalf by his father.

5. Mercy petitions to the president punctuated the court proceedings but they too were turned down. The convict, nevertheless, clung on and, as stated earlier, his pathetic persistence in the plea for commutation has been passed before us by counsel on two scores. He has urged that a decision of this Court in Shanta Singh v. State of Punjab, Criminal Appeal No.230 of 1976, Dt. 17-8-1976 (reported in AIR 1976 SC 2386) of which he was not aware at the earlier stages entitled him to a remand to the Sessions Court for reconsideration of the sentence of death. Secondly, he has also pressed upon us personal and social circumstances which have received judicial approval as justifying the imposition of the lesser sentence of life imprisonment even where the offence of murder has been made out.

6. In the ordinary course, the supplicant's forensic battle for life must be repelled by us since this Court has refused leave, rejected review petitions and denied reconsideration. Even so, realising that by this prolonging proceedings he is longing for dear life and clutching at legal straws, we have desisted from a dramatic rejection of the petition outright, anxious to see if there be some tenable ground which reasonably warrants judicial interdicts to halt the hangman's halter. We were willing to strain, within permissible limits, to blend leniency with legality. 'The last breath' is the last hold of the law on the living to do justice and at that point judges, while hating the crime, do not hate the

man who committed it, such being the humanism of penal justice. Circuit Judge Christmas Humphreys told the B.B.C Reporter recently that a judge looks "at the man in the dock in a different way; not just a criminal to be punished, but a fellow human being, another form of life who is also a form of the same one life as oneself.' In the context of Karuna and punishment for Karma the same Judge said:

"The two things are not incompatible. You do punish him for what he did, but you bring in a quality of what is sometimes called mercy, rather than an emotional hate against the man for doing something harmful. You feel with him; that is what compassion means."

(The Listener, D/- 23-11-1976, page 692).

But if the harsh frontiers of the criminal law are clearly drawn, to travel beyond is out of bounds for the Court.

Farewell to death sentence is my final conviction. Perhaps, a minimal exception may be made in the case of blood thirsty economic mafia who inflict on whole communities starvation, rape, robbery and other anti-social offences. Even they must be spared their life if they can be transformed into safe human beings through penological therapeutics. From the Buddha and Jesus down to Gandhi and Jayaprakash Narayan, we have one great lesson to learn from our cultural heritage; Thou shall not kill.

# 13
# Separate Shamsher Singh Opinion—A Hospital Telephone Call

A land of settled government,
A land of just and old renown,
Where Freedom slowly broadens down,
From precedent to precedent

If India is to be a land of settled Government, judicial precedent must slowly broaden down the fundamental freedoms of the people. One such notable precedent is Shamsher Singh case (1974 S.C P-2192). A bench of seven judges heard the case. The leading judgment having been delivered by Ray C.J, a separate judgment focussing emphatic attention on the constitutional law of Cabinet Government was delivered by Bhagavati and Krishna Iyer J. Why was it that a separate judgment was delivered laying down the law of Cabinet system whereunder the President (Governor) reigns but the Prime (Chief) Minister and his colleagues rule. The quintessence of our parliamentary system consists in this supremacy although in verbal wonder, the plenary executive head is the President or the Governor as the case may be. This constitutional point of grave import arose for consideration in Shamsher Singh case. While the seven judges who sat on the bench broadly agreed to the law, the separate opinion expounded the constitutional law at great length and still remains the clearest exposition of the Indian Cabinet Government within substantially the same parameters prevail in England.

Shamsher Singh was delivered in 1974 and the separate opinion was handed down by Justice Bhagavati on behalf of himself and myself (Krishna Iyer J).

In 1957 I became a minister holding the portfolio of law and home, in the State of Kerala. I had no doubt even at that time that the Governor had to act on the advice of his ministers, although in form the constitutional text reads as if the Minister advise and the President decides. The law is the other way about. As a young minister but sure of my constitutional law I once drew the attention of the Governor to the fact that I had as Home Minister decided on a commutation of a sentence and therefore the Governor need not exercise himself reading through the expensive deposition in the case. The Governor agreed about the law and signed the commutation. Decades later, I had occasion, in my leading judgment in *Maru Ram* case to examine and lay down the law of commutation of death sentence on the same lines. The power belongs to the Cabinet, though not exercisable arbitrarily; the Governor, as constitutional head, had to accept the advice and duly sign the commutation order. If I may say so with a sense of satisfaction, the law of the constitution as I learnt from experience as minister, stood me in good position while functioning as judge. To work the constitution teaches better than by reading the text lexicon in hand. On critical occasions, I have had the advantage of confidently taking decision without the formal concurrence of the Governor. I must caution, however, that if the minister is illiterate in constitutional law and violate cabinet responsibility, he may be like a bull in a China shop and practice the grammar of anarchy, doing what he should not do and failing to act where he had to.

Fifteen years after I ceased to be a minister, I heard arguments in Shamsher Singh case on the power of the President and the Governor. All the seven judges on the Bench took the same view, but then I felt strongly that the euphemism of the Constitution might be misleading unless clarified luminously. The totality of executive power textually vests in the Governor but on more than one occasion he is more or less a glorified cipher with power to advise, not decide. To avoid confusion, and to make the law unmincingly explicit I thought it is a good opportunity to explain emphatically the power of the Governor vis-a-vis the Chief Minister. Ray C. J had briefly dealt with the matter but, the exhaustive discussion the subject deserved, especially because of the ambiguity of the language used in the Constitution was my justification. Should I write a separate judgement? I decided I should, but circumstances made this a hard choice. My wife had already undergone a heart surgery, but needed another which we thought could be done better in the United States. My son Ramesh was working in Milwaukee and there was an excellent heart hospital there. So we resolved to fly to the U.S as soon as the court vacation began. But that left hardly a few days for me to prepare the judgment. The importance of the points at issue and the constitutional researches I had on my table made brevity an impossibility. Therefore hard-pressed for time I did dictate at a stretch my opinion which has to be corrected and completed, before I left on my long trip. My Private Secretary Chandramouli was quite efficient and finished my long judgment in the shortest possible time. The draft opinion was lying on my table.

My wife was a political science student and knew the rudiments of Indian Constitutional Law. She casually glanced at the judgment lying on the table, was fascinated by the diction and the scholarly presentation. I gathered later that she was deeply impressed by the learning in the judgment and liked the opinion as a lovely piece. Anyway, leaving the corrected draft of the judgment with my Secretary, who kept confidentiality strictly, we flew to Milwaukee. There she was admitted into the hospital and the date for heart surgery was fixed. What would happen? Would she survive? Hope and despair alternated in our bosom. Then came a special messenger from the Indian Embassy in Washington D.C. with a copy of the Chief Justice's draft judgment. There was a letter by Ray C.J to me indicating that since a couple of months or so had already elapsed after the case was closed, the judgment had to be delivered without delay. The Chief asked me either to sign in approval of his judgment or to produce at once a separate judgment, if I had any. There was a sense of urgency in the Chief's note. I was perplexed and felt unhappy that the Chief Justice was not willing to wait till I returned from America. I was left with no option. My draft judgment was in Delhi, not in the hospital in Milwaukee. In that helpless plight, anxious about the outcome of the next day's surgery, I wrote my approval of the Chief Justice's judgment, hunded over to the messenger and left and I sighed relief. Was the delivery of my concurring judgment more important when confronted by the crisis of the impending heart operation? No.

My wife was lying in the intensive care room watching my worried face. Misery and gloom were writ large on my face and so my wife asked me what it was all about. I told her about the Chief Justice's messenger and the message. Having no option left I told my wife that I had signed my consent to the Chief Justice's opinion. Let my draft text on the table of 2, Teenmurti Marg slumber for ever! What is more valuable *in your life*? This was a tearful moment when, forgetting her critical state of health, Sarada my wife asserted that my draft opinion should be delivered as my separate judgment as it was a good piece, fine precedent and would be long remembered for its language and the law. She added firmly that I telephone Justice Bhagavati *from the hospital* to collect my judgment from Chandramouli and deliver it as my separate opinion. If he agreed with me, the judgment may be delivered on behalf of both of us. Bhagavati and I were very close friends. From the hospital I telephoned him and he readily agreed to pronounce the opinion as *our* separate judgment. So it was that in Shamsher Singh's case, my judgment was delivered on behalf of Justice Bhagavati and myself. I am ever grateful to my learned brother for this act of courtesy. My wife passed away the next day as the surgery failed, but my judgment in Shamsher Singh's case survived with an obituary touch.

The great constitutional savant Seervai, who never missed an opportunity to criticise my judgments and my English, did make an exception while commenting on my separate opinion in Shamsher Singh case.

The Chief Justice pressed me for an early approval

because he could not wait longer. After all, only two or three months alone had passed after the arguments where closed. The case had been heard at length and covered a constitutional issue of consequence. Were two months too long a delay. Later years have revealed that a large number of judges of the Supreme Court and the High Courts have been indefensible dilatory and perfunctory in pronouncement of judgements. If you collect statistics, many judges of the High Courts will be guilty of procrastinatory delinquency, allowing months and years to pass after the arguments have wound up. A code of conduct for judges insisting on early pronouncement of judgment is a felt necessity if audi auteram partem, in the dimension of promptitude of delivery of judgement after hearing, were to be a binding rule. Nor, indeed, is the Supreme Court a model for prompt pronouncement of judgments. *'ye are the salt of the earth; but if the salt have lost his savour, wherewith shall it be salted?'*

Leaving judges and their long delayed pronouncements in contrast to the quick judgements delivered during my time, let me conclude this piece with what Seervai in his classic work on the Constitution critically observed about my separate opinion in Shamsher Singh's case:

> 18.26 To those who are not put off by an highly ornamental and emotional style of legal exposition, the concurring judgment of Krishna Iyer J. makes interesting reading. Stripped of ornament and emotion the judgment comes to this: Krishna Iyer J. agreed with Ray C.J. that under our Constitution the President and the Governors are constitutional heads of government since the Constitution has adopted a Cabinet or parliamentary form of government. This is clear from the opening paragraph of his judgment:
>
> "These two appeals, by a couple of small judicial officers whose probation has been terminated by orders of concerned Ministers in conformity with the recommendations of the High Court, have projected constitutional issues whose profound import and broad impact, if accepted, may shake

up or re-shape the parliamentary cornerstone of our nation. Great deference and complete concurrence would have otherwise left us merely to say 'we agree' to what has fallen from the learned Chief Justice just now, but when basic principles are assailed with textual support, academic backing and judicial dicta, speech, not silence, is our option"

The "thesis" of the judgment is:

"Not the Potomac, but the Thames, fertilises the flow of the Yamuna, if we may adopt a riverine imagery. In this thesis we are fortified by precedents of this Court, strengthened by Constituent Assembly proceedings and reinforced by the actual working of the organs involved for about a 'silver jubilee' span of time."

Following the sound advice to translate the out-of-the-way into the every day, the thesis of the judgment is that judicial precedents, debates in the Constituent Assembly and the actual working of our Constitution for nearly 25 years, show that our Constitution has adopted the British Parliamentary and Cabinet form of government, as opposed to the Presidential form of government adopted in the United States Constitution, so that the President of India, and the Governors of the States are, like the sovereign of the United Kingdom, constitutional heads of government.

Thus ends the Shamsher Singh episode which is now more a sad recollection for me than a powerful pronouncement of Constitutional Law.

# 14
# The Story behind the Ratlam Case

A white man taught me the Law.

Way back in 1940 the seed of the Ratlam Municipality case, decided in 1980 by the Supreme Court, was sown in my brain by a European Sub Collector J.I. Wood I.C.S who presided over the Joint Magistrate's Court in Tellicherry (Malabar) at that time. How did this happen? I was quite a young lawyer ambitiously crossing swords in court with self-confidence. I had a client Viswanathan, the proprietor of the Madras Cafe in Cannanore within J.L.Wood's jurisdiction. This prosperous hotelier fell out with his landlord, a simple sait who owned the building but was artless in dealing with tough tenants. The landlord lived behind the hotel but the access for scavenging was common for landlord and tenant. When the tenant fell out with the landlord he hit upon a vicious idea of closing the door which provided the common access through which the scavenger was to enter to clean up the landlord's latrine. When the door was closed the scavenger could not go in and the latrine of the landlord began stinking. This was an insufferably noxious situation. The naïve sait slipped out of his house at dawn and drove up to the Sub Collector's House 15 miles away, narrated to him his pathetic plight and his tenant holding him to ransom. Mr. J.I. Wood was a humane 'CIVILIAN', jumped into his car and himself drove down to Cannanore. He visited the noxious scene, was satisfied that the nuisance should be abated and on the spot issued an order to keep the scavenger's access open until further orders. He exercised his power under section 133 Cr.P. Code and served the order instantly on the tenant. Viswanathan, the tenant, frightened and defeated, rushed to my place asking me to appear for him before the Joint Magistrate to get the ex-parte order cancelled. I got ready with my law and reached the court in time to get the Magistrate's first attention. J.I. Wood I.C.S was no wooden bureaucrat but a sensitive executive magistrate. My law books and learned arguments could not move the young 'CIVILIAN'. 'Your argument is ingenious, but your inference is not inevitable. I have made personal inspection and am convinced about the nuisance. Argument halts where experience negates. Therefore, I confirm the order'. This, in brief, was section 133 in practical application, free from legalese. The life of the law is not logic but experience. I learnt the lesson of public nuisance and the law, although I lost my case without adequate 'audi alteram partem'.

One may lose a legal battle but win a social war. That is the story of Ratlam (AIR 1980 SC 1622). That small Cannanore case, decided by a mere Joint Magistrate, was the seed which blossomed forty years later into a leading case on environmental law decided by a bench over which I presided by accident. Look at the comparable condition between Ratlam and Cannanore. I quote what the court spelt out in the case:

> The key question we have to answer is whether by affirmative action a court can compel a statutory body to carry out its duty to the community by constructing sanitation facilities at great cost and on a time-bound basis. At issue is the coming of age of that branch of public law bearing on community actions and the court's power to force public bodies under public duties to implement specific plans in response to public grievances.
>
> (The court described conditions of filth and stench resulting from the absence of public sanitation facilities or drains.)
>
> The Sub-Divisional Magistrate, Ratlam, was moved to

take action under S. 133 Cr. P.C. to abate the nuisance by ordering the municipality to construct drain pipes with flow of water to wash the filth and stop the stench. The Magistrate found the facts proved, made the direction sought and scared by the prospect of prosecution under Section 188 I.P.C. for violation of the order under S. 133 Cr.P.C., the municipality rushed from court to court till, at last, years after, it reached this court as the last refuge of lost causes. Had the municipal council and its executive officers spent half this litigative zeal on cleaning up the street and constructing the drains by rousing the people's sramdan resources and laying out the city's limited financial resources, the people's needs might have been largely met long ago.

The Magistrate, whose activist application of S. q133, Cr. The larger purpose of making the Ratlam municipal body do its duty and abate the nuisance by affirmative action, has our appreciation. (The court reproduced lengthy extracts from the Magistrate's order describing the extremely unhygenic and insanitary conditions in a locality of Ratlam and the unsuccessful efforts of tormented residents to activate the municipality.)

The Magistrate held in the end:

Thus after perusing the evidence I come to this conclusion and after perusing the applications submitted by the persons residing on the New Road area from time to time to draw the attention of the non-applicants to remove the nuisance, the non-applicants have taken no steps whatsoever to remove all these public nuisances.

He issued the following order which was wrongly found unjustified by the Sessions court, but rightly upheld by the High Court:

Therefore, for the health and convenience of the people residing in that particular area all the nuisance must be removed and for that the following order is hereby passed.

The Supreme Court laid down the law forty years after an intelligent, imaginative magistrate of Malabar had ruled much to my disappointment in the case but very much to the advancement of the law of environment and public nuisance. A learned American Author, commenting on Ratlam, has observed:

Environmental pollution in Ratlam affected a large community of poor people and arose from a combination of diffuse causes: private polluters, slack and under-financed enforcement agencies, and haphazard town planning. In view of these peculiarities, the court tailored the existing public nuisance remedy to provide relief.

The judgment explicitly recognizes the impact of a deteriorating urban environment on the poor, and links the provision of basic public health facilities to both human rights and the directive principles in the Constitution. The court commends an activist judiciary to compel municipalities to provide proper sanitation and drainage, thereby enabling the poor to live with dignity.

Although the language of Justice Krishna Iyer is flowery in parts, the judgment is notable for the principles it enunciates. Notice the court's interpretation of the nature of a magistrate's power under section 133; the court's response to the municipality's plea of budgetary constraints; and the relief granted by the court.

Vehement submissions addressed before me did not shake the environmental humanism indelibly writ into my sensitive soul by a long ago magistrate of common sense. Our Justice System must jettison the baggage of judicialism and act with instant wisdom liberated from procedural pettifoggary dressed in learned length of arcane jurisprudence.

# 15

# The Independent Initiative— Two Episodes

While a slew of invitations to deliver addresses and lead secular organizations greeted me on retirement, one of the voluntary social instruments which I fondly founded (and remained as president for long) was the Independent Initiative (for short, The Initiative). It was geared to dynamic social, cultural and political goals. We had, as catalysts and collaborators, outstanding intellectuals and social activists with great credentials and non-party conditionalities like the rare-thinker Dr. Rajni Kothari, the former Auditor General) Dr. Chaturvedi (who resigned when he joined the BJP) the sweet yet redoubtable visionary Nikhil Chakravarti, the intrepidly surpassing Swami Agnivesh, the doyen among Journalists B.G. Verghese, that statesmanly Justice Rajindar Sachar, the widely travelled Justice Hari Swaroop, a superannuated civil service supremo Nirmal Mukherjee, who later became Punjab Governor and other equally distinguished personalities whose luminous names, amnesia hides from my memory. Prasant Bhushan, that creative advocate and relentless crusader against corruption was a source of strength. We had mass-action programs such as doing observer functions at elections, invigilation against booth capturing, campaigning against corruption in public life and so on. High-level echelons without cadres ready for fieldwork, may flop and be merely ornamental. The most celebrated constellation of leaders may be functional futility, absent energetic youth with yen for public causes. Luckily, we had in our fold such committed delegates as S.K. Ananth,

Dr. Vinod Sethi, Chandramouli who were the backbone of our secretariat and the brain of our operations. A crowd of names rushes in for mention in this context but suffice it to say we were able to attract University students, young lawyers, senior citizens with a militant disposition to serve, public workers and journalists who shared our ideals and objectives. No politician or member of a communal body was eligible since our projects had to be above board from a secular, democratic dimension and social justice was our signature tune. Financial resources were scarce but we survived with voluntary contributions and free venue. A certain militancy, aloofness from the Establishment and a campaigning spirit made the Initiative an instrument of elite influence, popular acceptance and moral authority. The Election Commission (of the pre-Seshan sensational era) gave observer status to our members, listened to their complaints about abuses at the polls and gained popularity for integrity in many states. Popular participation of that dynamic order makes democracy a dialectical reality.

I will do well to illustrate with a few anecdotes the tasks which engaged the Independent Initiative. During the sensational general elections where Prime Minister Rajiv Gandhi, with all might and main, led the Congress campaign with no holds barred and the Opposition Janata Dal, led by V.P. Singh, fought hard, mustering support from every source which demanded change from the Congress with Bofors scam. The Independent Initiative's observers brought to the Election Commission reports of Congress violence at the hustings. I met the C.E.O and urged him to order re-poll. The Election Commission initiated action after its own enquiry and in several cases, directed fresh polling. To mobilise the people, geared to safeguard the purity of the polls, is no mean matter. In Karnataka our observer team was led by the great (late) Rev. M.A. Thomas and the now centenarian and former Chief Justice Nittoor Srinivasa Rao. In Andhra Pradesh we secured the services of a retired Chief Justice who organised a good team. Our Former Chief Justice (late) K.B.N. Singh organised observers in Bihar. In Kerala, a respected retired judge Chandrasekhara Menon and other public figures offered their services.

Senior citizens, seasoned in public activities in younger

years, offering their experience and spare time for socially strategic causes and freely guiding organizations with dignity and selfless straight-forwardness are a precious asset to the nation. And when they are able to inspire a generation with a sense of idealism there emerges true democracy in locomotion in a different dimension from drawing salaries and disposing of files. The Independent Initiative was a paradigm of social sensitivity, of collective wisdom and seasoned intelligence in altruistic action. Life's evening for me, spent on people's causes, was the true pursuit of higher happiness. Good Samaritan jurisprudence while on the bench and social justice in action on superannuation makes life worthwhile.

An exciting anecdote which rewards recounting may be a finer footnote to Operation Independent Initiative. After Indira Gandhi's ghastly assassination, Rajiv Gandhi ascended the gaddi with a record victory. Rajiv Gandhi, the ebullient field marshal who led the Congress Party in its 'do or die' campaign in the next General Elections, left no stone unturned in winning the polls despite scams haunting him. Various Opposition Parties gave a good fight. V.P. Singh of the Janata Dal emerged as a national rival. The polls are a political process where the little Indian with a little voice moves into a little booth to make a little mark on a little ballot to settle, in a little measure, the fate pro tem of the governance of the nation or province. Great was Nehru but Rajiv never rose to that stature and lost the General Elections although, after Indira Gandhi's assassination he was returned with a stupendous majority. 'The world is weary of statesman whom democracy has degraded into politicians'. Rajiv, however, showed great qualities at times but in this election his party lost at the hustings. The Independent Initiative took no sides with parties but opposed and exposed malpractices. The cleaner contest was by V.P. Singh's conglomeration. The Independent Initiative expected Rajiv to be replaced by V.P. Singh as a national choice although he was fresh at the national level and other veterans with less glamour and dubious record had won Opposition seats.

Frankly, the Initiative, knowing the mood of the people and the message of the polls welcomed the Janata Dal as salutary alternative. I met N.T. Rama Rao, the leader from

Andhra Pradesh, and he left me in no doubt that V.P. Singh should be the choice for Prime Ministership. I argued, and he agreed that the Nation had two persons from whom to choose: Rajiv Gandhi or V.P. Singh. The people had chosen the latter. So the Initiative summoned a public meeting to felicitate V.P.Singh as the country's leader to be in power. Not because we had any political partisanship but because the plurality of votes had settled the issue. A huge crowd attended our meeting in the Constitution Club. Dr. Rajni Kothari presided. We had gathered to greet the announcement to be formally made from Janata Dal quarters. We waited till late in the evening, but there was a disquieting absence of information. What was happening? Was there a last minute hitch? We were worried about some unexpected frustrations. Some silly slip between the lip and the cup. Has it not been well said by W.E. Hearst: A politician will do anything to keep his job—even become a patriot. Therefore, even as the meeting went on I left for the A.P. House to ascertain whether any misadventure had upset the people's verdict. Although N.T.R assured me that there was no problem, shrewder Karunanidhi, who was sitting next to him, suggested that I had better proceed to the Haryana House to verify personally whether any imbroglio had cropped up. I rushed to the Haryana House where, behind closed doors, hot discussions were going on. The man at the door was told by me, seeing the melee-like debate, that I wanted to speak to I.K. Gujral, a most respected leader whom I knew well. He came out and I gathered that Chandrasekhar, the seasoned political leader was staking a claim. I pleaded with Inder to mention to Chandrasekhar that I was urgently wanting to have a word with him. Good Luck. Chandrasekhar came out and I took him to a lonely room. We had known each other for long and had mutual respect. That was the only investment in our personal relationship. Chandrasekhar with long political experience, told me that he had been hurt by a group of people demonstrating in front of his house against his leadership. He mentioned some big names in the group. Naturally provoked by this indiscreet and offensive conduct he felt like asserting his right to be the leader. May be, Chandrasekhar was an astute politician of long standing but at the hustings the national image of V.P. Singh was what won the people's franchise. My persuasion prevailed, my credentials were those of the Independent initiative. Devilal, a veteran politician, was also in the contest. He too withdrew. Thus the mantle of Prime Ministership fell on V.P. Singh. At the public meeting the next day, Dr. Kothari rejoiced to announce the choice as the success of the people. Not that the Independent Initiative, influenced the selection, but a gentle and timely move softened feelings and hastened the conclusion of the election process. A little timely act did help a happy conclusion. This is only a narration, never a claim to tilt even a wee-bit the political gambit that ushered in the Janata Dal Regime. We are too insignificant to shape history's dialectical process.

Another event which could have been a matter of great moment may, nevertheless, be briefly set out here, not as an achievement of the Initiative—which it was not—but as an stance of the wider concerns which became part of the Initiative's profound pursuits. One of the major tensions which shook the nation at that time was the Babari Masjid issue. It deeply affected two communities and their religious sentiments. Had it been solved with grace through a national dialogue an indelible stain and incurable wound could have been pre-empted. The general body of the Initiative set up a small committee with me as President and Swamy Agnivesh and Sri B.G. Verghese as the two other members. Our assignment was simple. We take no sides, adopt a secular attitude and show a disposition of national concern. The sole object was to bring together the Hindu and the Muslim sections and factions who had ranged themselves on either side of the Ram Janmabhumi conflict. We had no axe to grind, no gains to make, no cause to promote, no game plan to execute and no victory to win, save a satisfactory solution whereby two large communities may, on terms of amity, arrive at a formula of peaceful co-existence. It is so satisfying to recall how our credentials were accepted when we invited several groups of Hindus and Muslims who had stakes in the dispute and acrimonious voice to express. Our sole motive viewpoints was promotive of a better understanding and resolution of the estrangement which had explosive potential. We sat and met numberless times and the response from both sides was positive. There was agreement to bring down tension and not to aggravate the prevalent anger. Muslims clamed that the Mosque was of longstanding and should remain as such in a society of religious freedom but they were willing to consider whether there was any evidence of the Mosque having been constructed on a non-Muslim land. In case there was an impartial and authoritative finding that the Mosque stood in a place which did not belong to a Muslim, it was haram and contrary to Islam. In that event, Muslim leaders would explain to the entire Islamic constituency that the Mosque having been built on non-Islamic venue should be removed without any order of court, communal intimidation or governmental intervention. But there should be a clear and unbiased pronouncement by some acceptable authority to this effect and, in case there was proof that the Mosque stood on terrain which did belong to a Muslim, the Hindu community should allow the Mosque to continue. The Muslims were willing to accept an advisory opinion of the Supreme Court or like body of high standing. This central issue found broad agreement between the two groups and the best solution could have been a reference under Article 143 of the Constitution for the advisory opinion of the Supreme Court. There were other subsidiary and ancillary issue on which also general consensus was reached. At this point our committee of the Initiative felt that the matter could be referred to the Prime Minister for immediate action because a looming disaster or brooding danger could be obviated by timely action agreeable to both sides. From the Kerala House where the committee met I telephoned Prime Minister Chandrasekhar and sought an immediate interview on this issue. With statesmanship he responded and all three of us drove up to the Prime Minister's office, gave him a nine point (?) formula and pleaded with him to act with creative celerity and without dawdling spoiling the solution.

The Prime Minister was agreeably surprised and promised action forthwith. He would have a word with Attorney General and refer the matter to the Supreme Court under Article 143, he told us. I met Soli Sorabjee, the Attorney General, and he agreed with my view that the advisory opinion would, under the circumstances, be an answer to an intractable problem.

There is a destiny which takes its on course and shapes history according to dialectical materialism beyond our control or cognition. In this case, the expectations raised ended in frustration because for some reason difficult to comprehend Sri Rajiv Gandhi opposed the idea of references to the Supreme Court of this simple issue. He suggested a Judicial Commission of the Supreme Court. So the whole scheme was sabotaged. Rajiv's support made Chandrasekhar survive. A month later when I met the former Prime Minister Rajiv and asked him why he did not agree to a reference under Article 143, he said he had committed a blunder, a frank young man who acts impulsively and regrets belatedly. Anyway, the Initiative scheme did not materialise. The later developments are a disastrous chapter of Indian History.

# 16

# A Kerala Karseva Chronicle

T.V. Puram is a pretty small town in Kerala around thirty miles off Kochi, the central city of the State. Like most places in South Kerala T.V. Puram too is green country, densely populated and has heavy Hindu and Christian presence in peaceful co-existence. While India is the hallowed land of the Upanishads, Kerala is where Adi Sankara, the greatest exponent of Vedanta, was born and St. Thomas the direct disciple of Jesus Christ, lauded and spread his message. This peninsular wonder and its religious pluralism had harmony writ large over the centuries but communal lunacy and religious rivalry did not spare Kerala geography and history. There arose, however, a sublime soul, humble of origin but universal in his teaching, walking and talking, conscientising. Malayalee humanity, lifting the lowly to a new sense of dignity, divinising the diverse castes and communities through a unifying process of dynamic fraternity and advaita philosophy. He was the spiritual revolutionary Sree Narayana Guru with global and local relevance and impact.

T.V. Puram had a parish church and at some distance a chapel too. The priest kept the flock together, attended to the ceremonial needs of life and death. The dead had to be buried, a cemetery in the chapel precincts had become a religious urgency and so, the church functionaries moved the civil authorities and secured sanction for construction of a cemetery at a chosen site in chapel premises.

The dead do give problems to the living and religious skirmishes aggravate tension, seeming secularism and simmering acerbity may flare up as communal scrimmage, especially if there is a rival shrine in the neighbourhood and supportive population to respond. Once tantrums erupt, they feed on themselves and are hard to extinguish. Such a scenario emerged when steps to build the cemetery were set in motion. The Ezhava community awoke to the situation and protested in minatory numbers against the prospect of Christian cadavers being carried into the cemetery since there was a school nearby, a temple in the neighbourhood and Hindu residents in the locality. The Church countered this hostility by flaunting the official sanction and seeking police assistance to remove the SNDP demonstrators. The SNDP is a powerful Sree Narayana Guru organization. (Now, a split has diminished its glory). The escalation of the estrangement, what with police entry on the Christian side embittering the Hindu side, reached explosive dimension and extreme militancy. Shock and awe struck the scene and a tense stalemate, with violent potential, became a grave prospect. The collector was worried, the Government could not resolve the crisis. The Marxist led Left Front was concerned with the political balance sheet, not with the merits of the cemetery issue. Communal momentum cannot be smothered by the locomotive of secular sanity or the lathi and custody tactics of the constabulary. Police remedy often aggravates the socio-political malady. This happened in the T.V. Puram communal pathology.

I had no idea whatever of this brewing malaise until when one morning in June 1996 two young advocates James Kadavan and Shajan Mannali walked into my office without notice. I knew them both but was surprised at their unannounced entry. What brought you here in a hurry without even an appointment, I queried. They sought forgiveness but pleaded they had come on an urgent errand where my mediatory mission was needed right now. They explained the tragic climax raging in T.V. Puram. What can I do to deflate this terrorist development, knowing neither side nor leaders and cadres of the Church or SNDP, I asked. How dare I use my good offices when I have no judicial office, having retired as early as 1980, when I have no political clout having kept away from all political parties with critical, sceptical independence, having no social position or organisational control sufficient to influence fighting parties? They countered me flatteringly. Your credentials, integrity, independent judgement and decades of selfless service to society and high position in Indian national life warrant the assumption that your word will be listened to without hesitation. The authorities also will heed your advice since you are on good terms with all political parties and personalities. These highly complimentary words did not make me vain nor persuade me to summon both sides for a conciliatory dialogue. Give me the opportunity to ascertain whether they would care for my mediatory effort, I posed. The young advocate agreed with my fair proposal, contacted the local SNDP militant and the high church dignitaries at Cochin. The Cardinal and the Arch Bishop respected me and readily consented to co-operate in a negotiation through me. Despite the angry mood, the local SNDP stalwarts responded favourably. Initially, the hot temper and sense of injustice of the SNDP youths, wounded as they were by the police action of the State and the Collector's insistence that what has been already sanctioned shall come to pass, made me feel that my move would end in futility. They would rather fight and lose their life than surrender to the dead bodies of Christians being buried in the proximate chapel compound. The priestly adamancy was no less firm. The law is on our side, they said, the appropriate authority had approved the site of the cemetery. The police was there to protect their right and the work would go on. I pleaded with both again and again not to be intransigent. The Government was apparently for the implementation of the cemetery construction, but found the problem too tough to be tackled by official fiat. When my personal negotiation gained momentum and signs of reconciliation were in sight the minister concerned, as well as the Opposition leader, telephoned me to do all I could to negotiate and settle. The Collector, a well-meaning officer, concerned to bring about peace, came to me, participated in the discussion and made some useful proposals for an acceptable site for the cemetery. Plots were marked; lines were drawn, alternative sites were proposed and a spirit of give and take warmed up our nocturnal deliberations. With great patience I tried to sort out the differences. Both sides expressed willingness to abide by a just compromise. The Collector's presence was creative. Mr. James Kadavan and a highly accomplished advocate Mr. Kurian Joseph (Now elevated to the Bench of the Kerala High Court) helped a great deal in selling my point of view to the Arch Bishop although it meant a minor displacement of the location of the cemetery. On the other hand, the leader of the struggle on the spot Satyan and the then District SNDP President Mr. Premachandran softened the resistance with sweet reasonableness. At long last, the dissolution of the dispute was in sight. Both parties and the Collector were communal peace and a happy ending was likely to emerge. I toiled for hours because time was short for me. I had to be in Australia (Adelaide) to participate in a World Victimology Conference and the local controversy had to be settled before I left. Somehow, by persuasions and dissuasions, by imaginative shifting of the site meeting the objections of one side or the other, driving a sense of realism into the heads of both sides an accord was reached, a map was drawn and hostility yielded to goodwill. After all the Hindus and Christians all over Kerala had churches and temples in close proximity, festivals and offerings with mutual trust and cordiality had been the rule of life. The land of Adi Sankara and St. Thomas could not forsake the profound fusion of the fraternal faith once fundamentals were accepted. Above all, there was the great spiritual revolutionary, Sree Narayana Guru, who had spread the message of religious tolerance, unitive understanding and the credal glory Of one Caste, one Religion, one God for Man. The confluence of the temporal and the spiritual, the quintessence of great religions being the same and the application of vedanta in the pragmatism of worldly life were the spiritual splendour of Sree Narayana Dharma. What motivated me in spending three sleepless nights, negotiating with both sides assisted by the two young Christian advocates, the priestly representative of the Arch Bishop, the amiable Premachandran, the mellowed Satyan (SNDP) and Thomas the Collector of Kottayam coming in at the later stages, was not the material success of mutual settlement of a local confrontation. I was inspired by the invisible presence of Sree Narayana Guru. Another factor, which had a compelling influence on my soul as I ceaselessly talked to those with rival viewpoints, was beyond a cemetery construction or the adjustment of Hindu-Christian dispute. A new dynamism and co-operative effort in both the communities joining together in sacred mutuality to build each other's shrine would be a great beginning of cultural camaraderie in action. I regard it this Operation Karseva, where all people regardless of religious differences, join to put brick and pour cement as if they were constructing their common hallowed shrine. This would be a demonstration of communal amity which was more weighty than religious discourses and political claptrap.

I wanted a tremendous message to go from T.V. Puram, small town than it was, to the large country India, with its diversity and raging dissent over god. So I insisted before we drew up the settlement clauses, with all emphasizes, that two magnificent postulates should be included.

The two basic conditionalities, which were too fundamental to be negotiable, were specifically mentioned in the draft dispute settlement drawn up with the Collector (Sri. Thomas) and the Advocate General (Sri Damodaran) participating in the process. What a marvellous message it would be if Hindus and Christians, jettisoning their disputation, together put brick and mortar on the cemetery foundation as a unique example of communities uniting in Karseva! Luckily and enthusiastically, all parties agreed to this spiritually charged gesture. I had yet another condition to fulfill, as part of the project of T.V. Puram settlement. I insisted in principle, and all of us gathered at my residence in giving final touches to the compromise fell in, with the great idea that a lovely house of learning or library should be constructed in T.V. Puram with a magnificent arch in front on which will be inscribed a great teaching of Narayana Guru that this is a hallowed land free from caste differences, and religious feuds bonded together by universal brotherhood. On one side of the arch would be the divine statue of Jesus and on the other the inspirational statue of Sree Narayana Guru. The aura of this message was to be the soul of the settlement. Everybody gave assent to this lofty idea.

Thus ended the T.V. Puram cemetery conflict generating a settlement of refined values, accommodating every one's point of view and more than all, sending a transcendental message of Karseva, symbolic of religious symbiosis, and building a monumental house of learning with Jesus and Narayana Guru adorning the portals of the edifice. A day or two later, the Karseva was fixed, the cemetery construction was to commence, I visited the place, saw the priest and the State President of the SNDP (Dr. Rahulan). The Collector addressed the meeting expressed, his happiness because a law and order problem had ended in the noblest expression of human solidarity. He also said that he had located a suitable plot of land for the library which was contemplated in the settlement. Then followed the Karseva. I laid the first spatter of cement and the priest as well as Dr. Rahulan, the SNDP Yogam President, did the same. Others followed. We are witnesses to history because the spatter of cement jointly laid was sacred symbol of Indian fraternity.

The other component of the settlement was the construction of the library which was publicly promised and mentioned in the draft settlement. However, there was no *political* gain in a sacred symbol and so the political Government eliminated references to my central role in the settlement, in the conditionality of Karseva and *Grandhalaya*. Why? Politics, perhaps. The ruling front was fighting an election at Tellicherry. It should be a great gain to assert with secular success that Government, on its own, had successfully solved a communal imbroglio. To dilute it with names of other activist in reaching the remarkable result would be to whittle down the impact of the Left Front's achievement. Indeed, months later, when I casually met the Collector he told me that he had been advised by the political bosses in power to forget about Karseva and the Jesus-Narayana Guru Library. Politics is pachydermic.

Years later, a few days ago, I visited Vaikom a mini-city near T.V. Puram having been invited for the inauguration of a YMCA Centre; and there I met the old faces, Christian and Ezhava who had skirmishes over the cemetery. All of them whom I met, Christian and Hindu, remembered the cemetery struggle and warmly thanked me for the timely conflict resolution and restoration of absolute communal amity in the area. Political parties have short memories but sons of the native soil, indifferent to religious diversity, have long memories and deep gratitude—a value which I cherish more than Kudos from those in power.

This episodic narrative may perhaps suffer from lapses of memory since amnesia spares gerontics but the substance of the story is correct to the best of my knowledge and in my belief.

# 17

# Bhagawan Satya Sai Baba—Some Reflections

Some rationalists and several sceptics may ask whether spiritual therapy is credible at all in this world of materialist forces? Let me cite poetry de profundis to prove my point in the positive since, by flashes of light: Noble verses reveal truths too intangible for forceps, lancets and laboratories. Here is Lord Tennyson:

> More things are wrought by prayer
> Than this world dreams of. Wherefore, let thy voice
> Rise like a fountain for me night and day.
> For what are men better than sheep or goats
> That nourish a blind life within the brain,
> If, knowing God, they lift not hands of prayer
> Both for themselves and those who call them friend?
> For so the whole round earth is every way
> Bound by gold chains about the feet of God.

Mere materialist dogma cannot grasp the vistarama of truth.

> Our little systems have their day;
> They have their day and cease to be:
> They are but broken lights of thee,
> And thou, O Lord, art more than they.
> Let knowledge grow from more to more,
> But more of reverence in us dwell;
> That mind and soul according well,
> May make one music as before.

A larger vision of life and divinity makes God's presence a curative reality and God can, in the rarest of rare instances, move in human form, amidst us and give light and heal wounds in a manner temporal science cannot know but larger *saience* can demonstrate. Sai Science, the profound faith of millions, is this larger light one may call Saience, a beautiful blend of spiritual and material procedures, the twin sides of Truth not to see which in its wholeness is purblindness. Sai Wonder is a fact. I have experienced it and been entranced by the sublimity of it while preserving my stand as sceptic.

T.H. Huxley, the great thinker, in a letter to Charles Kingsley, wrote:

> Sit down before fact like a little child, and be prepared to give up every preconceived notion, follow humbly wherever and to whatever abysses Nature leads or you shall learn nothing. I have only begun to learn content and peace of mind since I have resolved at all risks to do this.

Science, in its humility and veracity, must bow before fact and search for answers and not reject with pusillanimity what fails to fit into prejudged but jejune ideas. Progress lies in courageous acceptance of the spiritual, if verifiable evidence is forthcoming.

Sri Sathya Sai Baba's dream hospital conducts hi-tech surgeries *for no cost to the patient.* Is this not a marvel in our materialist universe which looks to the purse for cure? Did not Shakespeare exclaim in Hamlet 'There are more things in heaven and earth, Horatio than are dreamt of in your philosophy'.

Who/what is Sai? Sai is the first name of two supra-human beings come in human form. The first Sai is Shirdi Baba of Maharashtra. The second Sai walks the earth as Sri Satya Sai Baba, born at Puttaparti and radiates light all over the Universe. Shirdi Baba was both 'Allah Malik' and 'Rama'; why, in his words "I am you, I am in the dog and the worm too".

> In a new book by Dr. Hiramalini on Saiscience she writes: Bhagawan Sri Satya Sai Baba says that the highest is achieved when head, heart and hand coordinate harmoniously. Modern medicine simply HAS to learn to open out its heart, for by responding to the call of the heart, modern medicine which is as of now rather head-hand oriented can become whole and complete; and then

it will truly be transformed into that great art of healing that it was always meant to be.

Incarnation, be he Rama or Krishna, Ramakrishna or Sai, has human limitations and divine potential. Of Sri Satya Sai Baba one may well say: where he walks is hallowed ground, where he talks is divine speech, where he sits is shrine.

Some rationalists and several sceptics may ask whether spiritual therapy is credible at all in this world of materialist forces? Let me cite poetry de profundis to prove my point in the positive, since by flashes of light, noble verses reveal truths too intangible for forceps, lancets and laboratories. Here is Lord Tennyson:

More things are wrought by prayer
Than this world dreams of. Wherefore, let thy voice
Rise like a fountain for me night and day.
For what are men better than sheep or goats
That nourish a blind life within the brain,
If, knowing God, they lift not hands of prayer
Both for themselves and those who call them friend?
For so the whole round earth is every way
Bound by gold chains about the feet of God.

There is a glorious institution in Puttaparti run by the Satya Sai Baba Trust—an unusual hospital with Baba therapeutics. But the Baba hospitals do everything free, too difficult to believe, too true to be denied, as you study the magnificent medical institution in Puttaparty. The finest hour of curative power arrives for every Baba lover when he reads the last paragraph of a medical book for which I wrote a foreword.

I adore the Power where the divine meets the human and life finds its highest fulfillment by the realisation that there is a divinity in everyone and therefore universality embraces all in one. Of Bhagawan Satya Sai Baba one may aptly quote what Albert Einstein said of Gandhiji : Generations to come will scarcely believe that such a one as this, ever in flesh and blood walked upon this earth.

# 18
# A Democratic Defeat without Personal Disappointment

## A Superannuated Man

My age of retirement as judge of the Supreme Court was 65. This happened in November 1980 when, sans robes of judicial office, I continued my commitment to society without the authority and insignia of official power. Not that I was tired—indeed few who retire are tired—but the command of date of birth and Art. 124 of the Constitution made me lay down office. Throughout my career on the Bench and the Bar, social activism in the larger sense has consumed my interest. Of course, at the Bar apart from court work, I was connected with quite a number of public organisations and spent a considerable part of my time in addressing public meetings of a miscellaneous sort. Fine Arts Associations and Sports Organisations too claimed my time. Assuming office as judge I did not jettison my association with people's organisations. Nor, indeed, did I give up public speaking under the auspices of legal and cultural bodies, taking care to see that I did not involve myself in issues which were likely to become problems in court. That would be an embarrassment to my office. Total insulation from public activities is not an obligation of the judicial office. In the words of Chief Justice Earl Warren 'Our judges are not monks or scientists, but participants in the living stream of our national life'.

Oftentimes experience in public life before elevation to the Bench may be an advantage, as the American judges from John Marshall to Earl Warren have demonstrated. The secluded life of judicial aloofness robs the functionary of the great advantage of activist involvement in national preoccupations. The rule of law and the rule of life run close together. I have found, speaking for myself, that my life as a minister, my membership of public organisations such as the Indian Association of Lawyers. All India Peace and Solidarity Council, Indo-Soviet Cultural Society and the Free Legal Services bodies to mention but a few, only enriched my capacity, deepened my people-oriented convictions and widened my vision of life in its larger dimension while sitting on the Bench. When superannuation overtook me, I did not find life empty. Because, even while I was judge, I continued to be associated with public bodies of a non-controversial nature with a socially useful agenda. True, the great satisfaction of exercising judicial power is not replaced by being President or Patron of any number of other organisations. To do justice in court is soulful joy, to be activist on the Bench is a remarkable self-fulfillment. The robe is more than a symbol and a judge, to be worthy of earning the appellation of justice, has to have wide experience, large learning

***(General Quotations-II P-534/535)***

Back to my retirement and the days thereafter

My public speeches were on the increase. my public engagements were diverse, my cultural pursuits were multiplied, my time was consumed by writing articles and delivering lectures. In that sense, shorn of Power though, I lived a fuller life. Of course, a great tragedy, my wife's demise, darkened my survival by the distress of separation of the dearest. Today, I can say as a poignant reality that there is no bar of limitation for the tears of separation. I search and research into life after death. Meanwhile, I remain immersed in the human issues engaging the nation and the world. I have often felt that an epitome of my autobiography was a pale but honest reflection of the answers to a questionnaire prepared by Marx's daughters. I reproduce it here because it brings out what I have lived for:

What is your favourite virtue? Simplicity.

Your outstanding characteristic? Singleness of purpose.

Your idea of happiness? To struggle.

The vice you detest most? Servility.

Your favourite maxim?

I am a man and nothing pertaining to man is lien to me.

Your favourite motto?

One must doubt everything.

**(General Quotations P-646)**

I did frequent philosophers and saintly souls in search of profound light about life and after. Ranganadananda, J. Krishnamoorthy, Muktananda, Matha Amritanandamayi, Maharshi Mahesh Yogi and above all, Sree Satyasai Baba et al. Am I the wiser about life after death; even after sittings and seances and other experiments on communication with the dead? Some light I have derived. Sometimes I feel with Scott Fitzgerald 'in the real dark night on the soul it is always 3 o'clock'. Maybe, Edward Fitzgerald may also fit in, *though not wholly.*

Myself when young did eagerly frequent
Doctor and Saint, and heard great argument
About it and about; but evermore
Came out by the same Door as in I went.

**(Oxford Quotations P-212-20)**

I skip these sombre leaves of life since simultaneously I have been in the thick of public life, national issues and matters of common concern to humanity. I have written books, which are collections of writings, I have travelled and addressed lectures. With Edward Gibbon, I must reluctantly observe that two causes, 'the abbreviation of time, and the failure of hope, will always tinge with a browner shade the evening of life'.

Now I come to an episode which springs from my involvement in the political issues of our time. Long years ago, I did have political friends belonging to all parties; and public figures regardless of party affiliation have extended their friendship to me. This is due to a non-dogmatic and affable attitude, although I am generally and rightly known to have a slant to the Left. My integrity was generally accepted because I had no ambition for acquisition of wealth or position. Indeed, one of the early decisions I had taken on superannuation from the Supreme Court was to be totally free from the temptation for office or fabulous fee from consultation and arbitration income from which not many judges were exempt (and some have totally succumbed). How free I feel when lucrative lust fails to gain any purchase over my soul!

I had known Nehru with deep admiration and was reciprocated with a measure of affection. I had known Indira Gandhi while she was President of the Congress Party and I in the Opposition and later, when she was Prime Minister during two terms. Although as a judge I maintained the necessary propriety of aloofness I could still truthfully say that our relationship was good. Her assassination suddenly made Rajiv Gandhi, the Prime Minister of the country. I had seen him but not known him although in later years I had a few occasions of friendly meetings with him. Of course, by then I had retired from the bench. I had known with some degree of intimacy, Comrade Surjit of the C.P.I (Marxist). My cousin S.K. Ananth used to bring him to my room in the Kerala House whenever I was in Delhi. One of the items of casual conversation was the suggestion that I should contest the election when the Rashtrapati's office fell vacant. This was a few months ahead of the vacancy. As a realist I dismissed the idea as preposterous for two reasons. Firstly, I had not the remotest idea of running for an office whatever the prospect be. (I had once dismissed a Rojya Sabha suggestion during V.P. Singh's tenure as Prime Minister). That was no longer my cup of tea especially after my defeat in 1965 in the Kerala Assembly elections. Secondly, there was not the ghost of a chance for any candidate set up by Leftists who made national noises disproportionate to their electoral muscles. Surjit and Ananth gave up the proposal knowing my mind and firm resolution. Then came the expiry of the term of Rashtrapati R. Venkatraman. Rajiv Gandhi, though young, was resolute. His candidate, whoever he be, would win hands down. So in any contest for Presidentship, the rival to Rajiv's choice would fail utterly. Nevertheless, the idea was mooted that in the largest democracy in the world, it should not be that the election to the highest office should go without contest in spite of the fact that thee was a significant Opposition to the ruling party inside the House and outside. For these reasons, the diverse opposition groups toyed with the idea of setting up a rival candidate.

From now on, I speak from amnesic memory. One day while I was undergoing ayurvedic treatment at Kottakkal, my old friend, a C.P.I leader, the late N.E. Balaram, landed up made his way to my room where I was resting. When I warmly welcomed him as an old friend he puzzled me with a ludicrous proposal that I should run for Rastrapati's office. Balaram could advocate his cause cleverly. He tried his best to persuade me into an odd affirmation but I rejected as fantastic the proposal for candidature. When he found me diamond-hard, he left in disappointment. To wipe out the gossip of my being presidential candidate, I issued a clear press statement negating any such possibility. After my ayurvedic treatment, I returned to Kochi. One day while I was convalescing, the great E.M.S, who had given earlier intimation, sprang a surprise on me. He came all the way from Delhi and announced that the Opposition parties, many, though tiny, had collectively resolved that I should be their candidate. I had no hesitation to tell my respected friend Namboodiripad that I could not consider the opposition proposal. He insisted that he had come all the way from Delhi because that was a mandate entrusted to him and he had to carry it out. I had sanity enough to know the result of the election. I had resolution enough to remain firm on my decision. Namboodiripad, to our mutual embarrassment, returned to Delhi, although his errand proved to be a damp squib.

Let me correct my memory by reproducing the politically sensitive E.M.S. letter:

> "My dear Krishna Iyer,
>
> The three-man Committee (NTR, Chandra Sekhar and myself) met yesterday when I told them about my talks with you. My two colleagues are agreeable to your name provided (a) you give your consent, and (b) they want to consult parties like the BJP whom I am not prepared to

consult.

In the meanwhile, it is clear that there is no prospect of a consensus candidate. Rajiv is determined to push his party candidate, making it appear that he (or she) is a 'consensus candidate'. There is, therefore, no possibility of our (opposition) candidate winning the election; it is a fight on policies.

From this point of view, you are the best person to take up the challenge. Your widely-publicised article provides the political basis on which to fight. On the other hand, there is a real danger that, in case of your decision to stand down, the non-left opposition parties may float names which cannot be accepted.

I, therefore, plead with you that you should give your consent.

Yours sincerely,

E.M.S. Namboodiripad"

And now my reply personal:

"My dear Namboodiripad,

Your letter was delivered to me by Comrade Ramakrishnan at Calicut yesterday and I had a brief discussion on the subject with him but promised to send you a reply today. N.E. also met me and had a longer exchange of views. The issue of presidential candidature is one of decisive moment at this sensitive juncture of our country's democratic saga. I agree with you that the politics of that high office is not idle polemics but a facet of the dialectics of the current Indian crisis. Clarity is critical when confusion fertilises interested forces in their efforts to throw out polity into disarray.

I am heartened tat my jural-political approach to the President-Prime Minister problem receives your approbation as well as of many progressive jurists and political thinkers.

Any serious social realist studying the political scenario of India in the context of the presidential election will agree with the conclusion you have indicated that the Congress nominee will numerically (not ethically) win hands down. The dynamics of political forces may, (?) in its evolutionary process, wreak slow or sudden changes upsetting conservative conclusions. Even after making an allowance for such developments, one must realise that in the short term the command performance of the Congress electorate, may be as directed by the 3-line whip. It is fair to accept the position that a rival has no real chance in the present mood of the Prime Minister and his fiat. What is regrettable is that the illusion about a national consensus was cultivated by him cleverly but without authentic will.

Proceeding on the footing that the contestant to the Congress candidate has no prospect of success, the crucial question arises whether I should agree to be a candidate at all. My general disposition has been against being a candidate even if the prospects were rosy. My physical health leaves much to be desired. (I have just returned from the Manipal Hospital and am going into the Kottakkal Arya Vaidyasala for treatment a little later). However, I had not banged the door of my mind on account of certain persuasions from friends whom I respect, including you. But I had not any time consented to be a candidate of the Opposition, even in the absence of a consensus, a position which is clear from your letter. Nevertheless, a few newspapers erroneously published some days ago that I was an opposition candidate and my consent had been secured. There was no need for me, who had been keeping out of the fray, to go to the Press and contradict. I had never agreed for President.

While I agree with you about the analysis of the situation in the event of my declining to be a candidate and while I deplore the emergence of more than one candidate for the Opposition parties, I find myself unable to run for President. Your few sentences in the last part of the letter have moved me beyond words and touched me to tears. But emotional reactions do not solve problems. My negative subjectivism based upon several factors, unnecessary to be detailed here, persuade me to tell you reluctantly that I do not find my way to be a candidate for the presidential election. My indifferent health corroborates my mood. Of course, in a rapidly changing situation, it is political prudence to keep one's eye open.

Dear Namboodiripad, I am deeply grateful to you and all the other parties which have chosen to put faith in me in the present presidential electoral race. Yet, I am unable to agree, and plead with you to forgive me for saying so. I deeply respect your sentiments and request you to reciprocate it.

With kindest regards,

Yours sincerely,

V.R. Krishna Iyer"

***(Justice V.R. Krishna Iyer—A Living Legend P-251/252)***

I was the President of Indo Afghan Friendship Society at that time when that finest President Najibullah, a friend, governed the country admirably. The Vice President of Afghanistan was visiting Delhi and the Indo-Afghan Friendship Society decided to give him a warm reception. Necessarily, I had to be in Delhi for this purpose and I had a few other engagements. So I visited Delhi and stayed in the Kerala House. Sri. N.T. Rama Rao, a unique leader of Andhra Pradesh with large political support, was my affectionate friend and great admirer. He came to the Kerala House and pressured me to be the Opposition candidate. He assured me that all the Opposition parties would unite to support my candidature. I reluctantly surrendered and I was taken to the Andhra Bhavan where all the Opposition parties except the BJP had gathered to welcome me as their choice. N.T.R told me that the BJP had told him they would support me as an anti-congress candidate. Anyway, there was tumultuous announcement at the meeting of my choice as the opposition candidate. Democracy should not fail in India by not being able to find a candidate to contest the high office. This was the sentiment thrust on me. I do not think anyone had the illusion that I would win. What is more important than the victory is the principle of freedom to differ. Dean Inge is right:

> Democracy is only an experiment in government, and it has the obvious disadvantage of merely counting votes instead of weighing them. (Oxford Quotations P-270:7)

Next morning I filed my nomination with due attestation.

Thus did I enter the fray to fight on democratic credentials mindless of the eventual result. I began my campaign, but with total fidelity to the fair norms of elections. I was a little unhappy because Mr. Venkataram, the congress candidate, was my good friend and never expected that I would run against him. Alas! The political compulsions based on principles of democracy when pitted against personal friendship and lesser considerations, the former prevailed. I sighed like a friend but obeyed like a statesman. I too put up a manifesto where nothing but the truth was projected. I agreed in writing, followed by speeches in many centers, that a President in a parliamentary system of the Westminster pattern ordinarily *reigns*, but the Cabinet in daily governance *rules*. In exceptional circumstances, the President has supreme power and they are among the rare cases. While I was on the Bench of the Supreme Court, I had myself expounded every dimension of the status and powers of the President of India, so my mind was clear. My campaign was principled, my integrity unchallenged and my friend Venktaraman maintained perfect silence, his election campaign being left entirely to the mighty field marshal Rajiv Gandhi.

Nikhil Chakravarti inaugurated my battle for the ballot at Thiruvananthapuram, the Kerala State Capital. I gained national support in goodwill, not in more votes. N.T. Rama Rao introduced me to the MLAs at a large meeting in Hyderabad and sought their support. I too addressed the gathering Karunanidhi did the same thing in Chennai, Somnath Chatterjee brought the Left MLAs in Calcutta together and urged them in battle mood to back my candidature. In Bhubaneswar, the tall leader Biju Patnaik powerfully pleaded for me and Nandini Satpati promised her votes. The Chief Minister of Bihar, Devilal of Haryana and Barnala of Punjab movingly projected me as the best democratic symbol and I was deeply touched by their great gesture. Humility overwhelmed me and the prospect of defeat never disturbed me. I stood for a cause and every cause claims a martyr. Round the country I gyrated in a whirlwind campaign and my morale was high as I crossed the nation and felt the warmth of welcome. I knew my fate but how inspiring to behold India and be one with Bharat's elected surrogates!

An anecdotal divagation is of general interest. In one of my speeches, during the campaign, I explained that the Rashtrapati was not a glorified cipher but had strategic powers. One such sword in his armoury was to ask the Prime Minister to disclose or demand even the most embarrassing or confidential information, however secret it be. If the Prime Minister is implicated in a grave scam such as the Bofors swindle the President can compel full disclosure to him of reports on the alleged fraud although final action belongs to the province of the Cabinet. This point had a topical flavour at that time. To make it spicy I said in a vein of alliterative humour, 'If a big *Kumbakonam* shakes the nation the President cannot remain a sleepy *Kumbhakarna.*' What I meant was that when a large national financial scandal is reportedly alleged against the Government the President cannot sleep over it smugly but must alertly ask for full information and advise his Prime Minister. Kumbakonam is a well-known town in Tamil Nadu. But Kumbakonam had come to mean big fraud, a libelous insinuation about the people of that town. When my statement appeared in the press I received protest letters from Kumbakonam denizens against the defamatory innuendo. I wrote back saying that the Oxford English dictionary carried that meaning. The more knowledgeable Kumbhakonam citizens corrected me at once that on a protest from the City of Kumbakonam the Oxford Dictionary had, in its later editions, deleted this calumnious meaning. I withdrew and apologised my Kumbakonam illustration was proved wrong; my law about the President's powers stands good (vide Shamsher Singh's case).

Back to the ballot contest.

On 25th June, 1987 Krishna Iyer wrote a letter to all the MLAs and MPs, it read:

> Dear friend,
>
> A fateful hour of history has brought me suddenly close to you through this letter which I take the liberty to write. Kindly have the charity to consider what I have stated

here not as a personal plea but as a national appeal to your responsible role as a navigator of this dear motherland of ours.

Long years ago we made a trust with destiny, Pandit Nehru intoned from the Parliament House as India awoke to Freedom, and chose to redeem its pledge to the vast masses of the people, now 800 million strong. What was that profound promise, that solemn resolve which our Founding Fathers and architects of Independence made as the surrogates of the countless victims of feudal and imperial injustices? Mahatma Gandhi, that frail marvel who smbolised in his humane person the collective will of Indians sought to wage a ceaseless, conscientious war for the Dalits and the Soshits, for the women under gender discrimination and other minority segments and majority have-nots? Why are we, one nation, one people under one flag lost in communal commotion, regional tension and cultural fratricide burying the great traditions of our many religious and glorious legacy of historic reformers?

Our progress on many fronts has been proud and promising. Our scientific and technological advances have the potential to be the locomotives of social transformation. Our Constitution, with its Preambular commitment and Parliamentary imperatives, is a manifesto of justice to every citizen and especially those in the lowliest brackets.

There is, nevertheless, a paralysis, an instability, a political; dilemma and more dangerous than these, a constitutional crisis of menacing proportions which may throw out of gear our national direction and plunge the creative processes of State Power into constitutional chaos. Indeed, unless this will-lessness and wilderness, this constitutional imbroglio and consequent panic and deadlock are immediately arrested we, as a nation, may fail to overcome the crises that currently grip the political process.

Dr. Ambedkar, whose contribution to constitutional history and struggle for social liberation of large, suppressed sector of Indian humanity remains an angry interrogation to Bharat's engineers of State Power. Jawaharlal's humanism and socialist world view is a living force guiding us. We have had mighty spiritual giants operating for the truer principles of diversity and dignity of every human being and a harmonious, composite heritage of religious pluralism and commitment to the unity, integrity and strength of the country. Numberless martyrs, with their sacred blood and suffering, have sanctified the value-based sage of Brave New Bharat. But where are we today? How do we dare into the coming millenium with the grave challenges, internal and external which is in peril. The Constitution is on institutional trial. The pathological politics of President-Prime Minister estrangement at a critical phase of the nation's history can prove disastrous. If there is no time or temper in the highest functionaries like the President and the Prime Minister to consider many issues of communal holocaust, Punjab tragedy, military security, Sri Lanka policy, Pakistan's escalating arsenal, multinational infiltration, feudal-medieval fundamentalist epilepsies and so on, the future of India that is Bharat may be fractured. The current situation of President versus Prime Minister paralyses decision-making processes and hijacks the attention of Government to questions of negativity leaving the major problems of urgency to drift and inevitable collapse. Therefore, the Presidential Office and he electoral contest for it have come too critical to be routine, too grave to be treated as a mere matter of party loyalty, too historic to turn upon the prestige or permanence of a particular leader, who lives if India dies? Such is the crucial issue that revolves round the resolution of the constitutional confrontation which is the central question in the current presidential election.

Indubitably, high offices should have a harmonious equation based upon constitutional parameters laid down by our founding fathers. The Westminster pattern has been adopted and adapted and the Supreme Court has affirmed the cabinet system and the conventions which accompany it as basic to our constitutional order. The

President cannot arrogate to himself powers of Government but he is beyond question, the head of the nation, the symbol of its unity, the legal power in whose name the administration is run. H has the right to advise, to encourage and to warn his Ministers and, for this purpose, to claim the information that he needs from the Government. There is no iron curtain nor system or secrecy between the Prime Minister and the president. Likewise, the Cabinet headed by the Prime Minister has the plenary power to govern although the President may ask the Cabinet to reconsider, to take note of warnings, to shape its policies in the light of the wisdom he may impart. To transgress the limitations by either side is to create confusion and cloak the wheels of the political processess. I have explained this position while on the Bench as a Judge and later in articles in journals.

Today we need a President who will re-establish healthy relations with the Prime Minister by playing an independent role as advisor, as sentinel, as auditor and as engineer of certain powers exercisable in exceptional situations. He cannot sit with folded hands even without vital information, when the national scenario is showing serious shocks of corruption charges at the highest levels. Of course, he cannot rush into rash action but must use his good offices to see that confidence in the administration is sustained. May be, even parliamentary innovations in the committee system on a permanent basis may be considered. These are matters for future action, of course. He must, however, give respect to the plenary power of the Government under our Parliamentary system, and never take over any part of the administration lest he should become a despot, that is. Nor is he helpless if the Parliamentary system is subverted. We need a President who is neither a parrot nor a puppet nor even a mechanical ventriloquist but a person of higher authority and dignity commanding through his presence as Rashtrapati respect for the norms and imperatives of our Constitution and its destination as a Secular, Socialist, Democratic Republic. Pt. Jawaharlal Nehru asserted in the Constituent

Assembly that the President must be a person of high stature, independent authority and dignity and not merely the reflection of the party which has the majority in Parliament. Indeed, that is the reason why a broad-based constituency involving the entire nation and including every state legislature has been devised.

You, as an elector have the weighty responsibility in the fulfilment of the Constitution and its processes, including the important duty of choosing its highest functionary, the Rashtrapati. Ultimately, our accountability is to the Nation and we are all its servants. On this categorical imperative, I offer myself as a servant of India, as the servant of the humblest millions and its lowliest denizens. If you feel convinced that I have any claim on your confidence and judgement, you may render your verdict accordingly. If you feel otherwise surely you must act according to your wisdom.

May be, I will try to meet you personally but collectively if time permits. Whether we meet or not, I commend the nation's destiny to your navigational duty and best judgement.

With kindest regards,

Sincerely,

V.R. Krishna Iyer"

**(Justice V.R. Krishna Iyer—A Living Legend P-255/ 257)**

The poll day arrived. My opponent, the official candidate, taciturn to the last, won by a huge count while I lost horrendously although all my supporters duly cast their votes in my favour but the BJP maintained a mystic neutrality. L.K. Advani wrote to me what still is a riddle and an enigma:

You are a handmaiden of the Soviet Union and therefore we are not in a position to support you. But the leaders of the BJP units of Kerala and Maharashtra who met Krishna Iyer assured him that they would write to the party high command to stand by the decision taken earlier and support Krishna Iyer. BJP advocates in the Supreme Court also wrote to the high command but the

BJP did not change its stand.

Maneka Gandhi in her letter to Krishna Iyer wrote that there were a fewer number of MPs and MLAs in her party but all those in her party would vote for him. They also stood by this assurance and voted for the Opposition candidate.

(Justice V.R. Krishna Iyer—A Living Legend P-258)

To lose at the hustings is not to lose heart in life. Was not Winston Churchill, after World War victory, defeated? He writes in The Gathering Storm that when the enemy had surrendered 'I was immediately dismissed by the British electorate from all further conduct of their affairs'.

I am no politician and never was Life is an experiment and the Presidential election is an experience. Venkatraman has been my friend before and after. I spent very little money but did a lot of travel. I acquired rare friends and learnt the art of having no enemies.

The tranquillity of vanquishment has a spiritual value. I had no disappointment because, in this election, my rendezvous with destiny was defeat. What a heroic tryst with democratic might to dare and differ! The glamour of success brings material pleasure denied to one who at the polls has been the victim of macro-mathematical majority, but in the deeper measure of life Longfellow's lines strike the true note:

Not in the clamour of the crowded street,

Not in the shouts and plaudits of the throng,

But in ourselves, are triumph and defeat.

**Postscript**

The fury of canvassing, contesting, counting and collapsing was over but I had secured several votes by way of supports. I had to express gratitude to them and to the nation and so I wrote an open letter with which I conclude this Chapter:

The Presidential polls are over, the process of swearing in of the new Rashtrapati brings the chapter of contest to a close. On this occasion, I owe love and thanks to all those who have voted for me, and even those who have abstained or marked against me. My profound gratitude goes to those legislators, those in a sore minority, who have reposed confidence in me, despite powerful adverse winds. I stood for a democratic proposition, I campaigned for the Presidential right to information, I ran the country round to awaken the nation to the functional relevance, invigilatory importance and the authority and dignity of the head of the Republic in the very process of the Executive's ultimate accountability to the people of the country without in the least, disturbing the paramountcy of Parliament and the abundance of the Cabinet's governance. My numerical defeat notwithstanding, those who responded to my voice with their ballot, have placed me in a deep debt of gratitude. Even those who dismissed my candidacy have by their very taciturnity affirmed by thesis. Silence is implied assent where speech is occupational risk. Pressures and compulsions in tense situations may bend discretion to avert the displeasure of Power. To sacrifice secrecy, even though it be a constitutional guarantee, to avoid discovery and consequent sanctions is, perhaps, pardonable human frailty, I have no grievance whatever. On the contrary, the eloquence of silence on the part of those who opposed me is a significant victory for the validity of my presidential ideology. I have great personal regard for the leader of the abstentionists but feel sad when I read poet Dante who once said:

The hottest places in hell are reserved for those who, in a time of great moral crisis, maintain their neutrality.

While thanking those who voted for me and against me, I once again place before the people, our ultimate masters, the principle that the President matters and, within the parameters of the Cabinet system, ahs promises to keep. However camouflaged by demagoguery, never can the power process be left to one man, be he great or no, lest our system insidiously slip into freuhrerism. I conclude with a quote from John Stuart Mill:

A people may prefer a free government; but if from indolence, or carelessness, or cowardice, or want of public spirit, they are unequal to the exertions necessary for preserving it; if they can be deluded by the artifices used to cheat them out of it; if by momentary discouragement, or temporary panic or a fit of enthusiasm for an individual, they can be induced to lay their liberties at the feet of even a great man, or trust him with powers which enable him to subvert their institutions—in all these cases they are unfit for liberty.

Indians, I dare to hope, will prove worthy of the imperatives of Independence. My millions of thanks to my countless countrymen.

I wind up, as a little man from a long distance, with felicitations to Sri. Venkataraman as he fills his high office, but cannot help reminding him of what a great philosopher once said:

History has no other way of answering old questions than by putting new ones'.

# 19

# Parole Justice and Clemency Jurisprudence

Fifty-five years ago or so I was a prisoner for a brief while in the Cannanore Central Jail as detinue under a draconian detention law. That gave me deep insights into prisoner life and conscientised me about the compassionate justice of parole and release of sentencees before their full term had run out. Later I have had occasion to chair a committee to examine conditions of custodial justice to women, having been appointed by the Central Minister Margret Alva. That study also enlivened my consciousness about human rights of victims of State custody. Quite recently, I was requested by Chief Minister Antony of the Kerala State to head a committee to deal with the deeper issues of parole, emergency leave, furlough and grant of premature release from prison ahead of the full term of the sentence. Inevitably, I reflected on the last topic aided by my experience as a judge and as Minister for Prisons several decades earlier (1957-59). Those thoughts and ideas have been collected and presented by me in the following long essay titled *My Vision of Prison Justice vis-à-vis Parole and pre-term release.*

The human essence of prison jurisprudence consists in the presence of constitutional compassion as the ethos of jail justice, not etiolation of the person of the convict by a punitive regimen as implied in the judicial sentence. Indeed, human rights, in their plenitude, caged within the confines of the stone walls and iron bars but liberalised by the values of human dignity and developmental opportunity, are an inalienable part of the worth of the human person worshipped by our cultural heritage. No sentencee jettisons his humanity while being marched into the walled world but preserves and promotes it subject, of course, to the necessary limitations, the law imposes on incarceration. Judicial sentence is geared to social defence and towards this end, the benign transformation, through corrective operations, of the victims of punishment, is a purposeful measure. Thus Operation Correction is integral to prison process. Freedom behind bars carries with it creative methodologies whereby the offender becomes a finer non-offender and the safest social investment. Not crimogenic but curative, not pathological but therapeutic should be the dynamic approach to fulfill the goal of social justice, a fundamental of penology.

The basic philosophy of my thesis is that while retribution is savage and deterrence, if draconian, counter-productive, reformatory humanism must receive more emphasis. Ghandhiji wrote in Young India Weekly that jail environment hardens and humanitarian reform is the right direction. Nehru, quoted by the All India Committee on Jail Reforms (Vol. I P-iii) stresses this human element and the recognition of the fact that a criminal is largely created by social conditions and must be treated as for a disease. Rehabilitation is the radical recipe which can remedy the malady of criminality. Nehru, in Prison Land writes what is indelibly instructive for progressive jurists:

> High walls and iron gates cut off the little world of prison from the wide world outside. Here in this prison world everything is different; there are no colours, no changes, no movement, no hope, no joy for the long-term prisoner, the 'lifer'. Life runs its dull round with a terrible monotony; it is all flat desert land with no high points and no oases to quench one's thirst or shelter one from the burning heat. Days run into weeks and weeks into months and years till the sands of life run out.
>
> All the might of the State is against him and none of the ordinary checks are available. Even the voice of pain is hushed, the cry of agony cannot be heard beyond the high walls.

(v)

At p.142 of his book Nehru poignantly paints the lot of long-termers and lifers:

> Sentences of death and whipping impress us and pain us, but, after all, they affect only a very small number of the scores of thousands who are sentenced by our courts. The vast majority of these go to prison, mostly for long periods over which their punishment is spread out. It is a continuing torture, a never-ceasing pain, till mind itself grows dull and the body is blunted to sensation. The criminal type develops, the ugly fruit of our goals and our criminal law, and there is no fitting in then with the social machine outside. He is the square peg everywhere, with no roots, no home, suspicious of everybody, being suspected everywhere, till at last he comes back to his only true resting-place, the prison, and takes up again the tin or iron bowl, which is his faithful companion there. Do our judges ever trouble to think of cause and effect, of the inevitable consequences of an act or decision? Do they realize that their courts and the prisons are the principal factories for the production and stamping of the criminal type?

Reform, not revenge, is the central idea of criminal justice. Reverse despair and rekindle dignity, goodness and social commitment. Oscar Wilde poetised prison life thus:

> Something was dead in each of us,
> And what was dead was Hope.
>
> I know not whether Laws be right,
> Or whether Laws be wrong;
> All that we know who lie in gaol
> Is that the wall is strong;
> And that each day is like a year,
> A year whose days are long.

(Oxford Quotations P-572: 13:15)

The sentencing judiciary is no instrument of torture but a panacean process of healing discipline. Nor, indeed, is it true to assert 'Once a criminal, always a criminal'. On the contrary, every saint has a past and every sinner a future.

The great task of reform of the incarcerated convict is to recover the finer inner being lying latent in him. Nehru who has had long vicissitudinous jail suffering, argues in Prison Land:

> Why are punishments given—as society's or Government's revenge or with the object of reforming? "Do judges or prison officers ever think that the unhappy wretch before them should be made into a person capable of filling his place in society when he comes out of prison? It almost seems an impertinence to raise these questions, for how many people really care?"
>
> (Report of the All India Committee on Jail Reforms 1980-83 Volume-I p-xii)

In this context let me cite an educative paragraph from the All India Committee on Jail Reforms:

> Who are these murders? Instead of giving my reply to this question, I will first quote the answer given by the Royal Commission on Capital Punishment (1949-53) in its report at page 216, paragraph 617:
>
> There is a popular belief that prisoners serving a life sentence after conviction of murder form a specially troublesome and dangerous class. That is not so. Most find themselves in prison because they have yielded to temptation under the pressure of a combination of circumstances unlikely to recur. "Taking murderers as a class" said one witness, "there are a considerable number who are first offenders and who are not people of criminal tendencies. The murder is in many cases their first offence against the law. Previous to that they were law abiding citizens and their general tenor of life is still to be law abiding...." Many other witnesses with experience of prison conditions said the same thing. It is true that they were speaking of the state of affairs today, when the crimes of murderers serving sentences of imprisonment have all been of a sort that justified the commutation of the death sentence. But the Home Office, giving evidence to the Select Committee of 1930, expressed the opinion that, even if capital punishment were abolished, the greater

> number of prisoners 'who have not only committed murder but have been of criminal habits or tendencies, or are of a generally violent and insubordinate or sullen and morose temperament.' This accords with the experience of countries where capital punishment has been abolished; the evidence given to us in the countries we visited, and the information we received from others, were uniformly to the effect that murderers are no more likely than any other prisoners to commit acts of violence against officers or fellow prisoners or to attempt escape; on the contrary it would appear that in all countries murderers are, on the whole, better behaved than most prisoners. *It must be remembered too that prisoners serving life sentences have a special incentive to good behaviour, since the time they have in fact to serve depends so largely on it'*. (P-vi/vii)

"An offender is sent to prison *as a punishment* and *not for punishment*".

(Royal Commission P-xviii)

The reforming element, the compassionate component, has come to predominate, and the humane regimen has social justice content. Prisons are reformatories, not inflictive captivities.

There is an essential link between freedom behind bars and freedom *beyond* bars. The All India Jail Reforms Committee has expanded on this reformatory project:

Obviously, if after undergoing his term of punishment, a prisoner is going to take his place in society, it would be far easier to do so if his links with the outside world are not snapped. It is, therefore, imperative that his contacts with his relations and friends are not cut off and a reasonable opportunity should be given to him to maintain these ties during his term of imprisonment. In an extract of Pandit Nehru quoted above, the broad outlines of this treatment have already been given. The Committee has only enlarged this sphere according to present needs. *Greater latitude for his being released on parole, liberal permission for interviews (and these interviews not like mass interviews that exist today but separate interviews) and writing letters have to be given if continuous tension from their mind is to be removed.* The living conditions inside the jails should also appreciably improve and the hours when prisoners are kept locked up, therefore, must be reduced. The prisoners should also be permitted to pursue their reasonable hobbies, play games and indulge in social functions and thus an atmosphere should be created where there is greater relaxation and the prisoners are not keeping their hearts and minds locked. They should also be employed in some useful work which would benefit both the State and the prisoners themselves and which can secure employment for them when they go out of jails. Greater care should be taken about their physical and also mental health *so that they may not continue to brood but begin to feel that the string of life has not snapped for ever and they can pick it up again.* (P-xxiii)

If life in jail is not to snap social connections altogether, if prison cells are not to insulate and desiccate, by dehumanising solitude and iron drill, the person whose soul is very much alive and even luminous, it is appropriate to punctuate spells in jail with opportunity for being in society in such manner that experiment in re-socialisation will be a guarded operation, a disciplined exercise and a gradual re-entry into community life. Such is the philosophy and perspectival wisdom of parole, premature release, remissions and rewards. The goal is rekindling the sense of social responsibility and solidarity which promote the therapeutic objective of social defence. There are instances where persons, who have been in prison during the swaraj struggle, have later performed as excellent social and political leaders. Occasional discharge of prisoners into their familiar community milieu has also a penitential dimension so that when they return to prison premises an alchemy of the mind takes place. The moral-jural justification for periodic release into the open community under strict safeguards has been accepted by psychiatric and social scientists and therefore I am of the view, in agreement with the All India Jail Reform Committee and the Tamil Nadu Prison Reform Report, that a systematic regime of freedom *beyond bars*, regulated by correctional considerations of reform and social safety be experimented with.

Victimology is a developing branch of criminology. The

victims of crime, the witnesses who depose to the crime at the trial, the close relations of the murdered man and the people of the locality where, in a factions, fight or communal conflict, the crime has been committed leaving bitter feeling burning, have a voice in the criminal being out at large lest their safety be imperiled or even the offender's safety is in jeopardy out of reprisal. In such a view, it is but fair that these affected people are consulted before the crime-doer is enlarged on parole or otherwise. It is, therefore, just and fair that a probation officer enquires in the locality of the victim and reports to the jail authorities about the propriety of the release contemplated. Even the time of release may have to be carefully considered, lest a wholesome objective is defeated by a tactless step.

Let me pause here to *reemphasize* the rule of correctional justice, of punctuated and carefully guarded freedom *beyond* bars.

Here is a sum-up of the tentative propositions, I would consider the penologists to investigate. While deterrence has a role to play in penology the dominant principle is reformation, rehabilitation and social transformation. Progressive criminologists agree, even as Gandhiji, Nehru, the Royal Commission in England and the India Jail Reforms Committee take the view, that assimilation into society as safe and useful citizens requires constructive strategies which include a system of remission, leave and premature release. It is apt to cite the All-India Jail Reforms Committee:

> 20.1 The system governing remission, leave and premature release has been an integral part of our prison administration for over a century now. It has been functioning as a positive incentive to prisoners for good behaviour and work. The system came as a transitional step from mere custodial confinement to reformative treatment of offenders in which good behaviour and constructive work were considered essential pre-requisites for reducing the term of imprisonment on an individualised basis. In course of time, the concept was further enlarged and reinforced by introducing within the system certain new forms of special and State remissions.

> 20.2 Undoubtedly, the system of remission tends to bring in an element of flexibility in the determinateness of the sentence awarded to an offender so as to ensure, in consonance with his responsiveness to institutional treatment, his timely return to the community. The efficacy of the system has been reiterated by a number of expert bodies including the Indian Jails Committee 1919-20 the All India Jail Manual Committee 1957-59 and several state level Jail Reforms Committees/ Commissions. *It is fairly well established now that the remission system, if properly applied, encourages habits of industry and promotes good conduct among prisoners.* (Page 238)

Any benign system or salutory strategy is liable to abuse and therefore great circumspection is necessary while implementing Good Samaritan jurisprudence as part of prison justice so that abuse is pre-empted. One principle well established in our constitutional jurisprudence is that all power is a trust and *arbitrary exercise* is ultra vires. It follows that while the state may, under section 432 CrPC and Article 161 of the Constitution, enjoy the power to grant parole, partial release, remission, suspension and premature termination of imprisonment, this exercise must be *never arbitrary* and ever governed by sound guidelines. Indeed, the present essay itself is a product of a judicial direction by the High Court that paroles and remissions have been exercised arbitrarily, even absurdly, and so the state shall draw up definite rules and instructions to regulate and control grant of release from prison before the full term of the sentence runs out.

There is a different dichotomy confronting us when considering premature release of convicts. Lifers form one category and section 433A of the CrPC binds the State to keep in custody such sentencees for a minimum period of 14 years. In the case of others whose fate is a fixed jail term section 432 CrPC empowers the state to exercise the power without the precondition of 14 years custodial continuum. But as *Maruram* has elaborately explained (and *Balwan* has reaffirmed in 1999 VII 355 SCC) there is the paramount power to grant reprieve, respite or remission of punishment or to suspend, remit or commute the sentence of any person convicted of any offence falling within the State jurisdiction, untrammelled by statutory restraints. Even this plenary power is subject to the basic obligation of *non-arbitrariness* and relevant guidelines. In this view, the formulation of pertinent guidelines for the exercise of release by way of parole, premature release or otherwise becomes an unavoidable dimension of law. The grant of remission constitutes an area highly prone to corrupt and dubious practices if the discretion in this regard is not exercised *judiciously* but is left to the whim and humour of ministers or minions acting under delegation.

Since there are two sources of power for release, parole and the like, selective attention is needed in locating who can or should use the power. A mere parole, whether by way of emergency or periodic routine, can be exercised either by the Government directly or the Inspector General of Prisons or other delegate in the department. Being a statutory power, its delegation by Government will have to be by written rule, not by ad hoc instruction. Therefore, the grant of parole, to be legally valid, has to under section 432 CrPC and its exercise must be by the State Government itself, not by any officer under him in the prison department. If a certain category of parole can be disposed of at a lesser level, there must be a regulation or rule governing the situation. It is fair to remember that a delegate must operate within limited conditions. Release from prison of a person undergoing judicial sentence is a serious matter and hence the delegation has to be given to a responsible officer. I feel strongly that none lower than the D.I.G of Prisons should be entrusted with this power. Even the D.I.G must pass a *speaking order* giving cogent reasons relevant in law. What I mean is that even the D.I.G or I.G, while granting parole on an emergency basis or otherwise, must not act fancifully, ritually or fatuously. The ground must be good and sound, humanist and calculated to strengthen social relationship. For instance, parole cannot be granted merely for buying a lottery ticket or watching a pooram festival or cricket match or for a feast at home. On the contrary, responsible reasons, weighty enough from the angle of social sentiment or likely to promote the prisoner's humanisation vis-a-vis his family or group, may be all right. Here again, an emergency must be a *real* emergency, such as the grave or sudden illness of a very dear and near relative or the demise of one for whose funeral the presence of the prisoner is a necessary social obligation. One of the abuses of parole is flippant frequency and fallacious alibi in granting such liberal liberation. In fact, the period must be abridged to the minimum and the number of occasions of grant kept rare. Otherwise, prisoners will buy parole on some alibi using oblique influence and stultify the gravity of a court sentence. I would like to add when grounds are put forward for claiming parole, on-the-spot verification of their veracity by a probation officer or other credible agent may be a good restraint. During the sojourn when the prisoner is out of the gate, he must be under surveillance because he must be under close watch not to misuse the privilege. The prisoner will be *deemed to be vicariously in prison.* In short, he should be deemed to be in custody, in the sense that his movements are not fully free but under police surveillance or probation officer's scrutiny. These aspects must be governed by rule and the parolee must accept the condition when set free, so that on breach he can be re-arrested and brought back and even forfeit earned reward or remission. Parole has a humanist purpose, but indulgence in easy exit may defeat the therapeutic object. Moreover, the system will be corrupted if political or opulent influence or other vices creep in, to frustrate the ethical foundation of the parole system.

At the risk of repetition, realising the emphasis needed for proposition I deal with the jurisprudence of discretionary power again:

**The Role of Discretion in Parole—Reprieve and Allied Exercises**

Power postulates discretion in the depositary and unless guided by broad directions in its exercise, tyranny may be the price even in the case of the judiciary, vastly more so in the hands of the Executive, administrative bodies or quasi-judicial tribunals. Great care, indeed central concern, is thus necessary in controlling discretionary power vested in para-curial institutions with advisory functions. The great U.S. judge Frankfurter (344 U.S. 443) tersely observed:

'Discretion without a criterion for its exercise is authorization of arbitrariness. Therefore, the cardinal role of guidelines in the grant of any form of out-of-prison excursion cannot be exaggerated.

What then are cancalising conditions on the premature release of prisoners even by the Executive Head? Since personal freedom is dear, high voltage pressure for gaining a holiday from prison is natural. To forbid departure from due process, many experiments have been tried. Let us look at some.

Before entering into a detailed discussion of the conditions for liberations for short or long periods or for final release before the sentence has run out, we may briefly deal with parole which is of two kinds. Speaking generally, parole is a conditional release given to a prisoner who is still regarded as a prisoner and while out of jail is supervised by a probation officer or police personnel. A parolee as mentioned by me earlier, is never really free and his movements are subject to limitations. There is a public feeling that influential prisoners manipulate parole release from day one and by legal cunning, escape the rigours of imprisonment, reducing to impotence judicial sentence. The rules imposed therefore must be strict, specific and beyond evasion. Even so, there may be unpredictable circumstances which may compel a prisoner to seek brief release. It would be heartless to reject a plea for parole if the conditions are crying for compassion. That is why this class of leave from jail is called emergency leave. A sudden state of danger at home requiring the prisoner's immediate presence, a grave situation, quite unanticipated, may arise where refusal of a few free days to attend to the sudden exigency may be inhuman. At the same time, if the situation has arisen *before* the sentence was pronounced, emergency parole cannot be granted. Only if it is a post-conviction misfortune that one can earn emergency leave. Ordinarily, even emergency leave should not be granted for the first six months of the sentence except in the rarest of rare cases. The more powerful the prisoner and socially manipulable the situation, the sterner should be the criterion for release under this head. It must be subject to police surveillance so that the parole may not outwit the law. Lesser emergencies must meet with refusal and must be treated as mishaps incidental to imprisonment. Life in a prison, consequent on a judicial sentence, is not a holiday in a country club to leave and return as you please. This sense of gravity also requires the endorsement by a senior prison officer not below the rank of D.I.G. There must also be surprise verification of the alleged emergency by a local police officer. I suggest that the sessions judge who is a *visitor* to the prison concerned (under the rules) may periodically invigilate the grant of parole, its frequency and seriousness of the grounds, to check misuse.

The more standarised system of parole is awarded to an offender so as to ensure his salutary responsiveness to institutional treatment may well be called furlough. This enables a periodic return to the community and its efficacy in reforming the character has been reiterated by a number of expert bodies, including more than one Indian jail committee. To quote Mullah 'it is fairly well established now that the remission system, if properly applied encourages habits of industry and promote good conduct among prisoners'. Every incentive aimed at improvement of the inner being of the prisoner makes for raising the level of social consciousness and for that reason must be a strategy the state must adopt inside central prisons. The system must generate expectation but resist dubious recurrence. That is why a minimum of one year in prison should be condition precedent to a parole for a month. The recommendation must be by the Superintendent, must be based an objective appreciation of the conduct and character of the inmates and must be based on a written record of his impression. This report must be confidentially verified by the D.I.G who should, if satisfied, grant release for a period not exceeding one month. He should also pass a speaking order, so that later the advisory body and the sessions judge as visitor may review the use of the power. Indeed, there must be occasional reports by the intelligence wing of the police about the out of jail conduct and social behaviour of the prisoner. In case there is any complaint about a parolee's conduct, immediate information should be conveyed to the prison superintendent and power must be vested in the officer concerned to cancel the conditional release. There must be provision in the rule for the police to re-arrest the parolee under such circumstances. On enquiry, if the visitor, may be session judge, is satisfied that there has been breach of conduct on the part of the parolee, while conditionally free, he should pass orders canceling rewards and remissions and forfeiting other advantages. Parole must be liberal but the abuse by the beneficiary should be visited by condign penalty.

Emergency leave is eligibility for prisoners when sudden tragedies spring a sad surprise summoning their urgent presence at home. But there is another class of parole which appears to have been an established practice in Kerala for long years and has worked well in moulding the character and improving the behaviour of culprits in custody. Schools and colleges, court and tribunals enjoy vacation for a certain fixed period after a year's work, but such a standard vacation for prisoners who have worked for a year has no rationale. Can holidays, as bonanza, to murderers, dacoits and dreaded criminals be granted? Prima facie it sounds like a bizarre conundrum! But wait. If a convict while in custody shows signs of turning a new leaf, there may be justification for rewarding him with a bonus of a few weeks of free family life beyond bars. We cannot standardize such earned leave and make the prisoner look at that prospect as a *right.* I am of the view that it is good to reward good behaviour of an enduring nature by parole for say a month in a year although one can't be rigid about the practice. One has to be careful to see that many a prisoner may play the flunkey to please the boss and claim reward or remission. In fact, such a scheme may be promotive of servility, make-believe good behaviour. Therefore a prisoner wearing the mask or pretence of good behaviour should not get away with it. So I suggest that we prescribe a superior prison official making confidential enquiry about prisoners, independently of the Superintendent in immediate charge. While it is desirable to motivate a prisoner to become better behaved, more socially sensitive and generally worthy of trust as good citizen this benefit of 'earned' furlough should be granted after cross-checking of *apparent* good conduct. Higher level invigilation of behavioral betterment makes assurance doubly sure. Perhaps, if the system has worked well in the past, as was represented by the senior prison officials, there may be no serious flaw in framing a scheme of standard furlough, reviewed periodically, with built-in confidential enquiries about the use and misuse of a fixed term of furlough for a good prisoner who has served a standard period, say of one year. This annual expectation may be a sound inducement for the prisoner to change his conduct for the better and acquire a habit of social responsibility.

Furlough or standard parole, as distinguished from emergency leave, may therefore be regularised by rules and schematised where considerations of scrutiny, safety while at large, reporting to the police periodically, surveillance by the probation officer and local reports may be incorporated. Here again, the view I have earlier expressed about *victims* having a voice before release of the prisoner, even for a brief while, may have to be taken into account.

Remission may be earned by well-behaved prisoners. In fact, leadership qualities, educational attainments, cultural activities and even cultivation of aesthetic propensities may be given full opportunity for development, so that the incarcerated human being gets a fair deal for a finer future. The same consideration must apply in promoting sports and games, athletic achievements and the like. In all these matters it is a safe risk to take to allow teams and groups to be formed and give performances outside prison walls. Imagine a young prisoner earning a high distinction in the University or literary award in a competition! Similarly, a team of players within the prison, a group playing a music concert or displaying innovative skill and new discovery, may be a welcome incentive rewarded by remission. These and many other creative schemes may go a long way in transforming offenders and making them an asset to society. Stone walls do not a prison make, nor iron bars a cage, if the spirit of man is given scope to score higher or win laurels for proven work. This is a flexible field where imaginative projects can always be experimented with. Life is a liberal experiment. You can make a Gandhi out of goof or goon by corrective prison therapy, a Valmiki out of a robber in custody, a great singer inside a cell and a fine batsman, given the environment. Such a person may be given remission and considered seriously for premature release.

The touchstone is not the term suffered in jail, but the talent cultivated and the luminous change achieved.

**Remission System**

The remission system is a high-risk area of release *before time,* of prisoners under tough sentence. The jurisdiction is slippery and the operation is fraught with opportunism, corruption and an element of gambling uncertainty. The All India Jail Reforms Committee has sounded a warning which I may quote as caveat:

20.4. The system of grant of remission varies from State to State. There is no uniformity in the quantum of remission granted to inmates on various counts. Although the Model Prison Manual containing inter-alia guidelines in this respect was circulated to all States and Union Territories as long back as in 1960, there has not been any uniformity in the grant of remissions in the country. There is also a wide-spread feeling that remission system is generally operated upon in an arbitrary manner with little regard to the individual differences and merits of the case. There have been complaints by the prisoners about the manner and mode of granting remission in several places. It is alleged that the grant of remission is guided by the whims and fancies of the persons competent to grant it, and as such crafty prisoners manoeuvre the system to their advantage. The grant of remission constitutes an area highly prone to corrupt practices if the discretion in this regard is not exercised judiciously.

20.5. There is no uniformity of principles for grant of State Remission as well. The Committee has been given to understand that State Governments have been granting remissions even on occasions which normally do not justify such awards. It has come to the notice of the Committee that remission was granted to the inmates of a particular institution on one occasion only to mark the visit of a VIP. Grant of such remission is not only unwarranted but also purposeless so far as reformation is concerned.

The emphasis, therefore, is on preemption of abuse by

appropriate machinery for supervision. I agree with the jail reform committee that the system of remission as an instrument to alchemise the mind and humanise the soul of the convict in custody is a liberal tool of correction. There are four type of remission of sentences considered by the All India Committee. It may be a useful guide for us to adopt. They are (1) Ordinary remission. (2) Annual good conduct remission. (3) Special remission and (4) State remission. The criteria for eligibility must remove even traces of arbitrary antic from the system. The Justice Mullah Commission has ruled out the following categories of prisoners from the beneficiary ambit of the ordinary remission system. Broadly speaking, I agree with it, making it clear that habitual convicts are a high risk for remission. While excluding habituals, we may also have to consider eschewal of persons who are kept in confinement under the provisions of Chapter VIII CrPC (security for keeping the peace and for good behaviour). Even in these cases, however, we need not abolish remission altogether but may keep it as an exceptional option, provided there is exemplary good conduct on the part of the prisoner, which negatives the suspicion of misuse of remission. Justice Mullah Committee enumerates the following exclusionary types of prisoners:

20.7.2 The following types of prisoners should not be eligible for ordinary remission:

(i) Prisoners having substantive sentence of less than 2 months;
(ii) Prisoners sentenced in default of payment of fine only;
(iii) Prisoners whose sentence is reduced to less than 2 months (In such cases remission already earned, if any, should stand forfeited);
(iv) Prisoners transferred from one prison to another on disciplinary grounds during the period of their stay in the latter prison;
(v) Prisoners removed from remission system as punishment;
(vi) Prisoners specifically debarred from remission system under any law or rule; and
(vii) Prisoners out on special leave for the duration of such leave.

Sentences for short term up to six months need not be

considered for remission because of the brevity of the period. In special cases of alleviation, parole will take care of the situation.

I agree with the Mullah Committee that ordinary remission may be extended to sentencess with one year punishment and who have not committed a prison offence and may be awarded *thirty days* annual good conduct remission. There is a measure of ad hocism whichever way we prescribe the rate of remission or the grounds thereof. In human affairs, discretion distinguished from nepotism, depends on proper exercise and an amount of trust in the custodian of power can be the only guarantee. Meritorious work, defined as precisely as possible and related to local conditions, may be considered for a reward—may be as special remission, in addition to the annual good conduct remission, so as to create a spirit of healthy competition among prisoners. The All India Report is found generally satisfactory by me and I adopted the suggestion of a ceiling on special remission not exceeding 45 days in a year. The practice of granting remission on occasions or for reasons not justifiable by rational criteria should be immediately stopped.

If our jails fail to breathe humanism 'the vilest deeds like poison weeds bloom well in prison air'. We have to take great care by processes of parole, pre-term release and other creative projects that the personality of the prisoner, with his full potential in blossom, is allowed to unfold. Otherwise, we will prove the pessimism of Oscar Wilde in the Ballard of Reading 'it is only what is good in Man that wastes and withers there'. Our endeavour have to be to reverse this curse. I have seen in a Stockholm jail, prisoners allowed to be with their families for a day, every week, thus keeping up the family. While within the tall walls, I have seen in Newzealand a rapist sentenced to long imprisonment, regretting his mistake and taking to a creative sculptor's pursuit, convert a block of wood into a marvellous wood work worth ten thousand dollars by painstaking artistic wonder. He was no longer a wretch in prison, but a noble creator of a lovely piece of art to be revered in his new incarnation. Such is my vision of potential transformation of a convict into a Picasso or an Aurobindo!

Now comes another significant administrative problem. Who will advise on parole and release since that instrumentality must be above board, able to judge the consequences of release and be responsible to the Constitution and the court? Every aberrant who was benefited by a premature release is a censure by society on the advisory body.

Before going further into the question of the advisory ensemble, we must be clear about the constitutional dimension of release of lifers who have not served fourteen years as required by section 433A, CrPC Release in such cases is possible only under Article 161 which is the power of a Governor. This power shall be exercised *only* on the advice of the Home Minister and therefore every order of release under Article 161 has to be at the level of Government, not of the Prison echelons. Perhaps, parole by way of emergency leave or furlough may be so encumbered with conditions of surveillance and reporting to the police that it may be declared 'deemed imprisonment'. The prisoner is out but *not free*. He moves around but his mobility is conditional. In this view, orders of grant of parole may be passed, by appropriate delegation by Government through rules under section 432 CrPC and the Prisons Act, by an empowered officer of the prison department.

Rewards and Remissions are but recommendations and vest no enforceable *right* to release in the prisoner. They are matters to be considered by the advisory board or the Governor when an order of release is being made. The title to release, prematurely under Article 161 or section 432, CrPC springs into existence with the *appropriate signature* of government. However, government acts on expert advice. For this purpose a high-level versatile authority reprocessing many disciplines may be necessary. In my view, a judicial presence elevates the authority and stature of the Advisory Body. May be, a retired judge of the High Court will fill the bill. A senior medical officer or physiotherapist may add competence to the committee. A retired D.G.P, with familiarity in the field of prison management, will enhance the worth of the advisory body. Of course, the Government Secretaries of Home and Law must sit on the Committee with the judge as chairperson.

The United States is the land of *'due process'*. But India has advanced beyond the U.S and the U.K in certain dimensions of administrative law. After Maru Ram, why even before and after, the exercise of pardon power and of commutation in India is subject to de facto due process in the sense of reasonableness in exercise of power and guidelines governing even presidential clemency. By contrast, we may have a look at this branch of American jurisprudence. Sheldon Krantz, in his authoritative book Corrections and Prisoner's Rights writes:

The most common method of restoration in most jurisdictions is the executive pardon. There are many problems with the pardoning process, however. First of all, pardons are normally entirely discretionary with a governor (or President), and therefore, are not subject to judicial review. See, e.g., Murphy v. Ford, 390F.Supp.1372 (W.D.Mich.1975). Also, given the lack of guidelines, pardons provide an erratic and irrational method for restoring the rights of convicted offenders. President's Crime Commission, Task Force Report: Corrections 91 (1967). (Page 324)

The expression parole is used in a wider sense in American jurisprudence. The same learned author notes that in the American criminal justice process no point offers more opportunity for abusive and arbitrary power than does the parole-release decision. Until quite recently the courts had taken a "hands off" attitude towards this decision, primarily on the basis that parole release was a privilege and not a right'.

Indeed, parole proceedings were treated as an aspect of prison discipline, not an adjudication of rights in an adversary proceeding, and does not entitle a prisoner to notice therein, or specification of the grounds and underlying facts upon which the determination was based. Of course, a contrary note has also been struck in some cases. Sheldon Krantz observes:

Since the early 1980's, there has been an explosion in

caselaw on the parole release decision which potentially promises far greater accountability in this process. Most of the cases have involved attacks on the procedures (or lack thereof) of the United States Board of Parole. Others have involved similar attacks on state parole boards under the year 1983. The primary issue in most of these cases has been the applicability of the Due Process Clause to the granting or denial of parole. Many cases also have attacked parole release procedures of the United States Board of Parole on the grounds that they violate the Federal Administrative Procedure Act.

Although various cases had made small inroads on the up-to-then unlimited discretionary power of parole boards, the most significant decision to date has been Childs v. United States Board of Parole, 511 F.2d 1270(D.C.Cir. 1974). In Childs, over ninety federal prisoners brought a class action against the Federal Parole Board claiming that their rights to due process had been violated by the Board's failure to reveal the basis for denials of applications for parole. (Corrections and Prisoner's Rights Pages 295/296).

Now, however, a change has been chiseled. The law there is that there is a requirement of reasons for decision on parole or revocation thereof on due process grounds. The current status of the law is that sufficiency of reasons must be available for judicial scrutiny. Grant and deprivation of parole, according to the U.S. Supreme Court as of now, must be supported by reason and arbitrariness invites invalidation. The American law is best summarised thus:

The court determined that the reason was insufficient after applying this test:

Can such a reason be so meaningful that a reviewing court can determine whether the Board has adopted and followed criteria that are appropriate, rational and consistent, and does it protect the inmate against arbitrary and capricious decisions or actions based upon impermissible considerations? 389 F. Supp. At 409.

Thus, it appears that the giving of reasons requires both explicit criteria and facts indicating why the criteria were applied in a given way. This area obviously is in need of further development, however. It is clear that the giving of very general or abstract reasons would result in Childs amounting to a meaningless victory.

(Corrections and Prisoner's Rights Page 299).

Indian Criminal jurisprudence has crystallized the law of parole and release whether it be under statute or in exercise of clemency jurisprudence and therefore just, fair and reasonable exercise is now integral to parole—release jurisprudence. Fundamental fairness—the touchstone of due process—obligates the State to ground its decision on relevant, rational material with nexus to the objective of the parole-release-remis

# 20
# An American Trip that did not Click

Two American professors, a lady and a gentleman, telephoned me one day last year from Delhi and desired to meet me in Kochi. Why? I queried curiously. I live alone, have no high office nor official commission, have nothing to give nor take. Then why? They insisted that they had heard about me, had read my judgments and books and would feel their visit to India complete only if they met me—just a courtesy call, a friendly hour. O.K. I said. They came—Prof. John Bonine and Prof. Svitlana. The finest moments of one's life are when, out of sweet spontaneous sentiment nice persons engage you in lovely conversation without motive save the pleasure of exchanging views, taking a sip tea and greeting each other in a relaxed mood. We talked about India and America and John asked me whether I was likely to visit his great country. Would you come to the University of Oregon—wonderful place, good academic atmosphere and excellent campus. Maybe we will invite you if you are inclined to respond. What a charming gesture! I recollected my visit to Eugene (Oregon) in 1965 when my sister, a marine biologist, was working there as a researcher. She had a good and hospitable friend Tom Phillip, living close to the campus. I recalled that trip when my wife, who always gave meaning to my life, was with me, I was not yet fifty and was fighting fit. Challenge is writ large on one's mind and mien when bursting with the faculties of life's best years. But now that I am alone, alone, at age eightyeight, a weary world weighs me down, appetite for travel, lecture and glory wanes and the wonder of the mysterious universe withers away. And yet, my habits are simple, my vision of humanity is luminous and the battle for a better social order is invigorating. So I told John and Svitlana that I would consider to cross the pacific and enjoy their University hospitality when the invitation came. How fascinating the company, how fruitful the conversation and in retrospect, how predictive the sequel! We did cover Public Interest Litigation, Environmental law and Human Rights jurisprudence in the two hours of homely, happy gossip.

John and Svitlana, a loving pair, intellectual comrades and academic associates, left for Oregon and I was immensely pleased with my newly acquired friends. I did not expect an invitation to their university and I was not, at my advanced age, avid to grab a visit to that distant, though marvellous country. The abbreviation of time left in this life and the waning humanism in a sordid planet where American Might "doth bestride the narrow world like a Colossus and we petty men walk under its huge legs"—these two causes tinged with a browner shade the approaching sunset of my years. And yet the elan in me was not extinguished, the concerns and commitments which my soul cherished, never vanished. So when the invitation from John Bonine did come I was ambivalent. Although I did agree in the beginning, hoping to give myself time to say 'no' if I so felt later. After obtaining my informal consent Svitlana and John wrote on behalf of the University of Oregon formally inviting me to give a key note address to the Twentyfirst Annual Public Interest Environmental Law Conference on March 6$^{th}$ to 9$^{th}$ 2003 and to give a week of lectures at the University of Oregon from March 10$^{th}$ to 14$^{th}$, inter alia stating that my visit would be under the auspices of the 'Human Rights for All' programme.

'We are both incredibly honoured by your kind agreement to come to Oregon.'

All the time, I was in two minds or rather many minds, for one thing what heavily weighed on me was the lonely long long air journey, switching flights en-route. I had to plan a break of journey to make the travel feasible. Since I had friends in Hong Kong and the flight to Oregon was to be via the Pacific, I explored the possibility of breaking journey in Hong Kong. Basil Fernando, the key figure in the Asian Human Rights organisation with headquarters in Hong Kong, was close to me, close associate of Asian Human Rights and undertook to arrange for my stay for three days on my way. Although the University had offered not merely business class travel facility, but also comfortable accommodation I decided to stay at Eugune with my friend Tom Phillip who had a large house close associate of Asian Human rights, to the University and would look after me like a son. I needed personal attention since my health was poor, my vision gave problems and frequent medicines had to be taken. The best hotel cannot provide the personal attention an old man needs when he is in indifferent health and is under medication. Eugene, where the University is situated, is a beautiful place and I thought I would enjoy a holiday, since delivering lectures was a light operation, habituated as I was to the topic for discussion and for public speaking. An academic crowd is an innocent gathering for one used to noisy political meetings and daily Bench-Bar cross-fire. Meanwhile, another development took place. My young friend Rajkumar, who was formerly a student in Harvard and is now lecturing in Hong Kong had informed my long-standing friend Prof. Steiner of the Harvard University, about my visit to the U.S. So, Steiner readily informed me how glad he was that I was visiting America. He invited me to Harvard for a day's lecture and made available all the travel and accommodation facilities. This was a great bonanza, because a law lecture at Harvard and meeting the intellectual company there was a most stimulative pleasure. Indeed, Harvard still remains the 'Mecca' of legal learning and every time I have been there, has been a rewarding pilgrimage. Prof. Steiner is a superb human rights lover and a great teacher. To meet him and spend a day there was a worthwhile experience. I planned my programme meticulously and informed Basil of Hong Kong, John Bonine of Eugene, Prof. Steiner of Harvard, and my Son Ramesh Krishnaier, an American citizen in Fort Lauderdale. What a perfect project, if everything went through all right!

'There is a divinity that shapes our edge, rough-hew them how we will'. Some deeper issues were disturbing my soul.

President Bush and his imperial, aggressive intimidation of Iraq was intensifying day by day. I was fundamentally opposed to the bravado of bully Bush invasionary intransigence bypassing the United Nations, impotentising the security council and playing the role of self appointed global field marshal. I hated his arrogant assertion that Iraq had mass destruction equipment denied by the U.N. inspectorate and after all, the terrorist U.S., more than all of the nations put together, had the largest universal arsenal of nuclear weapons enough for annihilation of humanity. Neither the World Legal Order nor the U.N principles of International Law would contemplate a Power deciding for itself who should be President of another country and who should be installed in his place. Indeed, I wrote to Prof. Bonine and Svitlana that I was opposed in principle to the Bush-Blair Axis. America is a free country, and so, Prof. Bonine countered my argument by saying that I was welcome to Oregon and expresses my views freely. So I was silenced on that score although I was filled with wonder that Yankee authoritarianism did not extinguish free speech even in an hour of crisis, absent clear and present danger.

Supposing the war brakes out, will I not get stuck in a foreign country with my baggage of old age? So I consulted, on the telephone, Prime Minister Vajpayee at a personal level. This I did to get assured about my safety while abroad. Prime Minister Vajpayee, a fine person, frank and friendly, gently advised me *in all humility* that I had better avoid a trip to the United States until the Iraq imbroglio was over. Sinha, the Foreign Minister, gave me similar advice. Even so, in the light of assurances by Oregon friends that inside America I would be safe, I did not abandon my U.S trip or jettison the promise of being in Oregon.

This was not the end. My eyesight, for long in pathological condition, began to protest. I had also concern about weather conditions since friends from the States e-mailed me that there was unusual snowstorm this year and I would be frozen even with the best of woollen. I wrote to Prof. Steiner whether reports were true that Boston was ice-bound and if so I would have to cancel my warm visit to Harvard. As a realist he agreed and said that the winter was terrible, that some occasion may still arise when I could address his law school on Human Rights. Of course, one of my major attractions was Harvard and once that programme was off, my enthusiasm fell. Even so, I wanted to keep my word with the Professors in Oregon. So I wanted to be assured that my general health was sound. A thorough medical check up was done and there was nothing seriously worrisome. Even so, the doctors were divided in their opinion. The heart specialist said that while there was nothing wrong to be upset, he would advise me not to venture on a tiresome travel which would exhaust even younger persons. But my ortho specialist, who had been attending on my fracture in the vertebra, was more encouraging. 'Sir, your challenging spirit and general condition of health will overpower obstacles on the way. Therefore, do make the dauntless journey'. This advice did not quite convince me as the fatigue of age frequently reminded me of the advancing evening of life. However, I kept my mind open and wrote to the American Professors that I was not giving up the trip. In preparation for the keynote address I put down my talk in a paper of academic standard. John Bonine wanted footnote references, which I furnished to their satisfaction. To understand the depth of feeling behind John Bonine's great desire that I should participate in the Conference, I reproduce his letter of January 15th 2003 in full:

> The organizers of the Public Interest Environmental Law Conference (PIELC) asked us just two days ago about the prospect of your keynote address. We shall send them the latest draft of your paper now! We are encouraged to believe that all the planets will line up to guarantee your ability to travel here for your Visiting Scholar appointment!
>
> Meanwhile, here in Oregon the Secretariat of our international public interest network, the Environmental Law Alliance Worldwide (E-LAW), is hard at work in making arrangements for our E-LAW Annual Meeting, which will take place just before the PIELC. The importance of that?
>
> A large number of the finest public interest environmental lawyers from all continents will descend upon Eugene

for the private E-LAW meeting to discuss strategies and skills, and then they will all participate in the PIELC. They are truly a core (and corps) of hope and dedication. For example, M.C. Mehta of Delhi has confirmed attendance. Some others from India, Sri Lanka, Nepal, and Bangladesh will join terrific pioneering public interest advocates from Russia, Ukraine, Tanzania, Kenya, Chile, Argentina, U.K., and so many other places. We know that it will be exciting for you, as it is for them, to have some time to interact during the PIELC, to inspire, to commune.

We will, as mentioned earlier, arrange for medical insurance for your visit, and a schedule that does not tire you. We imagine that one of our tasks will simply be holding you back from too much participation in events that will feed your soul with hope and enthusiasm!

Have you obtained your visa, or do you already have a long-term B visa?

All along, some overly trepidant hesitancy was haunting me despite the affection showered on me from every side. The maladies of old age are not what words can explain. It is psychic, parasenile.(?) So I was punctuating my correspondence with sentiments indicative of my dubitation. One of the few letters reflecting this mood I reproduce for the reader to get a probe into my mind. Here is my letter dt. Nov. 26 2002:

Dear Prof. John Bonine/Svltana,

Never have I received so much warmth of welcome and affectionate assurance of care and concern for my sojourn as from you both. Never have I been in such an emotional see-saw, tossed between the deep wish to accept your invitation and the serious health hazzards standing in the way of my journey as now. Had my eye problem shown improvement and other bodily condition less diffident my decision gladly to be in Eugene with you early in March would have been clear and firm. So much is my keen desire to participate in the intellectual festival where you have kindly assigned to me a great role to play. But I am caught up in a crisis of conflicting medical opinions about crossing the hemisphere and addressing the conference, mindless of the cold weather and other changes difficult to negotiate at my age of eighty-eight. You have made my conditions of stay cordial and offered even medical insurance. What a hospitable gesture have you extended to me as if you were my brother and sister.

I have been through a round of medical consultations and have to go through a few more checks and tests. I can make up my mind for sure only after that process is gone through. The journey is long, but I am in a mood to take up the challenge. For the nonce, I keep my judgement in suspense although I know I am annoying you by this uncertainty. But life is a riddle wrapped in a mystery and simple solutions of easy negotiability may be baffling. I plead with you both to give me time. I entreat you to overlook my hesitancy. I request you to have compassion and receive my final choice, when I make it, as the best under the circumstances.

Whether I come or not, one thing I have gained since your visit to Cochin and your letters from Eugene. I have acquired the profound friendship of two souls John & Svltana. This will remain an abiding asset for the rest of my life. Do forgive me for the delay in replying to you. Do put me in the wait list in the great expectation that we will meet.

With warm regards,

Yours sincerely,

V.R. KRISHNA IYER

I had complained of my eyesight problem but John, with brotherly concern, wanted to take me to the best eye specialist, free of cost. So I wrote to him on January 21, 2003 in reply to his letter of January 20th which contains the following compassionate statement:

Your resistless affection manifests itself in every letter that you send. The last one being so magnetic in its appeal that I find myself helpless in striking a negative note. The truth is that while my general health is reasonably good for my age, my system is unable to cope with the exertions such as are involved in a journey to the other hemisphere. My eyesight is unpredictable but you have an answer for it. I will keep myself prepared to travel although my medical advisors in the leading hospital in Cochin will further examine me for my poor vision and sense of exhaustion. The spirit is willing but the flesh is weak? Let me be ready to be in Oregon. Your charming invitation may ultimately win, although I am sure in case I am disabled from travelling taking an overall view, you will in your characteristic indulgence forgive me this time. I am still hopeful and so I am sending all the particulars you have desired.

I must confess that John and Svitlana were no more mere American friends. They were my brother and sister whose concern for me made my eyes moist. Who can resist the emotion-packed epistle which runs thus:

Regarding your eyesight, it appears from my searching on the Web (Internet) that "macular generation" is a broad term for a number of different diseases. *http://www.eyesight.org/*. Also, "cornea defect" seems a very general term. It may be that, in addition to consulting a top-notch opthalmologist in Cochin, you will want to have an assessment here. I may be able to arrange that without cost. We are confident that all problems can be solved and that you can come.

The two of us spent the weekend on the beautiful Oregon Coast, walking on the beach, hiking to a 500-year old tree, listening to the crashing surf. We would love it if you can also see and hear and feel the incredible State of Oregon!

Best Wishes

John and Svitlana

In the light of my firmer stand that my eye specialists had strongly advised me against long air travel they knew better and I had to remember that my eyesight must survive the Eugene visit, John relented. Again at the end of February, comes the response of John Bonine pressing me for a reconsideration of my initial judgment. Said John on February 28, 2003:

The basis for this request comes from a careful reading

of the medical opinion attached below to your message, and your own reasons. The medical opinion stresses the risk of traveling alone because of the need to instill eye drops regularly. Your own message stresses the risks of falling, or not seeing clearly. All but the last can be overcome with a traveling companion! And we know that, even if you were completely blind, you "see clearly" more than 99.99 percent of the population, because your vision of mind is like its own moral and philosophical lamp!

This proposal, while doubtlessly surprising, and perhaps even irritating to you because of our persistence, is not impossible. M.C. Mehta has not yet left India, and will be traveling in the company of a scientist. He would guide as if you were his own father. A colleague and remarkable younger lawyer in Chennai, T. Mohan, might be willing to come (but the question is whether he has a current visa).

Why would we push like this? Frankly, it is because one of us (John) lives life in such a mode. "Pushy" is practically my middle name. But more importantly, this is the year when the 50 environmental lawyers from around the world are in Oregon for the Conference. This occurs only every second year. Whereas the Public Interest Environmental Law Conference takes place each year, and yes, we can plan for next year, and it will involve many public interest lawyers. But we would really like you to meet the ones from 40 other countries, and to inspire them. They — the members of our E-LAW network — are the most important.

So we will accept whatever, but I do want to look into this idea of joint travel!!!

I never realised that human relations, with instant spontaneity, would go so deep as did happen in the John-Krishna instance. How profound can humanism be, how loving, regardless of country and colour can human bonds be.

Prose in tears is poetry:

For Mercy has a human heart,

Pity a human face,

And love, the human form divine,

And Peace, the human dress. (Blake)

The problem of VISA, with brooding Iraq conflict delaying things, was readily solved by Prof. John Bonine speaking to his Congressman who in turn talked to the Madras Consulate of the U.S., with instant issuance of the VISA. Democracy and bureaucracy are not often on easy speaking terms, but when the American congressman spoke the bureau end in Madras acted quick. That democracy is best where people's representative have authority enough to be heard without paper-logging dialatoriness when a Congressman's voice is on the phone, not for any oblique objective but for a blitz performance of what should be done at once, but is often slowed down by the tardy processes of the system.

From an objective angle, everything was ready for my trip. A VISA valid for ten years was with me. Arrangements for a Hong Kong brake of the journey were ready. Tom Phillip of Eugene was willing to pick me up from the airport to his home. The University was in a hospitable mood and I was ready with my speech. and yet the trip was scotched.

Why and how? My eye specialist were firm that the risk would be great if I recklessly ignored their advice. I was eighty-eight years of declining days and my health left much to be desired. Age and infirmities in the evening of life, aggravated by poor eyesight, compelled me to take a decision quickly. I told John and Svitlana about my predicament and sent them two medical reports. After all, a judge has to judge and not vacillate. The hour to take a decision had come since I was already on the Ist of March. I knew the pressure on me from Eugene. I knew the disappointment if I said no. But I pronounced against my trip taking into consideration the insanely escalating Iraq situation. My host finally consented and emailed as follows:

Dear Justice Iyer,

I feel badly that I have pressed you so much — even attempting to reverse your final-final decision.

Thank you for faxing the medical reports. I did not need any proof at all, but it shows the depth of your own regret.

Please forgive me for pushing so hard.

With best and most personal regards,

John

Thus the long and anxious story ended and my trip was cancelled. I concluded it with a simple message to the generous Professors:

At this hour and through out the conference, I am with you all in spirit, anxious to share the wisdom of the jurists who must have thronged to participate in the scholarly deliberations. I am sad I am away but what cannot be helped must be endured. When the Conference is over and the conclusions condensed I hope you will send me an abridged version. Maybe, we may meet again when I am better in my vision and my health stands a long journey.

I greet every member assembled in the conference. I felicitate the organizers for the wonderful contribution they are making to global jurisprudence in dimensions which make the world legal order comport with the dignity and worth of the human person.

Did I act right? Perhaps yes. The weather was unkind, the travel was far too long for me to stake. My mind was darkened by despair because my soul was choked with the exasperation of humanity watching in vain a proximate carnage of imperial invasion with the United Nations and peoples everywhere making sound and fury ignored by the one Super-Power in our unipolar world. Anyway, my visit to the U.S did not click. The war against Iraq is savagely swift. Human numbers are dying and yet an exceedingly well-organised, thoughtfully planned conference was being conducted as beautiful Oregon by 'Human Rights for All'. What an irony that Human Rights should be at the vanishing point of jurisprudence and ghastly jurisprudence of 'Shock and Awe' with its nidus in the White House should triumph! Operation Shock and Awe ordered by President Bush is a violent violation of the U.N Charter, of the United Nations and of universal laws.

# 21
# Marad Massacre—A National Alarm

The Marad beach, a fisher folk's small colony a few miles off Calicut, has lovely sands and salubrious breeze, the Arabian Sea making the ambience of the place so soothing that people, not putting out to sea, are tempted at sunset to sit and gossip until yawning hours of night. Two communities, Hindu and Muslim, live in proximity and seeming amity and their hefty oarsmen's occupation is coastal fishing. There is a temple near by and so too a mosque. Speaking generally, no overt communal rivalry marred the peace of the locality nor was there provocative pugnacity between the Arayas (Hindu fishing community) and their Muslim counterpart. But there did break out in January 2002 a sudden breach of the peace which had no antecedent communal tension on the surface; but five people died, three Muslim and two Hindu and it was a Hindu-Muslim scrimmage too violently planned to be dismissed as a spontaneous eruption. The methodology suggested the presence of outside elements in the perpetration of the crime. There was a terrible outcry about this communal carnage. Many, including me, visited the scene and measures to mollify, grant relief and restore peaceful coexistence were undertaken. Apparent calm came to prevail although only a small police outpost and some relief measures in separate centres made symbolic State presence. The indolent investigation where a clash and carnage with grave portents gored the locality, did not result in a charge-sheet till *May next year.* Who will police the police? Remember, if the culprits are not brought to book with blitz speed reprisals and bitter fall-outs will breed revenge. No alibi avails the State in procrastination of investigation and inaction in intensification of invigilation. Anyway, for well over a year the fishermen's boats were busy occupationally and the people of Kerala slumbered assuming that life was normal. Terrorism dies hard and eternal vigilance is the desideratum of communal pacifism. The embers burn beneath, the surface quietude deceives. When external forces have access, ad hoc exercises are self-delusive. Deeper probes, more fundamental therapies, more perennial fraternization alone can counter Hindu-Muslim alienation, which may look local, but the groups hardly bury the hatchet. A hard look at the etiology of underground strategies of communal extremists reveals that mere monetary compensation to victims and formation of all-party conciliation committees are short-run anodynes while subterranean sinister indoctrination and invisible infiltration of fundamentalist operators remain undetected. Trained police intelligence capable of gathering light about subversive planning is a professional job of which the clumsy lathi-happy swaggering police force, easy at violence and facile with third degree crudities, are innocent.

It was Friday, 2nd May; the breeze was cool, the white sands, with a lovely view of the waves foamy blowing, were a refreshing rendezvous to relax and gossip in the evening. A group of simple Araya fishermen slipped and sat in the cushioned sand dunes and enjoyed idle conversation with the crimson sun beautifying the sky in the distance. The temple on the other side, at lamp-lighting time, found a few devotees around and otherwise Nature was calm, women were inside their humble homes and the scenic beach was brimful of rustic delight. And *then* swooped on the Araya innocents a savage brood of Islamic extremists with sharp weapons like swords or long curved knives with blood-thirsty blitz to unloose murder most foul, most treacherous, most barbaric. From more than one direction rushed this rabid rascal gang, with lethal arms and killer plan, stabbed the defenseless Araya gossip group, a devotee returning from the temple and a neighbouring petty tea shop dealer and spread terror by throwing bombs which did not explode. Had they burst, the number of the dead would have multiplied. Eight lost their lives and many more were wounded. One Muslim from the attacking raiders was hit by accident (?) and died in the melee. The glorious Marad sunset scene, in a few horrendous minutes, was drenched in blood and rent in cries and tears, with the police arriving after the savage carnage was committed and the terrorist felons had fled. Mobile phones were in action, the murders were perfectly organized, the villains made good their escape in vehicles waiting to operate the quick exit. A large cache of swords and knives were stored in the neighbouring masjid and the unholy heap of dastardly weapons were later siezed by the police. Beneath the heavy sands were hidden a large sabre stock ready as a reserve for a mass massacre. And the holy mosque, as a culpable custodian of weapons artful and asylum of assailants, betrayed an organised plot for a macro-scale gory modus operandi. The armed aggressors were not necessarily local Islamic hostiles retaliating the earlier year-old brutal battle—what is often referred to as Marad I. Maybe that too was a malignant motivation. Extraneous extremist infiltration and preparation, if true, make Marad II a darkly dangerous portent, not a mere coastal clash of Arayas and Mohallah fishing rivals. There is deeper ideological militancy, graver fundamentalist extremism, terribly more astute strategy and monetary investment; and Project Extermination outwitted Police Intelligence, political information and people's suspicion. Marad, with a little police outpost and no professional criminal intelligence mechanism, reveals the disastrous flop and tragic inefficiency of State and society in the preservation of secularity and security. If this happens in Kerala, the paradigm of political alertness, media ubiquity and communal harmony, what is the prospect of Indian humanity as a fraternity? *The Marad syndrome sounds a national alarm.* Beware!

Last week, in the company of leading social activists, I visited this coastal suburb, was enchanted by the charming azure expanse and wafting winds but as we entered the tiny homesteads where the Hindu victims of the killer villains had lived, cries of the bereaved changed our mood. What solace can you offer when the bread-winner of the family in the very flower of youth is brutally stabbed dead while sitting in the sunny sands relaxing and guilelessly gossiping? My eyes were wet and I was speechless as I heard the women sobbing and narrating. Grief from cottage to cottage! But yet the pity of it!—O, the pity of it! In helpless silence we listened and each widow added a new dimension to dastardly death. Then we heard the Araya Samaj President and Secretary who were tense and yet sombrely sober as they demanded from us not sympathy but justice. Sympathy is easy sentiment but justice is made of sterner stuff. Secular progressives merely condemn, in general neutrality, communal chauvinism. Hindu communalists, as majority communalists, are trenchantly stigmatized. But, the Araya leaders challengingly urged us why Islamic communalists who shoot and hate are not denounced harshly. They have a point, as I explained at an evening dialogue that day. They argued with agony that the mosque was the sanctuary of Islamic terrorists and nidus of weapons for Hindu slaughter. Then why should they not be taken over by the District Magistrate for the sake of law and order? Was not the Golden Temple, where Bindranwala sought refuge, the subject of Blue Star operation? Was not Sivagiri, sacred shrine of Narayana Guru glory, taken over by the District Magistrate? True, mosques or other shrines cannot be operational shelters of religious extremists for violent incitement or surprise siege? These issues are of national relevance, especially since sacerdotal bigotry, all religions included, has no territorial barrier. Blandly describing communal disturbances as obnoxious is different from zeroing-in on communal terrorism which is diabolic treachery. Deadly divisiveness is assuming apartheid dimensions. In Marad, the Araya Samaj told us, with burning rage, that the Muslim game plan is to drive out the Arayas from the entire Malabar sea coast to monopolise sea fishing for their community. This territorial terrorism is dangerous, if true, because this would lead to massive battles all along the West Coast and may spread to the East Coast. The pharmacopoeia of human solidarity must discover dynamic panacean processes if

Indian democracy is to survive. No serendipitous recipe is ready in the political repertoire. "We, the People of India" *as a dialectical reality and cultural fundamentality,* is dearer than party politics and regional or religious devotion. This is the first axiom of patriotism and the last testament of Hind Swaraj. A passionate nationalism, with paramountcy over party loyalty or paroctual obduracy, is high on the agenda of Indian integrity. Let us begin with this *mandate of Marad.* Who lives if India dies? That solemn summons, not one-up-manship in power-crazy politics, is the *yuga dharma* from classrooms to Houses of the Legislature and every public office in our native land. Kilkenny cat communalism can be conquered only by a profound, pervasive swaraj commitment in action and a tearing and raging campaign for an indivisible unity as the warp and woof of Indian humanity. All else comes next. Statesmen, do you listen?

The Marad massacre, as the victim families reminded us, proves that minority Islamic communalism, is as militantly blood-thirsty as majority communalism 'red in tooth and claw' as Hindutva extremism is—a la Gujarat. The voice of secularism cannot be soft towards either.

State action in countering communal explosion, tension and underground operation has been an exercise in futility all over the country, with political 'sound and fury signifying nothing'. Look at Marad—and there are Marads in every State—with a background of communal slaughter, and yet a mere police outpost! After the event, khaki uniforms and guns everywhere! I found the same dismal neglect in other communally explosive areas like Nadapuram. A new police road map is an urgent desideratum. Location of fully equipped police stations where simmering violence may burst aflame any moment, more technology and mobility, more special training and intelligence wings, more vigilance personnel and nocturnal rounds with focus sod attention on shrines, festivals and secret hide-outs, more scrutiny over religious classes and drills—these are 'more honoured in the breach than the observance'.

**Epilogue—The Lessons of Marad**

The first battle of Marad, a broad daylight lightning

attack with bleeding communal consequences, took fifteen months for the police to issue charge sheet giving dubious excuses. True Marad II, (by Islamic extremists) produced a better account of alert police operation. They rushed in number, searched and siezed from the sands and the Masjid huge quantities of arms and incriminatory articles, took into custody many suspects and got on to the trail of the culprits, although some of the key planners and cunning perpetrators are still to be tracked down. The Crime branch has done a good job despite the political—communal imbroglio and the complete discovery is yet distances away. Why? Terrorism, be it in Kashmir or Kerala, Assam or Tripura, often outwits the State machine in technology, strategy, mobility and celerity. Police reforms with creative cadres, talented and trained personnel, updated familiarity with technology, sociology and criminology to match the enemy, is a 'consummation devoutly to be wished'. A *miscellany* of policemen on traffic duty and V.I.P duty, on intelligence gathering and investigative functionalism can never be equal to the challenge of specialisation in each department sans which police efficiency is sure to be a uniformed futility and authoritarian illusion.

**One Final Plea**

Divided Marad is divided Bharat. Homogenise or perish! Therefore, the two communities in dynamic comity, with distinct identity but neighbourhood fraternity, must come together in moral and spiritual fellowship and material camaraderie. A tearing and raging campaign to extirpate violent extremism and terrorist godism is the only means of promoting civil society solidarity and preserving pluralist democracy. Rehabilitation of refugees, regardless of religion, by a process of communal symbiosis, organised as a non-discriminatory, people-oriented unititve project, is the beginning of a dynamic modus vivendi. That is the message and mandate of Marad.

I do not lend any credence whatever to the displacement bogey contrary to the fundamental freedom of residence for any Indian anywhere in the territory of India. Propagandist gambits, scary rumour and intimidatory stratagems must be dismissed as mischievous myth to unnerve the weaker Arayas by the local Mahal majority or as exaggerated imaginary communal concoctions by vicious vested interests. But rumours may inflame and spread and claim harmony as casualty unless timely joint vigilant action convincingly extinguishes the alarm.

# 22
# My Glimmering Evening of Life

The broad sunshine of life is when faculties flourish and the best opportunities for expression fulfill themselves. My life on the bench, leavened by the challenges of dispensing judicial justice, offered the most creative span in my variegated career although my socially sensitive and lucrative battles at the bar and the soulful satisfaction of implementation of people-oriented political and economic projects as valiant minister in the State of Kerala were thrilling and triumphant chapters of middle age. Lawyering and politics have their chills and charms. But marvels of judgements, if one has the good fortune to deliver a few, have no parallel in other occupations and so, I rejoiced on the rare occasions when fine pronouncements issued from my pen.

My judicial life, a great promise I looked for, darkened in the days since early 1974 because the glorious stimulant, one's inspiring partner's companionship, suddenly collapsed. My wife Sarada who had versatile interest in life fell victim to cardiac surgery in Milwaukee, an American City in Lincon Country with the fastest heart surgeon trained under the legendary Dr. Denten Cooley. I fainted that night and felt that all was lost. Life became empty and I returned from America with an urn of ashes reminding me of the cremated sharer of life's undying love. I survived, although statistically it has been found that between intimate spouses, when one suddenly departs, the other follows the footsteps of the departed one in around a year. Even Karl Marx, the great materialist, was broken when his beloved wife passed away and lived in deep grief till he himself passed away after a little over a year. Death leaves a gashing wound and there is no bar of limitation for the poignant pain of parting. Nearly thirty years have rolled by and my sombre memory has not faded a wee-bit. Indeed, from 12[th] August 1974 I am a different man with a chastened vision of life seeking solace in bringing solace to others. My later years sensitised me to the pain of those who were writhing in sorrow. To an extent my mind and mood were moulded by the indelibly macabre misfortune. My judicial behaviour, I am sure, also had suffered leaving me more sympathetic to those who had a tale of misery and injustice. Yet another sharp shock to my attitude to life took place. I began questioning death and what it meant. I remembered Ingersoll 'every cradle asks us whence and every coffin whither'. What is the meaning of mortality? Is transmortal communication a feasible proposition? While in this pensive mood, my son Paramesh, sad that I was sad, came and told me that a saintly personality called Maharshi Mahesh Yogi was visiting Delhi and perhaps if I gained an interview and placed my fate before him, a supramental solution may perhaps be a bonanza. I dismissed no suggestion as too fantastic to believe because more things are brought by prayer than this world dreams of. I lost all fear of death since I had seen it naked. She bravely fought and passed over and a similar fate could, therefore, never frighten me. But deep within was a profoundly philosophical inquiry about the dimensions of death and after. The subject was strange but I did want an answer. So I sought an appointment with Maharshiji, who arrived in the Asoka Hotel. I explained to him my pathetic situation. He was a picture of patience and desired me to meet him the next morning to initiate me into Transcendental Meditation. With great hopes which would remind one of Nachiketas and his firm resolve to penetrate death, I paid homage to Maharshiji. In all solemnity he gave me a *mantra* and taught the technology of T.M. With great expectation I left; and began, with scientific precision, the process of meditation. My mind cleared and tranquility supervened. But my soul, which remained seared, did not light up in the sense of seeing through the mortal scream.

Maharshi Mahesh Yogi is an inspiring personality by lighting in his devotees, a vision of the universal process. His spiritual outfit the product of a creative contribution derived from Adi Sankara, the Jagat Guru, who was the most profound intellect and spiritual scientist India has seen during the millennia. Creative intelligence with an original dimension led Mahesh Yogi to his philosophy. 'The art of living and science of being' is a textbook authored by Maharshiji explaining in depth the scientific basis of Transcendental Meditation (T.M.). In search of Truth, I frequented his Ashram in Delhi and although not a formal disciple, I was fascinated by his teachings. There was an intellectual flavour about his teachings and his method of meditation was based on Patanjali Sutra. He was encircled by young intellectuals who became respectful associates of mine. One of them who was attached to me as a younger brother, as it were, was Ferroke. Anklasaria, a Barrister who gave up promise of practice in England to become a brilliant exponent. Maharshi took a liking for me and I used to stay once in a way in Switzerland, the headquarters of the T.M. Movement. I felt that T.M. has a tremendous curative power. The process deepens one's consciousness, tranquillises the inner self and catalyses the faculties. Beyond propaganda and publicity, there were demonstrable achievements flowing from constant practice of T.M. and its higher courses. Scientific tools were his forte. Maharshi was the founder of a university in Iova, USA and for a brief while nominated me to its board of management. I did lectures on the blessings of T.M. and beheld for myself how prisoners and hardened criminals had undergone moral metamorphosis. I found that certain trial court judges of America had successfully experimented with T.M. as a corrective sentence. When a person is transformed into a non-offender because of the alchemy of T.M. there is no reason why that methodology should not be given a reasonable chance to improve individuals with criminal sentences. While on the Supreme Court Bench I persuaded several of my friends including judges, to be initiated into T.M. I went to the extent of discussing in a judgement the advantages of T.M as a correctional sentence and my brother

Justice Goswami, sitting with me on the Bench, briefly agreed with my view. The Maharshi association took me to various parts of the world, since I was able to explain lucidly, without jargon, the psychic transformation produced by this form of meditation. At great expense T.M was being given as a course by many states in the U.S to prisoners who stood to gain by this spiritual technology. I toured Australia and Newzealand, South America and England, at the instance of Maharshi Mahesh Yogi, explaining convincingly the physical, mental, moral and spiritual changes wrought by this psychic technology. Having said all this and having acquired the abiding friendship of Farouk and other like T.M-trained academics, I still felt that my grand design of discovery of *life after death* remained unfulfilled. "T.M has wonders to perform, but to break through death and reach the 'undiscovered country' from whose bourn no traveller returned" still baffled me. Mahesh Yogi is a versatile experimentalist with roots in ancient Indian treasury of knowledge and modern scientific approach. But the post-Death perceptions are not in his repertory.

Swami Muktananda and a host of other preachers and teachers with occult powers and magnetic appeal did claim my time. They had great followers and welcomed me too, but I had a quasi-occult purpose with a dialectical dimension, as it were. I wanted to interrogate, critique, experiment with and be personally satisfied that the goal of trans-mortal communication will be reached. Alas, my ceaseless effort was a failure and I must confess that although these supra-mental pilgrimages were rewarding in other ways, my major objective remained frustrated. It may be cynical, but still veracious, to quote Fitzgerald:

> Myself when young did eagerly frequent
>
> Doctor and Saint, and heard great argument
>
> About it and about: but evermore
>
> Came out by the same Door as in I went.

It is not my intention to debunk the glory of the great spiritual leaders I have come across. Of them it could well be said in Longfellow's lines:

Lives of great men all remind us
We can make our lives sublime,
And, departing, leave behind us
Footprints on the sands of time.

I had a specific search in view. It was to unveil the 'life beyond' because I felt that something did survive the phenomenon we regard as death. Otherwise, life becomes meaningless, if at the end of the finest and noblest life spent everything becomes nothing. It is irrational and negative to dismiss earthly life as altogether an empty exercise the moment last breath leaves.

Out, out brief candle!
Life's but a walking shadow, a poor player,
That struts and frets his hour upon the stage,
And then is heard no more; it is a tale
Told by an idiot, full of sound and fury,
Signifying nothing.

I reject his Macbeth myth. So I persisted in my investigation dissatisfied with credulous answers and meaningless seances and insistent on my prima facie conviction that death is not the end and a different dimension of life survives. Fatalism is commonplace and negativity has been poetised in Fitzgerald:

The Moving Finger writes; and, having writ,
Moves on; nor all thy Piety nor Wit
Shall lure it back to cancel half a Line,
Nor all thy Tears wash out a Word of it.

Death bound littleness is not all that we are and fate bound extinction is not the last about life.

My wanderings in the wildernesses of philosophical wisdom did elevate a wee-bit my spiritual values and promote a sense of detachment. Mahesh Yogi, Muktananda, writings of Aurobindo, Yogananda, and Vivekananda deepened my understanding of the mysterious universe and my identification with Creation. Here is a passage from Maharshiji which kindled a new Realisation.

The omnipresence of eternal Being, unmanifested and absolute; Its status as That, even in the manifested diversity of creation; and the possibility of the realization of Being by any man in terms of himself—these are the great truths of the perennial philosophy of the Vedas. (Bhagavad Gita Preface)

The true measure of the moral stature of Man, I learnt, was the boundless selflessness one could practise.

An enduring association with the Brahmakumari Movement helped me look at life from the angle of love and renunciation. I was fascinated also by the Movement and its global amplitude, emphasis on *Shanthi* the world over and on the survival of the Soul in astral form. Indeed, I had a sitting with one of their well-known mediums which satisfied me *partly* that there was more than myth in their teachings. For years I have been involving myself in their broader teachings of Yoga, on Thyaga and rejection of Bhoga. Even now the impact of their teaching on the jurisprudence of global peace is a vital link between me and Dadiji, their leading light in Mount Abu.

Another shattering experience came to me from Kriya Yoga and the profound teachings of Paramahamsa Yogananda. That masterpiece Autobiography of a Yogi gave textual revelations of trans-mortal communication.

It is impossible to condense in a paragraph the pearls of teaching I gathered in moments of meditative silence. Some glimpses of the divine profundity left behind by the great Rishi enriched my mind and soul. Transformation is a process, is a verb, not a noun and I am content to say that the blue influence of the Infinite and the consciousness of Absolute Identity have just touched my individuality but I am far from home.

My judicial pre-occupations put limitation on my occult travels, but on superannuation I became a freer agent. Among the most Sublime Spirits I have come across in my temporal life is Bhagawan Satya Sai Baba whose presence and performance are unusually divine. I have once been his critic but in my evening mood I did seek *darshan* of this great soul preserving my skepticism and refusing to jettison the test of verified testimony before acceptance of any conclusion. I was uplifted and felt myself humble before his lofty personality. He did perform what others could never have done. I received a ring, more than one, as Baba waived in the air and produced the golden product. He gave gold chains and other wonderful objects to those who came as established devotees and had the privilege of darshan. But while these miracles were far more than magic and were *utterly real* beyond laws of Nature as we understand them, I have been stunned by his profound speeches. But my purpose was different. What is death? Where are we after death? Is there a communicable link between the living and the dead? What divine process can materialise this life—death continuum? At this threshold Satya Sai Baba has not yet taken me through. Message is for the living. They say that he can and indeed, if I can trust Dr. Malini of Madras, she has spoken to her deceased father at the instance of Baba himself. I suspend judgement although I have conducted my pursuits in other directions with mediums and met with some success in the field of communication with the dead. In a condensed version I had given long interviews to a Malayalam paper Manorama on my own evidentiary experiences, *short of personal communication.* I have recently written a book titled 'Death and After' collecting extraordinary materials and presenting them in a credible manner. Every word in every page all through the book has truth impressed on it. I am not able to assert that I had achieved the goal I set for myself. I have failed to communicate directly with my wife who dies in far off America. That, perhaps, may happen only when I became discarnate myself cease to be corporeal and live in those subtle dimensions and realms where the dead play their game of existence.

**Superannuation**

There is a temporal foundation for human life which unfolds stage by stage till youth and adulthood yield to the aging process. This invisible law of change eventuated in my case as student, lawyer, minister and judge of the highest court in the land. Superannuation is farewell to office except in the profession of politics. To be a politician requires a rubberised conscience, nay more. Ignorance must masquerade as Intelligence. Burnard Shaw did define this capacity partly: 'He knows nothing, he thinks he knows everything. That clearly points to a political career'. Why confine this curious virtue to politicians only? There are some 'robed brethren' who while on the bench possess the Shavian qualifications of a politician. That apart, on 15th November 1980, I disrobed myself from judicial office, lost my power, pomp and authority to adjudicate. But I gained a freedom from the trammels of office, leisure from the slavery to dockets and obligation to hear long lucubrative at times luminous submissions. I decided to be free from material glamour although I did find my learned brothers of yester years seeking avenues for commissions, arbitration and legal consultation as an occupation—all these operations were geared to making money, more money. For what, when you are near the sunset of life? For what, when your concerns and commitments pressurise your conscience to serve humanity in its toils and tears, in its struggle in pursuit of happiness? Then I wondered: Who am I to dogmatize? Each judge on retirement pursues his appetite and reaps the fruits of his karma. In my sombre evening, consumerism did not overcome me because of my background. Moreover, I thought for myself that life was too precious to be wasted on hunting for wealth, provided your pension took care of your needs and comforts. I turned my attention away from the lucrative lollipops, did not prefer to idle away my time. I threw myself actively into various social occupations untainted by monetary returns. Public addresses on issues of people's concern, lectures in Universities and other institutions on a hundred subjects of public importance, acceptance of Institutional Presidentship to the common benefit kept me fully engaged. While a vistarama of issues claim my time I work tirelessly, without thought of income and with focus on the finer values of life. Free from consumerism my body gave little purchase over my soul. I was approached for legal consultations on heavy fees. Arbitration offers encumbers every retired judge. Without hesitation I turned my face away from these temptations. I do not blame my brethren who yield to demands for their services when the function is judicial, but moderation and refusal to make unjust riches preserve the dignity of the judicial office which once they filled. Indeed, it is only because they were judges *once* that their services are sought *now* on heavy payment. Austerity is far from immoderate acquisition for during post-retiral judicial work. But acquisitiveness is the occupational disease of many other professions and now of retired judges too. Way back in 1974, I had known the emptiness of life and the futility of chase of pleasure. So my very despair became an education in Spartan simplicity. I was busy, terribly busy, but my business was of a different order. I have no regrets that I have not amassed a fortune. I have had awards and rewards in life without seeking them and that is the joy which I can share with everyone. Sunset summons me and the reminder is ill health and poor vision. Harken! Gitanjali, my favourate poetry, rings the alarm bell:

> On the day when death will knock at thy door what wilt thou offer to him?
>
> Oh, I will set before my guest the full vessel of my life— I will never let him go with empty hands.
>
> All the sweet vintage of all my autumn days and summer nights, all the earnings and gleanings of my busy life will I place before him at the close of my days when death will knock at my door. (P-60 XC).

Of course, in pensive mood I repeat "Oh thou the last fulfillment of life, Death, my Death, come and whisper to me"!

I have been among the busiest of persons with numberless public commitments. I have travelled all over the country in feverish haste to fulfill social engagements. Delhi has found me fairly frequently, all for public causes. So too, remote places of Kerala. I have been to the Soviet Union before its collapse several times as President of the Indo Soviet Cultural Society. The last of my visits to that great country was when Gorbochev was the President. I have been to the United States, visiting many Universities including Harvard and Stanford. I have written well over 70 books, many of them collections of writings. I have loved the fine arts and while in Delhi have been the President of the Kathakali Centre, Sree Narayana Guru Centre and the Kerala Association. Some of the lectures are: The Tagore Law Lecures, Calcutta, The Gajendragatkar Memorial Lecture, Bombay, The Dr. Ambedkar Memorial lectures, Madras, The Krishna Menon Memorial Lecture, Trivandrum and Delhi, The Asuthosh Mukherji Memorial Lecture, Calcutta. The Mahajan Memorial lectures, Chandigarh, Public Law Lectures, Cochin. The Gokhale Memorial lecture, Bangalore, Sri Alladi Krishnaswami Iyer Memorial Lecture, Hyderabad et al.

Indeed, crowded have been my days. But age claims its price and now I find myself stricken with infirmities but people inside Kerala and the country and abroad refuse to accept my alibi of physical handicaps. They insist that I am fit and must travel and lecture. I am, in one sense, a most wanted man but now I have learnt the art of refusal. For tribal causes I have delivered several addresses, so too for war against Iraq. I have campaigned incessantly for great judicial causes. On legal issues I have written and spoken for radical reforms. At the end of the day, what does it all amount to? Generation after Generation, values change for the worse, people become more unprincipled and the reward of a life of struggle is exasperation. No, there is still hope. Despair is disaster. Truth must triumph although in the short run I have met with disappointment. However, there is one treasure—one's soul which has not succumbed to the syndrome of defeat.

**Operation Nachikethas**

While I was preoccupied with judicial business before retirement and with battle of Public Interest after superannuation, I kept a parallel interest in searching for life after death. I came across American literature of Dr. Moody and several others on their experiments with death and the dying. I came across materials which disclose that the dead are not really dead and it is wrong to dismiss death itself as an impenetrable mystery. In London there was a great institution, probably founded by Sir Oliver Lodge, Sir Aurthor CannanDoyle and other great men whose names inspire confidence. I had sittings with mediums and some of them gave astonishingly credible evidence. I went to the U.S and had an hour long sitting with Anderson in the Three Mile Island. He reeled off information at the sitting as he got them from departed ones. What an experience it was! My departed wife, my brother who died sixty years ago, my brother in law who passed away a few years back, came and mentioned about matters so true, specific and beyond Anderson's comprehension. Indeed, I have collected volumes of literature on the subject which will fill a whole almirah. Dr. Ian Stevenson, a Professor in the Virginia University, experiments with re-birth and life after death. Dr. Pasricha of the NIMHANS (Bangalore) also has studied cases in this domain. What is most breathtaking is my wife, after her death, meeting with information meant for me, more than once Mrs Gupta, the wife of Justice R.C. Gupta. I had a unique instance of a sadhu coming to me and after nocturnal meditation revealing what my wife told him—information impossible for him to get elsewhere. Mrs Natwar Singh, the Delhi politician's wife, has also helped me in these mystic voyages. I have met Lady Dowding who told me that she married the Lord (her present husband) because her late husband told her to go ahead. Incredible are all these and I have collected them in my recent book *Death and After.* I am still a sceptic but hold that when indisputable facts, such as are revealed in R.K. Narayan's book The English Teacher (every word is true, assured the great writer when I asked him) find no other explanation except life after death, one must have the courage of accepting rational conviction. Never retreat in cowardice when truthful testimony, acceptable to reason, confront you.

**Finale**

While young, my wife and I have sat and enjoyed reading Gitanjali. One stanza, which we read together then, I read alone now:

> I know that the day will come when my sight of this earth shall be lost, and life will take its leave in silence,

drawing the last curtain over my eyes.

Yet stars will watch at night, and morning rise as before, and hours heave like sea waves casting up pleasures and pains.

When I think of this end of my moments, the barrier of the moments breaks and I see by the light of death thy world with its careless treasures. Rare is its lowliest seat, rare is its meanest of lives. (P-61 XCII).

# 23

# A Compassionate Gerontic Undertaking—For Jail Justice

A long span of twentytwo years has elapsed since my farewell to the high office of Supreme Court judgeship. Superannuation was not for me mere oblivion, sheer liberation nor vegetative inaction. Nor, indeed, did I become a victim of political ambition nor votary of any sadhu or guru nor surrender to a monopolist godman. A larger vision of Creation and higher liberation of humanity became my pre-occupation, not lost in passive meditation or materialist satiation but militantised by a compassionate commitment to those values which give meaning to the Universal Process. This was my eidos but my experiments with this higher conceptual quintessence were mere humble essays, never actual achievements. I mention this dimension of my post-retirement perspective to emphasize what I had rejected as a temptation to which I would not succumb? What was that superannuation syndrome of judges?

Great is the judicial profession sublime is the occupational search for truth, marvellous is a career on the bench in pursuit of justice without fear or favour, affection or illwill.

> In 1954 Sir Winston Churchill told the House of Commons that judges are required to conform to standards of the 'life and conduct far more severe and restricted than that of ordinary people'. 'What', the Prime Minister asked rhetorically, 'would be thought of a Lord Chief Justice if he won the Derby?'
>
> *(Judges-David Pannick P-11)*

Noble is the aloof, austere, insular life of a good judge. Lord Denning drove home the ethical dimension of the character of judges:

> They will not be diverted from their duty by any extraneous influences, not by hope of reward nor by the fear of penalties; not by flattering praise nor by indignant reproach. It is the sure knowledge of this that gives the people their confidence in the judges
>
> (Lord Denning in What next in the law, 1982, page 310)
>
> Do these pleasing sentiments hold good to-day?
>
> The present generation of lawyers and judges, with a considerable number of splendid exceptions, is moving downhill towards professionally amoral, even immoral mores; shocking revelations about judges, rare to begin with but recurring with unhappy frequency, make the pernicious praxis first a whisper, then a wild rumour and then, by deepening degrees, a proven deed, an investigated act, a vice in the womb of the robed fraternity! Many, most members are pure even now. The few are no longer few and are enough in numbers and deeds to debunk the credibility and liquidate the sublimity of the judiciary. The other joint tort-feasor, the dubious lawyer, who is the corrupter, the traitor, the enemy of the Bar, is surfacing in a swelling stream. (Judicial Justice In Action p-51)

My grievance begins here. Judges, while in service, show signs of delinquency, despite great traditions, happy emoluments, high prestige, vast powers and reasonable pensionary benefits. They need to be disciplined and held sternly to a severe code of conduct. But on retirement they should not cash in on their judicial past. Their status and stature as judges and Chief Justices are non-negotiable as source of income except where public interest demands their service for public causes; where their judicial experience is needed by State or society on just terms. Judicial office, before or after superannuation is a trust, never to be defiled as a commercial service. But what is happening today is somewhat saddening, sometimes racketeering and in a few discovered instances shady and in many cases verging on business. True, a retired judge has so much to offer by way of pro bono dedication. Public Lecturers, free legal services, writing books on law and justice, public enquiries into people's causes in a dignified honorary capacity, placing their learning and wisdom at juristic conferences and public hearings of social grievances—all free. The sky is the limit and high is the esteem in which the nation holds them. But when the august occupant of high judicial seat of yester years jettisons values of great but gratuitous work and with an acquisitive appetite, opens shop, runs 'consultation' business for fancy fees, undertakes, almost on business terms, arbitration with procrastination and fat remuneration, seeks positions in salaried commissions, national or provincial, which are the gift of governments, degeneracy sets in, lucrative adulteration creeps in and a down-hill descent unwittingly spoils the nobility and integrity of a sublime calling once gloriously filled. In moderation, a judge's availability for quasi-judicial operations like Commissions and arbitrations of high moment is a just and reasonably recompensed engagement. But signs of avarice, ceaseless pursuit of money-making vocations and scruple-free search for commissions, undermines the importance of the judicature as a whole and dubious practices are suspected. The day may not be distant when a demand for a code of conduct for retired judges is desiderated. A socialist, democratic Republic provided a profusion of public causes where retired judges have tireless challenges on their time since conscience and the Constitution, designed for liberation of the masses, is being violated by corporate power and ministers unaware of the parameters of their power, needs all the rich experience, all the invaluable wisdom, all the non-partisan assessment and audit of grave aberrations in the exercise of public authority—our nation's rare resource is judges who have a readiness, on retirement, to be at people's service and the nation's call. I must caution my reader that these observations are an intropsection guiding me to a personal resolution and casts no reflection on my distinguished colleagues who perform a wonderful job, after retirement as while in service. They are too great for me to cast a slur.

On my superannuation in November 1980, I was witness to retired judges avidly making income from consultation fee. Everything was prepared by the solicitor who briefed the retired judge and sought his autograph. The fee was high, the work was light, the consultation was a little more than formal and the signature of approval meant handsome money. Rich clients were in a queue and the effort was infinitely less taxing than the hard court work. Similarly judges (Rtd) had a sort of monopoly over Arbitration Litigation. Here again high fees were fixed by the Arbitrators, but the judicial time devoted for the job was attractively minimal. There were Commission under the Constitution, whose membership was largely a judicial monopoly. Political goodwill and clout with ministers mattered. There were excellent exceptions, but to my mind the whole process looked like exploitation of quondam judgeship. Many judicial retirees earned in a few years more fortunes than the salary they earned in their whole career. Maybe, this is an exaggeration. In a few cases there was accusation of misconduct against the judicial arbitrator. On the whole, my conviction crystalised into a decision to avoid consultation for fee and Arbitration as an income earning occupation. I have done a few *People's Commission* Missions free, for the love of the cause. Even when one or two official Commissions were chaired by me, the work was done in a purely honorary capacity. What a freedom I gained, what a satisfaction I derived by this resolution of self- abrogation! Yes, the price of this liberation from temptation was a life of frugal simplicity by choice. No longer a prisoner. Tagore's Gitanjali has a profound stanza which has moulded my moral-material perspective. I quote a part:

> 'Prisoner, tell me, who was it that wrought this unbreakable chain?'
>
> 'It was I,' said the prisoner, 'who forged this chain very carefully. I thought my invincible power would hold the world captive leaving me in a freedom undisturbed. This night and day I worked at the chain with huge fires and cruel hard strokes. When at last the work was done and the links were complete and unbreakable, I found that it held me in its grip'.

After a few years, since I laid down office I settled down in my own home in Cochin, where as a lawyer practicing in the High Court, I had built a sufficiently commodious but hardly posh building. I was busy all the time with public engagements, people's commitments and popular writing. One day, a few months back Mr. Antony, the chief Minister of Kerala, telephoned me with a pressing request, that I should head a Committee to examine the conditions of those in incarceration and their eligibility for enlargement and formulate the guidelines governing the grant by the State of parole, and remission relating to convict prisoners. I was a Minister for prisons in Kerala, way back in 1957, and had been interested in the rehabilitation of prisoners. I had been involved in a few important cases dealing with prisoners and their lot while on the Supreme Court. Why, I was myself a detinue for a month in 1948 in a Central prison (Kannur). So the subject was not merely familiar but close to my soul. So I orally agreed. The Chief Minister was pleased. Later I received a communication from the Government constituting a High Level Committee for the implementation of the directions of the High Court regarding the formulation of guidelines governing parole and remission of sentences of prisoners. I was appointed Chairman and the other members were two Secretaries to Government, one member of the Human Rights Commission and a senior police officer as well as Director General of prisons. All the members being virtually Government servants, had no special remuneration ab extra. But then this order stated "The Chairman will be paid a remuneration of Rs.30,000/- per month plus Ist Class Travelling Allowance (T.A) and Dearness Allowance (D.A) for the journeys involved". Never having received any remuneration for chairing a Commission and opposing it in principle all these years, I had not bargained for a salary to draw which went against my grain. So I wrote back to the Chief Minister a letter, which I reproduce here, rejecting the offer of salary.

January 13, 2003

Dear Sri. Antony,

Ref : G.O.(MS)NO.201/2002/HOME dt.10.12.2002.

When you asked me whether I would consent to help Government frame guidelines in the matter of remission of sentences in criminal convictions I agreed because that has been a subject which I have handled with compassionate success as a Minister of Jails in Kerala (1957-59) and as a judge of the Supreme Court later. Thereafter I had a communication, which merely indicated Government's pleasure in my consenting to help frame guidelines. I did not read it with close scrutiny.

Without the formality of a committee meeting involving expenditure of the members travelling to Cochin, I suggested to Mr. Ramakrishnan, Special Secretary (Home) that he may meet me at my residence for a preliminary discussion of the subject. He came on 10$^{th}$ January 2003. At that time he handed over to me a copy of a formal order of Government constituting a committee with me as Chairman issued under G.O.No. G.O(Rt)No.2003/2002/Home dated 9.10.2002. As I glanced through the paper I discovered that at the bottom of the page there was mention that Chairman (that is myself) would be paid a salary of Rs.30,000/- plus T.A and D.A. I expressed surprise to Mr. Ramakrishnan at this salary part. It has been my conviction that retired judges should do free service, if at all, and never receive salary as remuneration. I have therefore not accepted any commission chairmanship or membership. Indeed, in the one committee which I chaired at the personal request of Mrs. Margret Alva to report on custodial justice to women, *there was no salary* nor budget allotment and the committee made an excellent report.

I, therefore, emphatically impress upon you that I shall serve the State in formulating guidelines in the matter of sentencing remission. That is after my heart and is pursuant to the compassionate principles of the Constitution. I cannot and will not accept any salary. Therefore I request you to be kind enough to delete the salary part of the committee Chairmanship and reframe the order according to technical requirements. I thank you for the offer of salary but regret with pleasure the opportunity to reject the offer. Of course, I will serve and help, whatever the personal infirmities of old age may be, because the cause is noble and the service an obligation to the people.

With warmest regards,

To,

Sri. A.K. Antony,

Hon'ble Chief Minister of Kerala,

Government of Kerala

Secretariat

Trivandrum

Pursuant to this letter, Government passed a fresh order accepting my objection and deleting the provision of salary to me. Thankfully, the Chief Minister wrote to me a brief letter of gratitude which I reproduce here (for completeness of information):

18.01.2003

Respected Justice Krishna Iyer Swamy,

I am in receipt of your letter dated 13th January 2003 expressing willingness to help the government in framing guidelines in the matter of remission of sentences in criminal convictions.

I am greatly impressed by your noble gesture in refusing to accept salary from Government for this compassionate mission.

I am sure that your wide ranging experience and commitment to the human concerns would be of great help in accomplishing this mission.

With respectful regards,

Yours sincerely,

Sd/-

A.K.ANTONY

Justice V.R.Krishna Iyer,
Former Judge, Supreme Court
Satgamaya
M.G.Road
Ernakulam-11

The terms of reference related to guidelines for pardon, remit or commute sentences under Article 161 of the Constitution taking into account the inactment of Sec.433A of the Criminal Procedure Code which made an *actual term of fourteen years in prison* as the minimum for any lifer. There was also a reference to grant of parole and the parameters guiding such leave. The Government Order made pointed reference to *Maruram case*, a decision of the Supreme Court which dealt with Article 161 of the Constitution (where I had written the leading judgement). Of course, the whole project of the Committee was response to the directions of the High Court objecting to arbitrary exercise of parole and remission power. The High Level Committee met and settled down to work at Trivandrum. Meanwhile, I prepared a paper on the subject which I described as a prolegomenon. It was circulated to the members as a basic document which would inform the committee of *my fundamental approach*. The routine sittings and discussions took place but as a gesture of democratic functionalism, we decided upon two steps. I had in mind, guided by judicial instinct, the Roman adage 'whatever touches us all should be decided by all'. It was obviously impossible to consult everyone, but natural justice suggested that we consult the prisoners in the Central Prison and give an opportunity to the public to present their views to the Committee. Thus we moved into the Central Prison, heard the prisoners, received their representation and felt that their views deserved to be sympathetically considered. Likewise, we had a day set for hearing. All concerned persons in the State who had something worthwhile to say on the subject were welcome. Since public notice had been given, around one hundred persons turned up to offer views or ventilate grievances. A senior Professor of Criminology, a leading lawyer representing a social justice institution, and various spokesmen from social welfare institutions, including person presenting victimologists perceptions, gave evidence. Whether anything creative or novel emerged from this hearing or not, it gave a unique touch to the committee's hearing process. As Chairman, I resorted to a refreshingly unconventional step of addressing a letter to the Hon'ble Chief Justice with a view to elicit views of the learned judges on the issues involved which were serious matters of criminological jurisprudence. My letter to the Chief Justice runs as follows:

May 22, 2003

Respected Chief Justice,

Pursuant to the direction of the High Court a certain committee was appointed by the State Government to frame guidelines regarding *the grant of parole, suspension and remission in the case of prisoners.* At the Chief Minister's request, I agreed to be the *Honorary Chairman* of the committee set up in this behalf. Some deliberations have taken place and I have prepared what I have described as the Chairman's Prolegomenon which outlines the broad prospective and approach to the problem (copy enclosed). It is only a draft.

It is my conviction that, under your leadership, your colleagues will be concerned to express their views in their personal capacity on the subject indicated above. Indeed, it is a sharp and constructive judgement of your court bearing on the parole, remission etc that has led to the healthy proposal to abandon arbitrary exercise of power and abide by sensible, sensitive and salutary guidelines governing the exercise of power of pardon and commutation by the Governor.

May I, in all humility, beseech you and your colleagues to communicate, if you may your views of wisdom which are valuable to me and my committee far beyond being mere ipsi dixits. To learn from the judges is a new source of knowledge and experience so far as my committee is concerned. That is why I am making this request. The committee will be grateful, if in a week or two, the learned judges reply, if any, were communicated to me to the above mentioned address.

With kind regards,

Yours sincerely,
Sd/-
(V.R. KRISHNA IYER)

Encl : as above

To,

Hon'ble Chief Justice Jawahar Lal Gupta,
High Court of Kerala
Ernakulam, Cochin-682 031

Promptly came his reply showing his courtesy and concern which I deeply appreciate. It reads:

28th May 2003

My Lord!

Your Lordship's letter of May 22, 2003 (along with the Chairman's Prolegomenon) was delivered in my Office on the evening of May 26, 2003. These have been circulated to all the Judges of the High Court on May 27, 2003. I shall get back to your Lordship as soon as I get some response.

With profound regards,

Yours sincerely,
Sd/-
(Jawahar Lal Gupta)

Justice V.R. Krishna Iyer
(Former Judge, Supreme Court)
"Satgamaya"
M.G. Road, Ernakulam
Kochi-682 011

I close this criminological adventure by incorporating excerpts from the text of my prolegomenon which is more a vision statement. The High Level Committee will give its full consideration to the grave issues which affect the freedoms of the prisoners. That will be as official text which cannot form part of this autobiographical excursion:

***My Vision***

The basic philosophy of my thesis is that while retribution is savage and deterrence, if draconian, counter-productive, reformatory humanism must receive more emphasis. Ghandhiji wrote in Young India Weekly that jail environment hardens and humanitarian reform is the right direction. Nehru, quoted by the All India Committee on Jail Reforms (Vol. I P-iii) stresses this human element and the recognition of the fact that a criminal is largely created by social conditions and must be treated as for a disease. Rehabilitation is the radical recipe which can remedy the malady of criminality. Nehru, in Prison Land writes what is indelibly instructive for progressive jurists:

> High walls and iron gates cut off the little world of prison from the wide world outside. Here in this prison world everything is different; there are no colours, no changes, no movement, no hope, no joy for the long-term prisoner, the 'lifer'. Life runs its dull round with a terrible monotony; it is all flat desert land with no high points and no oases to quench one's thirst or shelter one from the burning heat. Days run into weeks and weeks into months and years till the sands of life run out.
>
> All the might of the State is against him and none of the ordinary checks are available. Even the voice of pain is hushed, the cry of agony cannot be heard beyond the high walls.

(v)

About life in Naini prison, Nehru wrote in his autobiography :

Lifers'—convicts sentenced for life—were common, Usually a life sentence was supposed to terminate after twenty years, or even less, but there were many in prison then who had served more tan twenty years already. I saw one very remarkable case in Naini. Prisoners carry about, attacked to their clothes at the shoulder, little wooden boards giving information about their convictions and mentioning the date when release was due. On the board of one prisoner I read that his date of release was 1961! He had already, in 1930, served out several years, and he was then a person of middle age. Probably he had been given several sentences and they had been added up one after the other; the total, I think, amounting to seventy-five years.

For years and years may of these lifers, do not see a child or woman, or even animals. They lose touch with the outside world completely, and have no human contacts left. They brood and wrap themselves in angry thoughts of fear and revenge and hatred; forger the good of the world, the kindness and joy, and live only wrapped up in the evil, till gradually even hatred loses its edge and life becomes a soulless thing, a machine – like routine. Like automatons they pass their days, each exactly like the other, and have few sensations, except one—fear! From time to time the prisoner's body is weighed and measured But themselves and wither away in this terrible atmosphere of oppression? People argue against the death penalty, and their arguments appeal to me greatly. But when I see the long drawn-out agomy, of a life speni in prison, I feel that it is perhaps better to have that penalty rather tan to kill a person slowly and by degrees. One o f the 'lifers' came up to me once and asked me. What of us lifers? Will Swaraj take us out of this hell?"

Who are these leers? Many of them come in gang cases, when serge numbers. As many as fifty or a hundred, may be convi8nced embolic. Some of these are probably guilty, but I doubt if most of those convicted are really guilty; it is easy to gei people involved in such case. An approver';s evidence, a little identification, is

> all that is needed. Dacoities are increasing nowadays and the prison population goes up year by year. If people starve, what are they to do? Judges ad magistrates wax eloquent about the increase of crime, but are blind to the obvious economic causes of it
>
> Then there are the agriculturists who have a little village riot over some land dispute, lathis fly about, and somebody dies—result, many people in goal for life or for a long term. Often all the menfolk in a family will be imprisoned in this way, leaving the women to carry on as t they can;. Not one of tees is a criminal type. Generally they are fine young men, considerably above the overage villager, both physically and mentally. A little training, some diversion of interest to other subjects and jobs, and these people would be valuable assets to the country. (P-219220)

Remission may be earned by well-behaved prisoners. In fact, leadership qualities, educational attainments, cultural activities and even cultivation of aesthetic propensities may be given full opportunity for development, so that the incarcerated human being gets a fair deal for a finer future. The same consideration must apply in promoting sports and games, athletic achievements and the like. In all these matters it is a safe risk to take to allow teams and groups to be formed and give performances outside prison walls. Imagine a young prisoner earning a high distinction in the University or literary award in a competition! Similarly, a team of players within the prison, a group playing a music concert or displaying innovative skill and new discovery, may be a welcome incentive rewarded by remission. These and many other creative schemes may go a long way in transforming offenders and making them an asset to society. Stone walls do not a prison make, nor iron bars a cage, if the spirit of man is given scope to score higher or win laurels for proven work. This is a flexible field where imaginative projects can always be experimented with. Life is a liberal experiment. You can make a Gandhi out of goof or goon by corrective prison therapy, a Valmiki out of a robber in custody, a great singer inside a cell and a fine batsman, given the environment. Such a person may be given remission and considered seriously for premature release. The touchstone is not the term suffered in jail, but the talent cultivated and the luminous change achieved.

Rewards and Remissions are but recommendations and vest no enforceable *right* to release in the prisoner. They are matters to be considered by the advisory board or the Governor when an order of release is being made. The title to release, prematurely under Article 161 or section 432 springs into existence with the *appropriate signature* of Governer. However, Governer acts on expert advice. For this purpose a high-level versatile authority reprocessing many disciplines may be necessary. In my view, a judicial presence elevates the authority and stature of the Advisory Body. Maybe, a retired judge of the High Court will fill the bill. A senior medical officer or physiotherapist may add competence to the committee. A retired D.G.P, with familiarity in the field of prison management, will enhance the worth of the advisory body. Of course, the Government Secretaries of Home and Law must sit on the Committee with the judge as chairperson.

The United States is the land of *'due process'*. But India has advanced beyond the U.S and the U.K in certain dimensions of administrative law. After Maru Ram, why even before and after, the exercise of pardon power and of commutation in India is subject to de facto due process in the sense of reasonableness in exercise of power and guidelines governing even presidential clemency. By contrast, we may have a look at this branch of American jurisprudence. Sheldon Krantz, in his authoritative book Corrections and Prisoner's Rights writes:

> The most common method of restoration in most jurisdictions is the executive pardon. There are many problems with the pardoning process, however. First of all, pardons are normally entirely discretionary with a governor (or President), and therefore, are not subject to judicial review. See, e.g., Murphy v. Ford, 390F.Supp.1372 (W.D.Mich.1975). Also, given the lack of guidelines, pardons provide an erratic and irrational

> method for restoring the rights of convicted offenders. President's Crime Commission, Task Force Report: Corrections 91 (1967). (Page 324)

The expression parole is used in a wider sense in American jurisprudence. The same learned author notes that in the American criminal justice process no point offers more opportunity for abusive and arbitrary power than does the parole-release decision. Until quite recently the courts had taken a "hands off" attitude towards this decision, primarily on the basis that, parole release was a privilege and not a right'.

Indeed, parole proceedings were treated as an aspect of prison discipline, not an adjudication of rights in an adversary proceedings, and does not entitle a prisoner to notice therein, or specification of the grounds and underlying facts upon which the determination was based. Of course, a contrary note has also been struck in some cases. Sheldon Krantz observes:

> Since the early 1980's, there has been an explosion in caselaw on the parole release decision which potentially promises far greater accountability in this process. Most of the cases have involved attacks on the procedures (or lack thereof) of the United States Board of Parole. Others have involved similar attacks on state parole boards under the year 1983. The primary issue in most of these cases has been the applicability of the Due Process Clause to the granting or denial of parole. Many cases also have attacked parole release procedures of the United States Board of Parole on the grounds that they violate the Federal Administrative Procedure Act.
>
> Although various cases had made small inroads on the up-to-then unlimited discretionary power of parole boards, the most significant decision to date has been Childs v. United States Board of Parole, 511 F.2d 1270(D.C.Cir. 1974). In Childs, over ninety federal prisoners brought a class action against the Federal parole Board claiming that their rights to due process had been violated by the Board's failure to reveal the

> basis for denials of applications for parole. (Corrections and Prisoner's Rights Page 295/296).

Now, however, a change has been chiseled. The law there is that there is a requirement of reasons for decision on parole or revocation thereof on due process grounds. The current status of the law is that sufficiency of reasons must be available for judicial scrutiny. Grant and deprivation of parole, according to the U.S. Supreme Court as of now, must be supported by reason and arbitrariness invites invalidation. The American law is best summarised thus:

> The court determined that the reason was insufficient after applying this test:
>
> Can such a reason be so meaningful that a reviewing court can determine whether the Board has adopted and followed criteria that are appropriate, rational and consistent, and does it protect the inmate against arbitrary and capricious decisions or actions based upon impermissible considerations? 389 F. Supp. At 409.
>
> Thus, it appears that the giving of reasons requires both explicit criteria and facts indicating why the criteria were applied in a given way. This area obviously is in need of further development, however. It is clear that the giving of very general or abstract reasons would result in Childs amounting to a meaningless victory.
>
> (Corrections and Prisoner's Rights Page 299).

Indian Criminal jurisprudence has crystallized the law of parole and release whether it be under statute or in exercise of clemency jurisprudence and therefore just, fair and reasonable exercise is now integral to parole—release jurisprudence. Fundamental fairness—the touchstone of due process—obligates the State to ground its decision on relevant, rational material with nexus to the objective of the parole-release-remission grant.

This long penological journey is undertaken in the spirit of a social duty, a national obligation and a rationalisation of prisoners' freedoms now remaining jurisprudentially blurred. The cause of freedom of any person is a fundamental commitment of every person. I end this experiment in compassion by a quote from Carl Schurz:

If you want to be free, there is but one way, it is to guarantee an equally full measure of liberty to all your neighbours. There is no other.

# Index

## C

## Q



## R